day trips® from
seattle

help us keep this guide up to date

We would love to hear from you concerning your experiences with this guide and how you feel it could be improved and kept up to date. Please send your comments and suggestions to:

editorial@GlobePequot.com

Thanks for your input, and happy travels!

day trips® series

day trips® from seattle

first edition

getaway ideas for the local traveler

chloë ernst

gpp®

travel

Guilford, Connecticut

All the information in this guidebook is subject to change. We recommend that you call ahead to obtain current information before traveling.

To buy books in quantity for corporate use
or incentives, call **(800) 962-0973**
or e-mail **premiums@GlobePequot.com**.

Day Trips is a registered trademark.

Editor: Kevin Sirois
Project Editor: Lynn Zelem
Layout: Mary Ballachino
Text Design: Linda R. Loiewski
Maps: James Fountain © Morris Book Publishing, LLC.
Spot photography throughout © Sheila Say/Shutterstock

Library of Congress Cataloging-in-Publication Data is available on file.

ISBN 978-0-7627-5959-0

Printed in the United States of America
10 9 8 7 6 5 4 3 2 1

>> about the author

While ranging through the Pacific Northwest, Chloë Ernst has skied on the slopes overlooking her home in Vancouver, British Columbia, hiked to hot springs in Olympic National Park, been awed by the panoramas of the Gorge Amphitheater on the Columbia River, and followed parts of Ezra Meeker's Oregon Trail. For this guide she covered more than 6,000 miles of Washington highways, byways, and gravel roads.

While she holds a Canadian passport, her affinity with the friendly folk of Washington State has only grown amidst lost wallets, missed turns, and late arrivals in small towns.

Chloë coauthored the Frommer's guide *Best Hiking Trips in British Columbia* (2009) and writes freelance articles for print and online magazines. She holds a bachelor's degree in journalism and Spanish from the University of King's College, Halifax, Nova Scotia, and particularly enjoys the freedom of solo travel. Find more about the travel journalist's adventures at www.chloeernst.com.

>> acknowledgments

Tourism bureaus, innkeepers, and locals have all provided amazing assistance as I lost and found my way in new and familiar places around Washington State.

Thank you to Julie Hill for your ever-timely responses and to senior editor Amy Lyons and the helpful staff at GPP Travel for your guidance.

Apologies and thanks to my family and friends who tolerated phone calls from a different place each week and whose messages went unanswered while I traveled and wrote. My greatest appreciation, however, goes to my travel partner Matti, who unhesitatingly embarked on unknown itineraries. I hugely value your support—thank you.

contents

northwest

>> introduction

From Yakima's 8 inches of annual rainfall to almost 12 feet in the rain forests of the Olympic Peninsula, it's hard to put the Evergreen State in any one category. Wineries, whale sightings, steam-powered railroads, and power-generating dams count amongst the attractions within a 2-hour drive of Seattle.

Three national parks—Olympic, Rainier, and the North Cascades—and one of the nation's most stunning national monuments, Mount St. Helens, all deliver high-altitude, snow-capped scenery. Out on the coast, waterfront and underwater parks venture below sea level. Forests cover about two-fifths of the state, and approximately half of that is in public ownership. It's no wonder, then, that in a state lassoed by nature outdoor activities rank as a favorite pastime for Washingtonians. There are opportunities for everything from hiking and kayaking to rock climbing, skiing, and windsurfing in the state.

Washington takes much of its shape from volcanic activity and the ice age. Heaving plates created the state's volcanoes, many of which remain active to this day. The state shares an international border with Canada at the 49th parallel to the north and is bordered by the states of Idaho to the east and Oregon to the south. The Pacific Ocean lies to the west.

In the northern coastal region, waterfront towns are filled with outdoor art and surrounded by lush farmlands that yield crops of flowers, fruit, and vegetables. Indeed, along the entire tangled coast of Puget Sound, the dense population clustering in the lowlands ensures a mixture of museums, vibrant arts, and busy festivals.

To the east of Seattle lies the imposing Cascade Range. Part of the Pacific Ring of Fire (the stretch of volcanoes and frequent seismic activity that nearly encircles the Pacific), the mountains include the state's tallest peak—Mount Rainier at 14,410 feet—as well as the imposing heights of Mounts Adams, Baker, and St. Helens. Further east the scenery transforms into the dry but rich agricultural lands of the Columbia Plateau, defined by the grand Columbia River.

The Cascades are the dividing line for the weather in the state. To the west you'll need umbrellas and rain gear to stay dry in a maritime climate that is defined by its mildness, cloud cover, and drizzle. East of the Cascades expect the hottest and coldest extremes in the state. With its generally sunny days and clear skies, eastern Washington is a favorite escape from Seattle's low cloud ceiling.

A westward journey ventures into the Olympic Mountains, Kitsap Peninsula, and islands. Rain shadows create hyperlocal climates, which means driving 20 minutes down the road puts you in a new world all together. This is also the region where the Washington

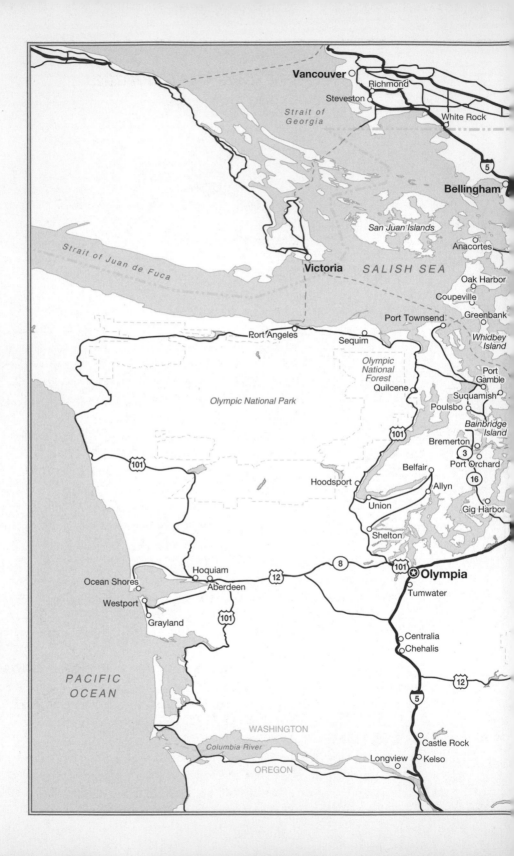

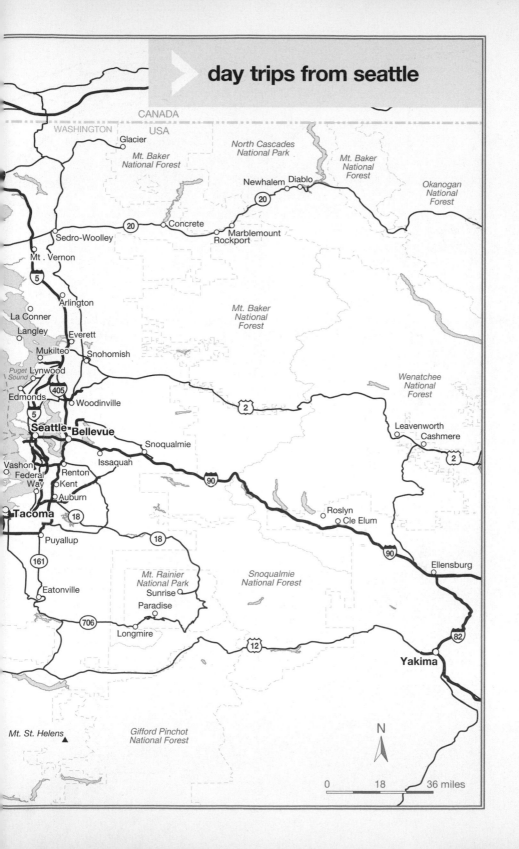

CANADA
WASHINGTON USA

Glacier

North Cascades
National Park

Mt. Baker
National Forest

Mt. Baker
National
Forest

Okanogan
National
Forest

Newhalem Diablo

20

Concrete

Sedro-Woolley   Marblemount
                       Rockport

Mt . Vernon

5

Arlington

La Conner

Langley   Everett

Mukilteo   Snohomish

Puget   Lynwood
Sound

405

Edmonds   Woodinville

5

Seattle Bellevue

            Snoqualmie

        Issaquah

Vashon
  Federal   Renton
  Way   Kent
       Auburn

Tacoma   18

Puyallup   18

161

Eatonville

706

Longmire

Mt. St. Helens ▲

Gifford Pinchot
National Forest

Mt. Baker
National
Forest

2

Wenatchee
National
Forest

Leavenworth
      Cashmere

2

90

Roslyn
  Cle Elum

90   Ellensburg

Mt. Rainier   Snoqualmie
National Park   National Forest
Sunrise
Paradise

12

82

Yakima

N

0   18   36 miles

State ferry system is most prevalent and provides travelers with access to the San Juan Islands, the far reaches of Kitsap Peninsula, and Canada.

Throughout the state you'll encounter the rich traditions and finely crafted art of Native American nations who have long called the Pacific Northwest their home. Several cities and towns in the state—Snoqualmie, Yakima, Chehalis, Puyallup—bear the names of these Native American nations. Many of the rivers, mountains, and natural features also take names from Native American languages. Not all appear on the map, however, such as Mount Tahoma—the Native American name for Mount Rainier.

Throughout the state, and particularly in the smaller towns, there's an enduring pioneer spirit—one that is preserved in re-created pioneer villages or in community-run museums. Local docents retell the days before and after Washington became a state in 1889.

We can also define the spirit of the state as festive. Faced by many a drizzly day, Washingtonians love nothing more that to get outdoors and celebrate the season. Whether that means partaking of the spring tulips in Skagit Valley, a late-summer fair in Puyallup, the fall grape crush at the wineries, autumn salmon-watching in Issaquah, or a winter cowboy gathering in Ellensburg, there's always something to see and do.

Expect traffic in and around Seattle, but a day trip out of the city will take you to places where the roads are open and the horizon beckoning. Washington—its mountains, valleys, activities, museums, history, and culture—is yours to explore.

>> using this guide

This guide is organized as the compass points lie. Deviations fall in line with major routes and highways so as not to separate neighboring destinations based on an arbitrary line.

Within each chapter, day trips are presented in a nearest-to-furthest order with those closest to Seattle appearing first. Those demanding more travel appear later in the section.

For each day trip we've offered up more than a day's worth of attractions and eateries. There are options for family getaways, romantic escapes, independent explorations, and historical tours. The intent is to provide diverse options so you can pick and choose from the listings to create an itinerary that suits your own style and interests.

All times and distances are given in relation to downtown Seattle. As you already know—or will quickly discover—being just a few miles outside of the traffic bottleneck will reduce travel time significantly, while hardly impacting the overall distance covered.

hours of operation, prices, credit cards

We've provided details on hours, pricing, and credit cards as they were at the time of publication. In the interest of accuracy, and because they are subject to continual change, hours of operation in particular are given in general terms. Please do always call ahead. Unless otherwise noted, all establishments listed accept major credit cards (Visa, MasterCard). If you have specific questions, please use the provided phone numbers and Web sites to contact the establishments directly—they will be able to provide the most current information.

pricing key

accommodations

The pricing code below reflects the average cost of a double-occupancy room during the peak-price period. Prices do not include state or local sales taxes, occupancy tax, or any other taxes and fees that will be included in a final bill. Always ask about special discounts, which can include AAA, military, senior, or corporate.

$ less than $80 for a double-occupancy room
$$ $80 to $130
$$$ $131 to $199
$$$$ $200 and up

restaurants

This code prices out the average cost of dinner entrees for two, not including drinks, wine, appetizers, desserts, taxes, and tip. In Washington, a 15 percent tip is customary, with more for exceptional service. Pricing for lunch and breakfast dishes, where applicable, usually falls in a lower price bracket.

$ less than $15 for two entrées
$$ $15 to $30
$$$ $31 to $59
$$$$ $60 and up

attractions

This code prices out the average adult entry cost to the listed attractions. Prices do not reflect the total including tax. Family pricing packages and discounts are often available.

$ under $5 for an adult entry ticket
$$ $5 to $10
$$$ more than $10

driving tips

With ferries, mountain passes, and major highways, a trip along a Washington roadway is no drive in the country. Rockslides, landslides, heavy snow, washed out roads, or ferries with mechanical troubles can all slow down a trip and provide a dose of the unexpected.

An undeniable fact is that it rains and rains a lot in the Northwest. Hydroplaning is a constant danger when the roads are wet. Slow down. Take a byway, not the highway. When roads are slick and water pools, it is easy to lose control of your vehicle.

State troopers are often out, ticketing those who exceed the posted speed limits. Watch your driving speed with particular attention on interstates where speed limits drop, such as the stretch of I-5 south of Bellingham where the limit drops from 70 mph to 60 mph. Fines double in construction zones.

I keep up-to-date on traffic reports by radio, particularly on I-5, I-90, and I-405 stretches around Seattle. The radio station 97.3 FM reports on traffic conditions every 10 minutes, as does 1000 AM.

Some highways that traverse mountain passes close in winter. Two such highways are SR 20 between Ross Lake in the North Cascades and Winthrop, and SR 410 from Cayuse Pass near Mount Rainier. Other high elevation roads may be closed or experience dangerous driving conditions such as landslides, rock falls, or washouts. Washington State Department of Transport (WSDOT) provides a traffic information line. Access it by dialing 511 on most phones or (800) 695-7623. Details are also available on the WSDOT Web site, www.wsdot.wa.gov/traffic.

Lastly, Washington State Ferries serves as a secondary, floating highway system for the state. But waiting in line patiently and smart planning are all part of the highway code. Ferries are charged with responding to Mayday calls, so journeys occasionally take a detour. Suffice it to say, plan on extra time as you negotiate the system.

highway designations

- Interstates are prefaced by "I" and are generally multilane, divided highways that are also known as freeways or expressways. There are seven in the state: I-5, I-82, I-90, I-182, I-205, I-405, and I-705.

- U.S. highways are mostly two- and three-lane undivided roads and prefaced by "US," although "Highway" is sometimes used locally, as in Highway 2 that runs through Leavenworth.

- State routes are paved and prefaced by "SR," although sometimes they are prefixed by "WA" instead.

highway quirks

State routes are often more commonly known by their destination rather than the number. Therefore routes such as SR 504 that heads up to Mount St. Helens is also called Spirit Lake Memorial Highway, and SR 542 is better known as Mount Baker Highway.

The occasional Forest Service Road is abbreviated as FSR—you'll mostly find these roads in or near national parks and forests.

Lastly, addresses given by milepost are abbreviated as MP.

travel tips

area codes

Traveling to most of these day trips will put you outside the 206 area code of Seattle. Area codes you'll encounter include:

- 253: Western Washington (Tacoma and area)

- 425: Western Washington (Bellevue and area)

- 360: Western Washington

- 509: Eastern Washington

Although not currently in effect, area code 564 will be used as the state gets low on available numbers. As the area code will be available in all of western Washington, it will switch the state over to ten-digit dialing.

For cell phones, be sure to check with your provider before dialing outside your local calling area—extra charges may apply.

sales tax

Statewide, you'll pay a sales tax on most items save food and prescription medications (6.5 percent in 2010). There are additional county taxes as well as a hotel occupancy tax. Expect to pay an additional 15 to 20 percent in taxes and fees on hotel rooms.

where to get more information

Day Trips attempts to cover a wide variety of attractions, but those looking for additional material can contact the following agencies by phone or the Web. Regarding the latter, there are increasing volumes of online reviews. Be aware these can be contradictory and conflicting as each person's experience is different. The Web provides a platform for all of these experiences to be publicized. Ratings such as AAA and Better Business Bureau offer a weightier authority.

Each region as well as larger cities and attractions all have their own tourism boards. In addition to these resources (which are too numerous to list here, although we've listed visitor centers with each of the day trips), a few other helpful sources include:

Amtrak
(800) 872-7245
www.amtrak.com

National Register of Historic Places
http://nrhp.focus.nps.gov

Washington Bed & Breakfast Guild
2442 Northwest Market St., PMB #355
Seattle, WA 98107
(800) 647-2918
www.wbbg.com

Washington State Ferries

(206) 464-6400 or (888) 808-7977

www.wsdot.wa.gov/ferries

Washington State Historical Society

1911 Pacific Ave.

Tacoma, WA 98402

(253) 272-9747 or (888) 238-4373

www.wshs.org

Washington State Parks

1111 Israel Rd. Southwest

Olympia, WA 98504-2650

(360) 902-8844 (information) or (888) 226-7688 (reservations)

infocent@parks.wa.gov (information)

www.parks.wa.gov

Washington State Tourism

(800) 544-1800

tourism@cted.wa.gov

www.experiencewa.com

Washington Trails Association

2019 Third Ave., Suite 100

Seattle, WA 98121

(206) 625-1367

www.wta.org

north

day trip 01

>>> **trams and planes:**
edmonds, lynnwood, everett

North of Seattle you'll find interactive museums, small-town shopping, and waterfront views all just a short drive up the interstate. Amble through Edmonds along streets lined with trees and independent merchants, where a slow-paced charm insulates visitors from the ever-close Seattle traffic. Then cut back towards I-5 to visit the tiny but historic Heritage Park and a mega shopping center in Lynnwood.

Sea and sky meet in Everett with an impressive trio of flight museums (including the must-see Future of Flight Aviation Center and Boeing Tour) and a lively waterfront district boasts a community-on-the-water feel and large marina. Add the bustling attractions of an AquaSox game or a concert at Comcast Arena and the wide streets with historic facades are the ideal place to spend a warm evening.

edmonds

Beyond the charm of the pedestrian-friendly main streets in Edmonds, its position on Puget Sound offers up frames of the Olympic Mountains from the city beaches. A central fountain, summer flower boxes, and a historic walking tour that includes more than twenty properties on its own Edmonds Register of Historic Places add an undeniable charm to a town that also boasts some quirkiness.

Formerly a mill town, Edmonds now serves as the departure point for daily ferries to Kingston—a gateway to the Kitsap Peninsula and Olympics beyond (see Day Trips West

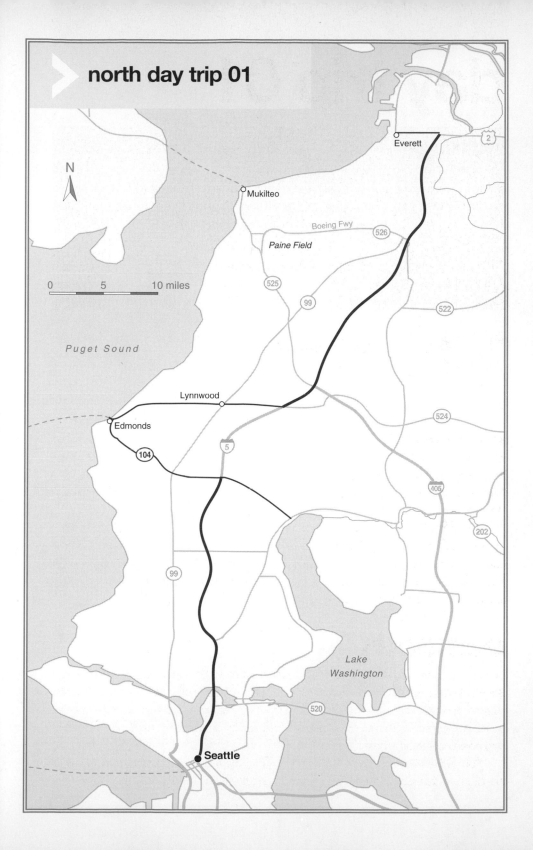

N

0   5   10 miles

Everett

Mukilteo

Boeing Fwy

526

Paine Field

525

99

522

Puget Sound

Lynnwood

524

Edmonds

5

104

405

99

202

Lake
Washington

520

Seattle

01 and 02, and Northwest 02 for attractions in the area). Nearby, venture to an underwater marine park where sunken boats become treasure for divers.

getting there

From Seattle, drive 10 miles north on I-5 taking exit 177 to Edmonds. SR 104 zips north-west to Edmonds, becoming Sunset Avenue and intersecting Main Street. The ferry and beaches lie on the shore to the west, while the shopping and museums are to the east. Total travel time is about 25 minutes, not accounting for heavy traffic.

where to go

Edmonds Visitor Bureau. 120 Fifth Ave. North, Edmonds; (425) 776-6711; www.every thingedmonds.com. Housed in the historic Hanley Cabin, the visitor bureau offers area information plus a dose of local history. In its former life this cabin was a home to various local families, the first of who were the Ganahls and the last the Hanleys. Open weekdays.

Edmonds Center for the Arts. 410 Fourth Ave. North, Edmonds; (425) 275-9595; www .ec4arts.org. Since hosting its first performance in 2006, the venue has become home to the Olympic Ballet Theater, Cascade Symphony Orchestra, and Sno-King Community Chorale. The center was once a school auditorium but has been completely remodeled. $$–$$$.

Edmonds Historical Museum. 118 Fifth Ave. North, Edmonds; (425) 774-0900; www .historicedmonds.org. Next door to the visitor center, the Carnegie Building houses the Edmonds Historical Museum. Once a library and city hall, the museum traces the roots of Edmonds back through its incorporation in 1890. Open afternoons Wed to Sun. $.

Edmonds Underwater Park. Brackett's Landing, foot of Main Street, Edmonds; www .ci.edmonds.wa.us/Discovery_programs_website/Underwater_Park.html. If giant Pacific

salish sea

Long has waged the debate over renaming the Pacific Northwest inland waters. The proposed area of the Salish Sea groups Puget Sound, the Strait of Juan de Fuca, and the Georgia Strait together. The new name recognizes its shared eco-system and Coast Salish heritage. As the waters include those of Canada and the United States, there are multiple official and self-appointed bodies involved in the discussion, including the Washington State Board on Geographic Names, which officially adopted the new name in late 2009.

Time to update your atlas?

octopi don't worry you, Edmonds Underwater Park makes a great diving destination. Beneath the waves divers will find sunken ships and diverse marine life. About two wooden boats are added to the park each year.

Marina Beach. Admiral Way, near Railroad Avenue at Dayton Street, Edmonds. On a windy day thrashing waves beat against the sandy shore. Between a fenced-in dog beach and an impressive marina and boatyard where shelves of boats stack three high, Marina Beach offers a vantage of the ferries. Picnic tables and views of Puget Sound provide a great spot to relax.

where to eat

Chanterelle, Specialty Foods. 316 Main St., Edmonds; (425) 774-0650; www.chanterelle wa.com. With a healthy share of well-priced yet creative comfort foods, this eatery will suffice whether you're looking for breakfast, lunch, or dinner. Start with a pear and Brie quesadilla, a medley of mussels and clams, or the famous tomato bisque. Then indulge in a simple meat loaf or a steaming dish of jambalaya or cioppino stew. Open daily 8 a.m. to 9 p.m.; closes at 1 p.m. on Sun. $$–$$$.

Daphnes. 415½ Main St., Edmonds; (425) 776-6402; www.daphnesbar.com. Tiny, intimate, and friendly, Daphnes is one of the most fun spots in Edmonds. With the tiny size of the venue (there are just two tables plus the bar), you can't help but meet the locals. Serving a selection of fine cheeses, meats, and chocolates, ravenous day-trippers may be best satisfied to make this a before- or after-dinner stop. Nevertheless, do enjoy a little food and a little wine in this lovely little find. Open daily 4 p.m. to midnight. $$.

The Resident Cheesemonger. 405 Main St., Edmonds; (425) 640-8949; www.resident cheesemonger.com. This is picnic central. Ripe cheeses, smoky cured meats, and olive-oil-drenched antipasti include some of the best selections locally available. The only downside is the pungent smell. Select a few items you love and a few undiscovered ones, then add a crusty baguette and take the cache to Marina Beach. Closed Mon. $$.

where to stay

The Maple Tree Bed and Breakfast. 18313 Olympic View Dr., Edmonds; (425) 774-8420; http://themapletreeb_b.home.comcast.net. Regulations in Edmonds limit bed-and-breakfasts to just one room. Therefore at the Maple Tree B&B you are The Guest—not one of many. Olympic View Drive curves along the coast, north of the downtown, leading to some water and mountain views at the B&B. But admiring the gardenscape and bird watching from the comfy solarium are equally as lovely as the peaking horizon. Credit cards not accepted. $$.

lynnwood

Originally established as the chicken-raising community of Alderwood, Lynnwood has since become a center for commerce. And although in some respects the highways dominate the city (it's at the junction of the state's most heavily trafficked interstates, I-5 and I-405), visitors will find hidden charm amidst the pavement. Discover the time capsule that is Heritage Park, where a telling exhibit on the Interurban tramway, friendly local ambassadors, and an absorbing genealogical society all make the park more than expected. Afterward head out to explore the shopping center at Alderwood Mall, one of the largest shopping complexes in the state.

getting there

Lynnwood lies just 3 miles east back toward I-5. From Main Street in Edmonds, head north on 9th Avenue North, bearing right onto Puget Drive. Follow the twisty route as it becomes 196th Street Southwest and heads into Lynnwood.

Or if heading straight to Lynnwood from Seattle, take I-5 exit 181B.

where to go

Heritage Park. 19921 Poplar Way, Lynnwood. The historic park offers a few heritage landmarks for a longer-than-expected stop. See the ornate stained glass of the **Interurban Car 55** (425-670-5502), search family history at the **Sno-Isle Genealogical Society Library** (425-775-6267), or time travel to the now completely transformed community of **Alderwood Manor at the Heritage Cottage** (425-775-4694). Mostly run by volunteers, the hours for each park attraction can vary greatly, so always call ahead. The park grounds, however, are open daily and parking is free.

South Snohomish County Visitor Information Center. 19921 Poplar Way, Heritage Park, Lynnwood; (425) 776-3977; www.snohomish.org. This visitor information center provides maps, brochures, and local insight. There's also a large photo exhibit detailing the history of the Interurban—including everything from its construction and the implementation of a "people catcher" to its deconstruction. Open daily.

where to shop

Alderwood Mall. 3000 184th St. Southwest, Lynnwood; (425) 771-1211; www.alderwood mall.com. Indoor and outdoor shops provide the sum total of more than 175 shopping experiences at Alderwood Mall. Fashion (Victoria's Secret to Lucky Brand Jeans to JCPenney), tasty treats (Sweet Factory to Godiva Chocolatier), bath and body (Sephora), accessories (Oakley "O" Store to Coach), and footwear (Foot Locker to ALDO) show the broad selection of mall tenants. Open daily.

everett

Air meets the ocean in Everett. The city makes a top destination for flight enthusiasts with a trio of museums dedicated to flying machines of all kinds. On the waterfront a ferry-accessed park, impressive marina, and requisite excellent sunsets connect the city to its coastal roots.

In downtown Everett wide main streets complement the many heritage-fronted commercial properties. Comcast Arena and Everett AquaSox games draw crowds into the downtown for concerts and sports events.

getting there

I-5 trims the eastern edge of Everett. If your plan includes visiting the flight museums or plane spotting at the airport, take exit 186 to 128th Street Southwest, which merges into Airport Road. Or turn at exit 189, which becomes the Boeing Freeway.

If a waterfront stroll and sipping a local brew on a patio are more your speed, follow I-5 to exit 193, leading onto Pacific Avenue and downtown Everett.

where to go

Everett Tourism and Visitor Services. 2000 Hewitt Ave., Suite 120, Everett; (425) 322-2658 or (800) 907-4765; www.snohomish.org. The bureau is located in Comcast Arena and is closed Sun.

Flying Heritage Collection. 3407 109th St. Southwest, Paine Field, Everett; (877) 342-3404; www.flyingheritage.com. World War II Allied and Axis aircraft form the bulk of this well-restored collection of prop planes acquired around the world by Paul G. Allen of Microsoft fame. Be sure to visit on a fly day when you can see the 1935–1945 vintage aircraft outside the hangar, soaring and roaring through the skies above Paine Airfield. Open daily from Memorial Day to Labor Day, closed Mon the rest of the year. $$–$$$.

Forest Park. 802 East Mukilteo Blvd., Everett; (425) 257-8300; www.everettwa.org. Everett's oldest park is a gem encompassing 197 acres of woodland. A summertime animal farm, forested trails, tennis courts, and indoor swimming pool make the park a perfect low-key day-trip destination. At the very least, take a drive along Mukilteo Boulevard and enjoy the route that winds down through the mossy groves. Open daily.

Future of Flight Aviation Center and Boeing Tour. 8415 Paine Field Blvd., Mukilteo; (425) 438-8100 or (800) 464-1476; www.futureofflight.org. By volume, the Boeing factory is the largest building in the world. The 90-minute tour takes visitors through the factory, where the majority of Boeing planes are constructed, including the latest of the Boeing line—the 787 Dreamliner. Extras like a flight simulator, design-your-own-jet program, gallery, and observation deck all add to the experience, making the factory a day trip in itself. There are some hard-and-fast rules: Children must be at least 4 feet tall, and no personal belongings are allowed on the tour (although there are lockers available). Either reserve tickets online for a small additional fee or plan to arrive early during the day as tickets sell out quickly, particularly on summer weekends. Open daily except for major holidays with tours starting on the hour. Military and senior discounts available. $$$.

Gallery at the Monte Cristo. 1507 Wall St., Everett; (425) 257-8380; www.artscouncilof snoco.org. In the historic opulence of the Monte Cristo Hotel, the Arts Council of Snohomish County welcomes visitors to six free exhibits each year. Open daily except Sun, although call ahead to check that the gallery isn't between exhibits. $.

Imagine Children's Museum. 1502 Wall St., Everett; (425) 258-1006; www.imaginecm .org. You'll find planes, trains, and automobiles at the Imagine Children's Museum, except these are mini sized and far less noisy. The museum is like the playroom every kid dreams of: an indoor tree house, pretend downtown Main Street, fire engine, walk-on ferry, and even a mountain. Closed Mon. $$.

Jetty Island. Ferries leave from Marine Park, 10th Street and West Marine View Drive, Everett; (425) 257-8305; www.everettwa.org/parks. Jetty Island is a human-made slice of sandy shore and a spitting-distance getaway. Free ferries leave every half hour from Marine Park, where there's also an expansive public boat launch. The summer schedule teems with events, particularly for families. Geocaching (hide-and-seek using GPS navigation), sunset tours, nature walks, and sand-castle-building contests are all part of the fun. Sitting on dry land at the 14th Street Yacht Basin near the ferry dock is the historic schooner *Equator*. The empty shell of the wooden boat hints at its one-time greatness as a trading ship. Jetty Island is open daily from July though Labor Day. $.

The Museum of Flight Restoration Center. 2909 100th St. Southwest, Everett; (425) 745-5150; www.museumofflight.org/restoration-center. In hangar C-72 there's some work going on: The restoration center refurbishes planes for the ever-popular Museum of Flight in Seattle. Various models of Boeings, a U.S. Marine Corps jet fighter, helicopters, and gliders can be viewed in various states of repair (and disrepair). Open Tues to Sat from June to Aug; Tues to Thurs and Sat from Sept to May. $$.

where to eat

Lombardi's. 1620 West Marine View Dr., Everett; (425) 252-1886; www.lombardisitalian .com. On the Everett waterfront sits this sleek restaurant. An outdoor patio complements the interior with lots of natural light—a bright spot to enjoy a rainy day. Head here for a plate of the area's rich ocean bounty: wild salmon or Dungeness crab. Open for summer brunch and year-round for lunch and dinner. $$–$$$.

The Vintage Cafe. 1508 Hewitt Ave., Everett; (425) 252-8224. Serving comfort food, the Vintage Cafe is a charming spot to chow down. Although focusing perhaps more on volume, the four-course dinner offered for about $13 will fill even the hungriest of bellies. Open daily for breakfast, lunch, and dinner. $–$$.

where to stay

Gaylord House. 3301 Grand Ave., Everett; (425) 339-9153 or (888) 507-7177; www .gaylordhouse.com. Gaylord House perfectly blends modern polish with the historic charm of a 1910 Craftsman-style home. Five rooms offer diverse ways to relax: from a soak in a claw-foot tub in the Lady Anne's Chambers room, a meditation in the Lotus Room, or the independence of a private entry and king-size bed in the Garden Terrace room. Set on a tree-lined street just off Rucker Avenue, this bed-and-breakfast makes an ideal central but hidden destination. Military, senior, and AAA discounts available. $$–$$$.

Inn at Port Gardner. 1700 West Marine View Dr., Everett; (425) 252-6779 or (888) 252-6779; www.innatportgardner.com. Few better locations exist. The Inn at Port Gardner overlooks the Everett Marina and offers a fun mix of nightlife and comfort. Thirty-three rooms all feature queen- or king-size beds, while the harbor view suites also offer soaking tubs, fireplaces, and decks or patios. Includes breakfast. $$–$$$.

day trip 02

north

>>> **tulips and turkeys:**
la conner, mount vernon,
chuckanut drive

The spring display of Washington's blooms is centered in the Skagit Valley. Usually in late March and April—or "according to Mother Nature" as the festival Web site puts it—daffodils, irises, and tulips brighten the local fields. But the region offers more than stunning blooms.

A favorite day-trip town, La Conner specializes in quaint—be it the roaming town turkeys, a rainbow-shaped bridge, or the roadside stands of fruit and local vegetables that operate on an honor system. Tucked in the saltwater Swinomish Channel that connects Padilla and Skagit Bays, with no speed limit topping 25 mph, time slows down in the village.

This route then heads along the coast through farmlands to stop in at tulip central: Mount Vernon. Further north, lucky travelers will follow the unrivaled Chuckanut Drive. The route, officially SR 11, connects the Samish farmlands, where hidden eateries are the norm, to cliff-side lookouts, where escarpments tower above the ever-tempestuous ocean. It's a narrow road that was one of Washington's first scenic drives, and it remains an all-time favorite.

la conner

This historic waterfront village warrants an on-foot exploration of quality shops and search for the local wild turkeys. As La Conner works its charm, stay longer and capture a waterfront vantage from the sculpture-adorned Gilkey Square or a restaurant patio while you tuck into a seafood feast of fresh Dungeness crab. During the Skagit Valley Tulip Festival, La

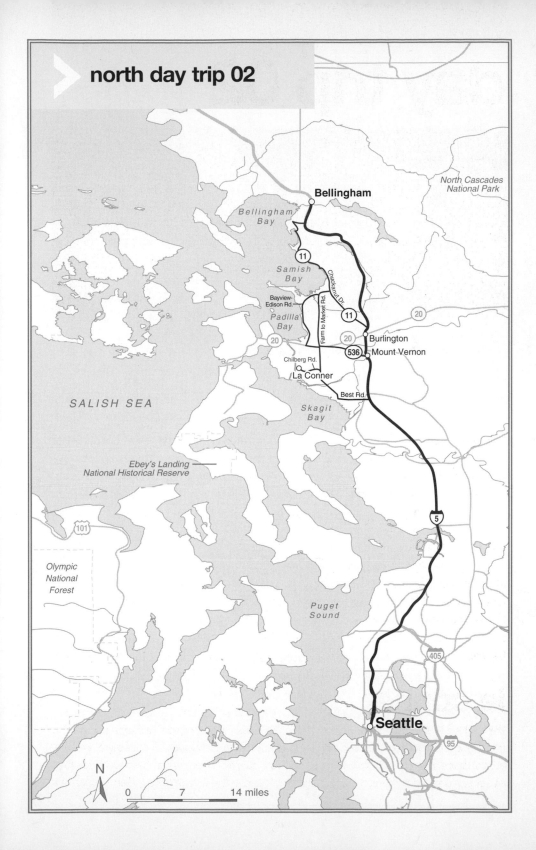

North Cascades
National Park

Bellingham

Bellingham
Bay

11

Samish
Bay

Chuckanut Dr.

Bayview-
Edison Rd.

Farm to Market Rd.

Padilla
Bay

11

20

20

Burlington

536

Mount Vernon

20

Chilberg Rd.

La Conner

Best Rd.

SALISH SEA

Skagit
Bay

5

Ebey's Landing
National Historical Reserve

Olympic
National
Forest

101

Puget
Sound

405

Seattle

95

N

0   7   14 miles

Conner becomes a top destination for enjoying the blooms and the refreshing spring days that accompany the festival.

If you're packing a picnic, be sure to bring some apples for the town gobblers.

getting there

To reach La Conner, take I-5 north to exit 221. Head west into Conway, taking Fir Island Road out of town and continuing west. Crossing the north fork of the Skagit River, the road becomes Best Road. Take Chilberg Road and watch for signs for La Conner (not, however, the La Conner–Whitney Road). Circle a roundabout, and follow the road as it becomes Morris Street and ends at the waterfront of the channel town.

where to go

Visitor Information Center. 606 Morris St., La Conner; (360) 466-4778 or (888) 642-9284; www.laconnerchamber.com. Located on the left when heading into town, the Visitor Information Center is open daily.

La Conner Quilt & Textile Museum. 703 South Second St., La Conner; (360) 466-4288; www.laconnerquilts.com. Fabrics weave many different stories at this La Conner museum. Housed in the 1891 Gaches Mansion—one of the town's oldest buildings—the exhibits fuse tradition with contemporary art. Open Wed to Sun. $$.

La Conner Volunteer Firefighters' Museum. 611 South First St., La Conner. As you amble along the vibrant stretch of First Street, stop in (if it's open) at the firefighters' museum. Displays trace firefighting back to horse-drawn fire carriages. Open by chance. $.

Museum of Northwest Art. 121 South First St., La Conner; (360) 466-4446; www.museumofnwart.org. There's a fusion of historic echoes and modern polish at the Museum of Northwest Art thanks to the beautiful cedar-and-hemlock-fronted building and the

turkey town

Since 1994 when the wild turkeys first appeared in La Conner, the gobblers have become the official town mascot, stopped traffic, pushed road-construction costs over budget, delighted children, and annoyed some locals.

The turkeys roam freely through town, protected by local laws. As the birds venture everywhere from the waterfront First Street to the county museum and beyond, be sure to keep a look out for them crossing the roads—they rarely yield to motorists.

exhibits' Northwest focus. The museum displays a permanent collection from Northwest artists dating from the 1900s onward. For shoppers, the gift shop stocks some of the best goods in town. Open daily. $$.

Skagit County Historical Museum. 501 South Fourth St., La Conner; (360) 466-3365; www.skagitcounty.net/museum. A bit tricky to find (Fourth Street only has two access points: Benton and Calhoun Streets that head uphill from Second Street), this county museum features a lovely observation deck looking out from the promontory location. The stories of farm life, Native Americans, and vintage toys all feature in the museum, which is open Tues to Sun. $.

where to shop

In the 1930s and 1940s, La Conner became a haven for artists. Today this creativity lives on and is yours to explore amongst the shopping opportunities on First Street. Including excellent quality crafts, functional pieces, and fine art, this First Street shopping tour represents the diversity you'll find in La Conner:

Earthenworks Gallery. 713 South First St., La Conner; (360) 466-4422; www.earthen worksgallery.com. From small jewelry items to larger home decor pieces, this gallery delivers stunning art and functional pieces.

Fairy Godmother's Unlimited. 705 South First St., La Conner; (360) 466-3340; www .fairygodmotherunlimited.com. A little escape from the main street, Fairy Godmother's Unlimited houses a glen of enchanting fairies in many forms. But the store also holds a cozy mix of gifts, baby wear, and art.

Organic Matters. 707 South First St., La Conner; (360) 466-4012; www.organic-matters .com. A wide selection of organic personal-care products, clothing, bedding, and gifts are all chemical free and natural. The house-special moisturizer delivers delicious but subtle scents like ginger, lavender, or vanilla. There's also an unscented version.

The Wood Merchant. 709 South First St., La Conner; (360) 466-4741; www.woodmerchant .com. A diverse selection of beautifully constructed, U.S.–made wood products shows the versatility of this natural material. Endless hours of woodworking create polished pieces that are thoughtful, natural, and appealing. The shop glows with the warm grains of maple, walnut, and pine patiently transformed into children's toys, serving dishes, and furniture.

where to eat

Kerstin's Restaurant. 505 South First St., La Conner; (360) 466-9111; www.kerstins restaurant.com. Featuring the best of land and sea, Kerstin's serves beef tenderloin, game hen, mussels, clams, oysters, and wild salmon. Quality, fresh, and natural ingredients are the focus, but that's not for you to worry about: Just enjoy the view from the second-floor dining room. Open Thurs to Mon for lunch. Open daily for dinner, except closed Sun. $$$–$$$$.

La Conner Brewing Company. 117 South First St., La Conner; (360) 466-1415; www .laconnerbrew.com. Walking into this brewery, the casual and warm atmosphere exudes the feel of a local favorite. It's hopping long before any other spot in town and serves a simple but quality selection of favorites that hit above the usual deep-fried nature of pub grub. Wood-fired pizzas, a prime-rib panini, warming soups, or local crab cakes strike a lovely complement to a pint of beer brewed mere feet away. Open daily for lunch and dinner. $$–$$$.

La Conner Seafood & Prime Rib House. 614 South First St., La Conner; (360) 466-4014; www.laconnerseafood.com. With debatably the best deck in town, the slow-roasted prime rib, Dungeness crab, scallops, and clam chowder have drawn patrons for more than twenty years. Situated on the Swinomish Channel waterfront, you'll take in views of the Rainbow Bridge and local boat traffic. For less-than-reliable West Coast days, the inside dining room places a close second to the deck for the best views. Open for lunch and dinner daily. $$$.

where to stay

Hotel Planter. 715 First St., La Conner; (360) 466-4710; www.hotelplanter.com. The location is unbeatable at this second-floor hotel on La Conner's main street. The views and amenities in all twelve rooms differ: Some include a Jacuzzi tub while others look out over the art-filled, hidden courtyard. A hotel hot tub tops the list of the best spots in town to relax after a day of exploring. If heading to La Conner in the low season (winter), ask about a frequent special that either provides the second night for free or at half price. $$–$$$.

La Conner Channel Lodge. 205 North First St., La Conner; (360) 466-1500 or (888) 466-4113; www.laconnerlodging.com. **La Conner Country Inn.** 107 South Second St., La Conner; (360) 466-3101. These two accommodation offerings are set apart from the bustle of town yet are still walking distance from La Conner's excellent restaurants and attractions. At the Country Inn, the decor blends a rustic country edge with a touch of history and cozy textiles. The Channel Lodge delivers the payoff waterfront views amidst clean, country styling. Over the two properties, rooms range widely in amenities and size—meaning there are options for most budgets. $$–$$$.

mount vernon

This is the heart of the Skagit Valley Tulip Festival, and spring is truly the best (and busiest) time to visit the area. Mount Vernon also offers rural delights like the iconic Roozengaarde gardens and a surprisingly fun theater scene.

getting there

From La Conner, head north on La Conner-Whitney Road to SR 20 east. From this stretch of the Cascade Loop Scenic Highway (which connects Puget Sound to the Columbia River Valley via the Cascade Range), head southeast on SR 536 or Memorial Highway to the center of Mount Vernon.

where to go

Mount Vernon Visitor Information Center. 105 East Kincaid St., Suite 101, Skagit Station, Mount Vernon; (360) 428-8547; www.mountvernonchamber.com/visitors. Head to Skagit Station for local scoop on attractions, tickets, accommodations, and dining. Open daily.

Lincoln Theatre. 712 South First St., Mount Vernon; (360) 336-8955; www.lincolntheatre .org. The 1920s theater emulates Spanish opulence. Well-preserved and treasured, the historic building is now home to concerts and movies. The theater's rare Wurlitzer organ gets a spin before most evening movie showings—a tradition retained from the early 1900s when organs added sound effects to silent films. Performances or showings run most evenings. $$–$$$.

Padilla Bay National Estuarine Research Reserve. 10441 Bayview-Edison Rd. (north of Bay View State Park), Mount Vernon; www.padillabay.gov. The muddy, flat bottom of Padilla Bay is the rooting ground for an eelgrass meadow that in turn provides a home to herons, eagles, fish, and other wildlife. The large and well-maintained Breazeale Interpretive Center offers information on bird watching as well as access to an observation deck and walking trails. Trails are open daily. The interpretive center is open Wed to Sun; closed holidays. $.

RiverBelle Dinner Theatre. 100 East Montgomery, Suite 240, Mount Vernon; (360) 336-3012; www.riverbelledinnertheatre.com. Improv and dinner theater combine in a historic setting to deliver a great show. Enjoy a full dinner or dessert alone while watching a dinner-theater comedy. Reservations needed for weekend evening shows; tickets start at about $20 per person. Performance schedules vary, so it's best to call ahead or check the RiverBelle Web site. $$$.

Roozengaarde. 15867 Beaver Marsh Rd., Mount Vernon; (360) 424-8531; www.tulips .com. Show gardens bloom each spring with bright-colored flowers from the Washington Bulb Company. Roozengaarde also sells bulbs. Open year-round. $.

where to eat

Calico Cupboard. 121 Freeway Dr., Suite B, Mount Vernon; (360) 336-3107; www.calico cupboardcafe.com. Visible from I-5, the old granary building sits below the Mount Vernon water tower. Soups, quiches, and sandwiches complement the simple entrees offered, including stir-fry, rice bowls, tacos, and potpies. The "lunchtime breakfast" is perfect for late starters. The warm atmosphere will combat any chilly spring morning. Open daily for breakfast and lunch. $–$$.

The Porterhouse. 416 West Gates St., Mount Vernon; (360) 336-9989; www.porterhouse pub.net. Celebrate the Northwest's brewing traditions with the twenty-one beers on tap at the Porterhouse. The menu mixes classic burgers, steaks, and veggie-loaded pastas with specialties like prosciutto-wrapped salmon. Open daily for lunch and dinner. $–$$$.

chuckanut drive

North of Mount Vernon, the grandeur of Chuckanut Drive twists along the coast, slipping between ocean's edge and mountain peaks. Frequent lookouts and the shoreline of Larrabee State Park provide excellent detours, along with refreshments at roadside eateries.

getting there

SR 11 officially begins at I-5 exit 231 in the north of Burlington and ends at exit 250 south of Bellingham.

where to go

Larrabee State Park. 245 Chuckanut Dr., Bellingham; (360) 902-8844 (Washington State Parks information line); www.parks.wa.gov. Ocean, lakes, and tide pools create a park with plenty of outdoor appeal. Larrabee was Washington's first state park and is now perhaps one of the best loved. Whether you head there to clam, crab, hike, camp, or bike, the park rates as the best stopping spot on Chuckanut Drive. Open year-round. $.

where to eat

The Oyster Bar. 2578 Chuckanut Dr., Bow; (360) 766-6185; www.theoysterbaronchuck anutdrive.com. Admiring a sunset over seafood and fine dessert may top the beauty of Chuckanut Drive. A tiny dining area in a building seemingly hovering over the ocean serves seafood at its freshest. Lovely variations on oysters plus mussels, salmon, abalone, halibut, and crab all feature for dinner. Lunch options are more casual, including fish tacos or a crab and cheddar melt. Reservations are recommended for dinner, although not necessary for lunch. Open daily for lunch and dinner. $$$–$$$$.

day trip 03

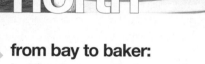

>>>

from bay to baker:
bellingham, glacier and mount
baker

In Whatcom County, a concentration of outdoor sculpture galleries and engaging museums are all located within sight of the soft curve of Bellingham Bay. Follow the shore south
along the South Bay Trail to reach Fairhaven. In the historic district south of downtown,
weekends are filled with visits to charming shops, community festivals, and a jazz-filled
nightlife.

Bellingham also marks the access point for a world-class scenic drive along Mount
Baker Highway (SR 542). At 10,781 feet, Mount Baker is the northern sentry of the Cascade
Range. It's also the snowiest spot in Washington, setting the record in 1998–1999 with a
snowfall measuring a whopping 95 feet. Good thing, then, that Mount Baker Highway cul-
minates in winter at a ski hill and in summer at the stunning panoramic viewpoint of Artist
Point.

bellingham

The Chuckanut Drive (see North Day Trip 02) scenic highway ends in Fairhaven, a historic
district south of Bellingham. There shops and festivals create a fun atmosphere to explore.
Just a short jaunt north, Bellingham rewards with museums, top-quality restaurants (or
cheap burrito stands, depending on your preference), and a university-fueled nightlife.

Spend a summer afternoon on the South Bay Trail, which connects Bellingham to
Fairhaven via Boulevard Park and a boardwalk where the ocean laps and shorebirds

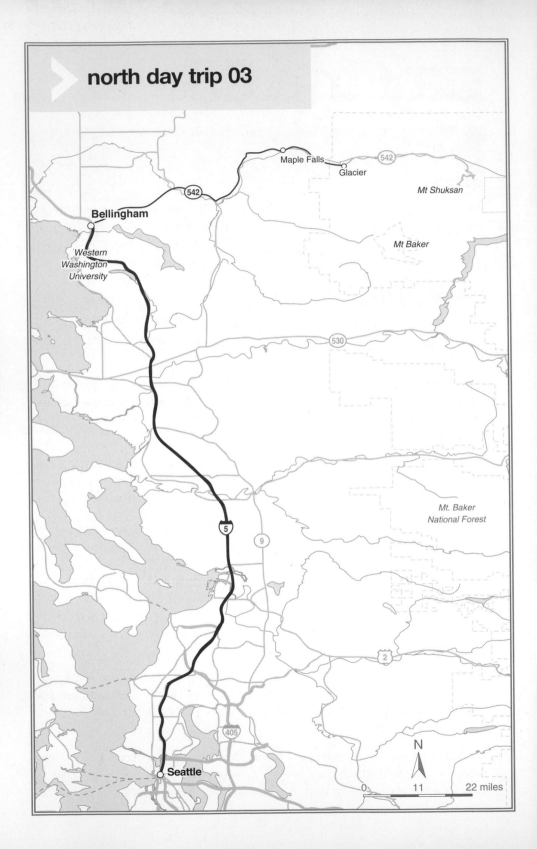

Maple Falls

542

Glacier

Mt Shuksan

542

Bellingham

Mt Baker

*Western
Washington
University*

530

Mt. Baker
National Forest

5

9

2

405

N

Seattle

0   11   22 miles

squawk on either side. Another favorite outdoor activity is a visit to the Western Washington University sculpture collection.

This hub of Whatcom County has also become a base camp for Mount Baker, a volcano in the Cascade Range.

getting there

From Seattle, travel north on I-5 for about 90 miles (1.5 hours). Take exit 250 for Fairhaven, exit 252 for Western Washington University, and exit 253 or 254 for downtown Bellingham.

Alternately, opt for a three-hour journey on the Amtrak Cascades train (800-872-7245; www.amtrak.com). The route is ideal for those spending a weekend in Bellingham.

where to go

Visitor Information Center. 904 Potter St., Bellingham; (360) 671-3990 or (800) 487-2032; www.bellingham.org. This visitor bureau provides information on Whatcom County as well as Bellingham. Open daily.

American Museum of Radio and Electricity. 1312 Bay St., Bellingham; (360) 738-3886; www.amre.us. As old tunes crackle out over the radio, the museum traces the source of electricity and the story of radio. Check out the broadcast on station 102.3 FM. Open Wed to Sun. $$.

Bellingham Railway Museum. 1320 Commercial St., Bellingham; (360) 393-7540; www.bellinghamrailwaymuseum.org. A train simulator takes you on a ride along the rails—and you're in the engineer's seat. Model train and antique railroad items make up a large collection. Call ahead to confirm hours and location as the museum has transitioned through different addresses over the years. At press time, open Tues and Thurs to Sat with a particularly affordable admission option for families. $.

Big Rock Garden Park. 2900 Sylvan St., Bellingham; (360) 778-7000 (Parks & Recreation); www.cob.org/services/recreation/parks-trails. Bellingham's lesser-known outdoor sculpture garden sits on the outskirts of the city near Lake Whatcom. The permanent collection features more than thirty pieces both large and small. Forested trails twist through the park offering many routes, scultpures, and benches to discover. Open year-round.

Mindport Exhibits. 210 West Holly St., Bellingham; (360) 647-5614; www.mindport.org. Interactive art exhibits are the highlight of this privately run gallery. Expect to be engaged by works that pique your curiosity and test your mind by blending light, touch, and sound. Open Wed to Sun. $.

Western Washington University's Outdoor Sculpture Collection. WWU Campus, Bellingham; (360) 650-3900; www.westerngallery.wwu.edu/sculpture.shtml. Perhaps the most appealing element of the WWU sculpture collection is how easy it is to engage with the pieces. Of course, standing under Isamu Noguchi's acclaimed *Skyviewing Sculpture* endures as a favorite, but so does an upward gaze to Mark di Suvero's *For Handel*, a seat on Scott Burton's *Two-Part Chairs*, or entering the metal walls of Richard Serra's *Wright's Triangle*. Take a wander through the sculptures on your own schedule, or plan a visit to coincide with a visit to the Western Gallery in the Fine Arts Complex. Pick up a photo guide to the sculpture collection and be sure to check in with campus parking, (360) 650-2945, and the visitor center at 2001 Bill McDonald Pkwy. Accessible year-round.

Whatcom Falls Park. Silver Beach Road (off Lakeway Drive) or 1401 Electric Ave., Bellingham; (360) 778-7000 (Parks & Recreation); www.cob.org/services/recreation/parks-trails. Flowing from Lake Whatcom, Whatcom Creek is the main vein of the park. The upper falls cascade heavily, and the 1939 sandstone bridge makes an excellent viewing point. A lesser-used fish hatchery, trails, and playground offer a lovely setting for a day spent parkside. Open daily year-round.

Whatcom Museum. 121 Prospect St., Bellingham; (360) 778-8930; www.whatcom museum.org. The Old City Hall building serves as the original flagship for this museum of art and history, although the new Lightcatcher building (250 Flora St.) opened in late 2009 and includes interactive family exhibits and art displays. The 1892 red brick of Old City Hall served as a landmark to sailors for many years. Collections reflect the rich culture and spirit-world art of the Northwest. Open Tues to Sun. $–$$$.

where to eat

Boundary Bay Brewery & Bistro. 1107 Railroad Ave., Bellingham; (360) 647-5593; www .bbaybrewery.com. A large selection of house-brewed beers complements a menu inspired by fresh foods. Best of all there's a house-made beer to complement each course—except you have to make the pairings. A row of small taster glasses or a recommendation from the (mostly) friendly staff members will do the trick. Serving lunch and dinner daily. $$–$$$.

Casa Que Pasa. 1415 Railroad Ave., Bellingham; (360) 756-8226. Casa Que Pasa's reputation for burritos is international in scope. Casa caters to a younger, thriftier crowd that doesn't worry about the rather basic seating as they emerge (stomachs grumbling) from the slopes of Mount Baker. The potato burrito in particular draws high honors. Open daily for lunch until late. $.

Nimbus. 119 North Commercial St., 14th floor, Bellingham; (360) 676-1307; www.nimbus restaurant.com. Washington loves its viewing towers (Seattle has three observation decks) and here is Bellingham's version: a restaurant with a creative menu and fantastic view on the fourteenth floor of the 1929 Bellingham Hotel. It's uncommon to see tofu on the menu at a nonvegetarian restaurant, but Nimbus includes a few soy offerings. Overall the menu shows the inventiveness of chef and owner Josh Silverman. Open daily for dinner. $$$.

Skylark's Hidden Cafe. 1308 11th St., Bellingham; (360) 715-3642; www.skylarks hiddencafe.com. Serving from breakfast through to dinner (with live jazz some evenings), this personality-filled restaurant offers a garden setting and historic style in the Fairhaven district. The menu encompasses both inexpensive and pricier entrees plus a budget menu for breakfast, lunch, and dinner priced at $4, $5, and $8 respectively. Open daily. $$–$$$.

where to stay

DeCann House Bed and Breakfast. 2610 Eldridge Ave., Bellingham; (360) 734-9172; www.decannhouse.com. This Victorian bed-and-breakfast offers antique charm with claw-foot tubs, heirloom furniture steeped with family history, and an antique pool table. Queen-size beds and private baths mean no comfort is sacrificed. Credit cards not accepted; discounts for stays longer than one night. $$–$$$.

Fairhaven Village Inn. 1200 10th St., Bellingham; (360) 733-1311 or (877) 733-1100; www.fairhavenvillageinn.com. Adjacent to the historic, quaint village of Fairhaven with views of Bellingham Bay, the Fairhaven Village Inn provides twenty-two contemporary rooms with excellent amenities. High-speed Internet, robes, continental breakfast, and a beautiful lobby all create a special destination. Choose from the bayside rooms with fireplaces and balconies, or the parkside rooms overlooking the lively village green. Includes breakfast. $$$–$$$$.

Hotel Bellwether. 1 Bellwether Way, Bellingham; (360) 392-3100; www.hotelbellwether .com. Sixty-five guest rooms plus the grand, free-standing lighthouse suite exude luxury and thoughtful presentation. Half offer waterfront views, fireplaces, balconies or patios, and jetted tubs. The on-site Harborside Restaurant provides gorgeous views of the marina, but as the hotel sits on a pier designed for conference guests, there are ample dining choices. For those arriving by boat, moorage is available, and the hotel is also float-plane accessible. For the rest of us, the hotel offers underground parking or a free airport shuttle. $$$–$$$$.

glacier and mount baker

Glacier is the feeder town to the volcanic peak and playground of Mount Baker. Filled with ski-bound traffic, shops, and après-ski eateries, the roadside village is more a departure point than a destination. Heading further east along the highway, the route climbs into the Mount Baker–Snoqualmie National Forest and winds along the Nooksack River towards Mount Baker ski hill and the end of the road at Artist Point.

Annual average snowfall at the ski hill measures nearly 54 feet; however, in the record-setting season of 1998–1999 the snowfall at Mount Baker measured a whopping 95 feet.

getting there

At exit 255, take SR 542 that cuts northeast from Bellingham to Mount Baker. The drive to Glacier takes under an hour along Mount Baker Highway, while Artist Point lies another 40 minutes east.

where to go

Artist Point. End of Mount Baker Highway, SR 542. This vantage has served as artistic inspiration for decades. Open July to Sept only; closed otherwise due to snow.

Glacier Public Service Center. 10091 Mount Baker Hwy., SR 542, east of Glacier; (360) 599-2714. For information on the national forest, stop at this roadside visitor center. Exhibits and information are plentiful. Grab a map and continue along the highway to enter the wilderness. Open daily in summer; weekends only in winter.

Mount Baker Ski Area. SR 542; (360) 671-0211 (snow phone); www.mtbaker.us. Skiing, sledding, snowmobiling, tubing, snowshoeing, and snowmobiling are all top winter activities. Summer brings hikers and photographers in large numbers to the peak. Day-pass lift tickets start at about $45. $$$.

where to eat

Graham's Restaurant. 9989 Mount Baker Hwy., Glacier; (360) 599-1964; www.grahams restaurant.com. Belly-filling eats include chicken, steaks, and burgers. The history of the restaurant goes back to its 1930s days as a general store and self-serve breakfast restaurant. Open daily for lunch and dinner during peak skiing and hiking seasons. $–$$$.

Il Caffe Rifugio. 5415 Mount Baker Hwy., Deming; (360) 592-2888; www.ilcafferifugio .com. With coffee that rivals any cup in Seattle, this little Italian-and-Northwest-style cafe is a not-to-miss spot at the start of the drive. If you're lucky, you'll arrive as fresh scones are coming out of the oven. Try a freshly grilled panini or one of the many house-baked, decadently presented goodies. Closed Mon. $.

where to stay

Mount Baker Lodging. Glacier; (360) 599-2453 or (800) 709-7669; www.mtbakerlodging .com. With access to dozens of properties, this rental company provides endless options for a stay in the Mount Baker area. Chalets, condos, and cabins sleep anywhere from two to twelve guests. Depending on the property, you can relax in a private hot tub, cross-country ski outside the door, or barbecue on your own deck. $$–$$$$.

day trip 04

>>> **canadian fishing villages:**
white rock, steveston, richmond

South of Vancouver, the cities of White Rock and Richmond blend urban with the historic. Although the White Rock Pier harks back to the city's fishing heritage, a lively waterfront district of packed patios and gelato shops modernizes the city. Yes, there's an impressively sized white rock, but you'll also discover a well-kept museum and perfect views from the promenade.

In Richmond, historic Steveston revives its fishing days while the rest of the city embraces an ever-evolving international feel. Here Olympic venues lie a short distance from Buddhist temples and malls that rival those in Hong Kong.

white rock

Just across the U.S.–Canada border, most visitors zip past White Rock on Hwy. 99 to Vancouver without stopping. In all fairness, though, you can't see the city's 5-mile beach, the pier inviting you for an evening stroll, or the walkable waterfront district of shops and restaurants from the highway. White Rock is a seaside getaway so close to the city—plus it sits in Canada's version of the banana belt, rewarding visitors with some Seattle-elusive sunshine.

getting there

Simply take I-5 north to the Peace Arch border crossing then continue on the Canadian Hwy 99. Exit almost immediately to White Rock, heading west on Eighth Avenue. Conveniently, Eighth Avenue turns into Marine Drive and follows the waterfront to the pier.

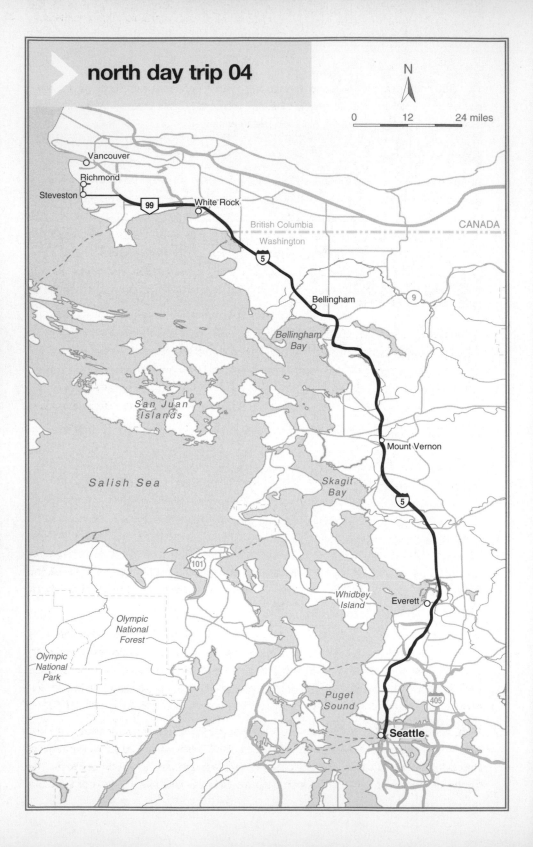

north day trip 04

N

0   12   24 miles

Vancouver

Richmond

Steveston

99   White Rock

British Columbia

Washington

5

CANADA

9

Bellingham

Bellingham
Bay

San Juan
Islands

Mount Vernon

Salish Sea

Skagit
Bay

5

101

Whidbey
Island

Everett

Olympic
National
Forest

Olympic
National
Park

Puget
Sound

405

Seattle

Waterfront paid parking starts at Finlay Street and continues west. Spots tend to fill up quickly on weekend nights, so grab the first one you see and then walk along the waterfront promenade to reach the beach, pier, and restaurants.

where to go

White Rock Beach, Pier, and Promenade. South of Marine Drive, White Rock. Of course, here is where you'll find the 486-ton white rock that gives the city its name. Although the rock was once bleached by bird guano (excrement), it now sports layers of white paint to cover the graffiti. As dusk settles, walk out under the lighted arches on the historic pier and take in the hill of crisp lights that define the shore. The promenade runs along a significant portion of the beach, connecting parking areas to local restaurants and the beach. Benches, safety lighting, and restrooms create a family-friendly destination. Open year-round.

White Rock Museum & Archives. 14970 Marine Dr., White Rock; (604) 541-2221; www .whiterock.museum.bc.ca. Located on the beach in the old White Rock railroad station, the White Rock Museum features a mix of railway, pioneer, First Nations, and local history, although that of the Great Northern Railway is most prevalent. See the rails that run right along the water and learn how the railroad helped shape the city. Open daily with reduced hours from Jan to May.

where to eat

The Boathouse Restaurant. 14935 Marine Dr., White Rock; (604) 536-7320; www.boat houserestaurants.ca. Seafood is the toast of the town at the Boathouse. The restaurant serves whichever seafood is in season: In spring you'll find shrimp; crab in fall; and lobster in winter. Summer brings an eclectic selection of halibut, salmon, and other feasts. A third-level patio offers a lower-priced menu, younger feel, and the best views, while a glassed-in second level provides a more upscale service and diverse menu. On the ground level, the Surfside Bar and Grill also serves ocean favorites. Open for weekend brunch and daily for lunch and dinner. $$–$$$$.

Giraffe Restaurant. 15053 Marine Dr., White Rock; (604) 538-6878; www.thegiraffe .com. Across from the historic White Rock Pier, the flower boxes and vine-wrapped patio of Giraffe inflect a touch of garden-tropical to this seaside stretch during summer. Seafood including sea bass, halibut, and Dungeness crab complement landlubber feasts and polished service. Open for lunch Thurs to Sat, for Sun brunch, and daily for dinner. $$–$$$.

Uli's. 15021 Marine Dr., White Rock; (604) 538-9373; www.ulisrestaurant.com. In a patio standoff, Uli's is in the running for its large deck. A diverse menu manages to encompass seafood (salmon), German cuisine (schnitzel), and pub favorites (bourbon chicken). The owner, Uli himself, is known to welcome guests, and the joint rates as one of the more economical choices on the strip. All this without sacrificing a sliver of view. Open Tues to Sun for lunch and dinner. $$–$$$.

where to stay

Dancing Firs. 13894 Terry Rd., White Rock; (604) 538-3835 or (888) 604-3835; www .dancingfirs.com. Private entrances make this hilltop retreat a true escape. Three rooms cater to those looking for quiet and relaxation with in-suite cappuccino machines, stocked pantries, fireplaces, and Nikken wellness systems that ensure excellent water, air, and rest. Lush Pacific Northwest gardens offer berries and panoramic vistas. The tall, top-heavy Douglas firs on the waterside of the property sway like a slow pendulum. And that feeling of time slowed down permeates the day, from the stunning views of soft sunrises to fiery sunsets. $$$$.

Sunset Harbour Bed and Breakfast. 1353 Everall St., White Rock; (604) 531-8353 or (888) 531-8353; www.sunsetharbourbb.com. Fives rooms, all with bathrooms, provide comfort with a twist of international decor. While the Canton Suite's rich colors are most popular, I prefer the lightness and finery of the elegant Bangkok Suite. A large common area includes couches and an outdoor patio. An elevator makes the guest areas accessible, while the views from the breakfast room shine on a clear day. $$$.

border crossing

U.S. citizens require a valid passport, NEXUS card, U.S. Passport Card, or enhanced driver's license to enter Canada. Keep in mind there are restrictions on the goods you can bring into the country—particularly when it comes to fruit, vegetables, dairy, and meat products. As different regulations surround firearms, leave guns in the United States, either at home or in a storage facility.

Taking a detour to the SR 543 border crossing, also known as the truck crossing, can often save minutes. Watch for highway signage giving updated border-crossing times or tune into local radio.

Heaviest weekend traffic is, predictably, from about 9 a.m. to 8 p.m. with the peak around noon. Southbound waits, according to WSDOT's average travel delays reports, are often longer than northbound. That means allowing extra time for the homeward journey.

steveston

Steveston delivers a grounded charm that only an oceanside town built around an industry, such as the fisheries, can offer. Fishing boats sell fresh catches from the village marina, restaurant patios line the waterfront, and there are parks and historic sites to visit. Although officially part of Richmond, Steveston is set apart as an entirely distinct village.

getting there

From White Rock, return along Marine Drive and Eighth Avenue to Hwy. 99. At exit 32, take the Steveston Highway west towards the village.

Alternately, head north along Johnston Road, which turns into 152nd Street before meeting with the 99. Cross farmlands and the Fraser River before reaching Richmond and taking the Steveston Highway west.

From the Steveston Highway, take a left onto the No. 1 Road and head south to the waterfront Bayview Street, for a total travel time of about 35 minutes.

where to go

Britannia Heritage Shipyard. 5180 Westwater Dr., Steveston; (604) 718-8050; www .britannia-hss.ca. Discover a historic collection of shipyards, old canneries, and stilt houses. See wooden vessels mid-restoration and birdlife from the shore while you walk the planks of an old boardwalk. Open Tues to Sun in summer; weekends only the remainder of the year. $.

Garry Point Park. 12011 7th Ave., Steveston; (604) 244-1208 (general parks line); www .richmond.ca/asp/parks/park.asp?ID=17. The park connects a waterfront walk to trails over marsh and dike lands. Summer weekends see the skies filled with kites, including those attached to zippy ground buggies. Although there is a nice sandy beach in the park, it is closed to swimmers.

Gulf of Georgia Cannery National Historic Site. 12138 Fourth Ave., Steveston; (604) 664-9009; www.gulfofgeorgiacannery.com. The smells of fish oil and engine grease still waft from the floorboards of this historic cannery. For decades the cannery produced herring meal and canned salmon. Today exhibits re-create the process using imagination and machinery left behind when the cannery was abandoned in the 1980s. Open daily May to Aug; call ahead for off-peak season hours. $$.

London Heritage Farm. 6511 Dyke Rd., Richmond; (604) 271-5220; www.londonheritage farm.ca. A farmhouse, gardens, and agricultural equipment take visitors back to the 1880s. Tea and scones in the tearoom make a snack to savor. Hours vary, but the farmhouse is generally open on weekends. Admission free, about $9 for tea and cakes. $$.

Steveston Museum and Post Office. 3811 Moncton St., Richmond; (604) 271-6868; www.richmond.ca/culture/sites/steveston.htm. The 1905 building has had many incarnations over the years: a bank, a doctor's office, and today a post office and museum. Too bad the museum doesn't have talking walls. Regardless, various displays on Steveston life tell the ever-changing tale of this waterfront village. Closed Sun.

where to eat

Blue Canoe Waterfront Restaurant. 140-3866 Bayview St.; (604) 275-7811; www.blue canoerestaurant.com. A step further and you'd be in the ocean. Blue Canoe delivers a hip atmosphere amidst steak and seafood favorites. A bonus: From the patio you can see the docked fishing boats selling the daily fresh catch. Open daily for lunch and dinner. $$–$$$.

Dave's Fish & Chips. 3460 Moncton St., Steveston; (604) 271-7555. There's an eternal local debate about the best fish-and-chips in town. Dave's chalks up a number of local readers' choice awards after more than three decades of battering. Have your pick of fish from salmon, cod, and halibut. Scallops, clams, and oysters are also available. Open daily. $$.

Pajo's the Wharf. The Wharf, Steveston; (604) 272-1588; www.pajos.com. The other front-runner in the great fish-and-chips debate, Pajo's has four locations, with two in Richmond. A nice option—for the very hungry—includes a piece each of cod, halibut, and salmon. The dock location is unbeatable, while the Garry Point Park location complements a walk in the park with fresh-air dining. No credit cards. Open daily in peak season and weather permitting the rest of the year. $$.

where to stay

Doorknocker Bed and Breakfast. 13211 Steveston Hwy., Steveston; (604) 277-8714 or (866) 877-8714; www.thedoorknocker.com. Three comfort-focused guest rooms exude an air of modern European styling. Beautiful and deluxe amenities worthy of coveting include a heated indoor pool, cedar sauna, and a hot tub. Hot breakfasts complement the owner's impressive, vibrant artworks. *Important note:* In late 2009, bylaws threw the operation of B&Bs in Richmond into question, demanding rezoning or reducing the number of guests to just two. As such, the Doorknocker may be closed, so please call ahead or check the Web site. $$$.

richmond

Head north from Steveston (in Vancouver that means driving towards the mountains) and you enter the bustle of a modern Chinatown. Markets, shopping centers, and Olympic venues are all top places to visit in Richmond, but the restaurants are perhaps the pick of the town. Endless varieties of Asian cuisine offer an immersion experience where menus are often written in both coarsely translated English and Chinese characters.

getting there

The shopping and dining areas of Richmond center around No. 3 Road. Travel east on the Steveston Highway then take the No. 3 Road north into the heart of Richmond—about 10 minutes from Steveston.

where to go

Richmond Olympic Oval. 6111 River Rd., Richmond; (778) 296-1400; www.richmond oval.ca. The Richmond Olympic Oval hosted speed skating events for the 2010 Olympic Winter Games and Paralympics. Its post-Games redesign includes two skating rinks and eight gymnasiums. The building alone is a marvel: The wave-design roof is constructed using wood damaged by the pine beetle. Drop-in day passes available. $$$.

Richmond Summer Night Market. 12631 Vulcan Way, Richmond; (604) 278-8000; www .summernightmarket.com. Enjoy all the bustle of a Hong Kong market without the price of the plane ticket. The night market runs on Fridays, Saturdays, Sundays, and holidays during the summer months; it features endless vendors selling gimmicks, gadgetry, and garments. Arrive with lots of time to browse and snack on the food.

where to shop

Aberdeen Centre. 4151 Hazelbridge Way, Richmond; (604) 270-1234; www.aberdeen centre.com. With stores like the legendary Daiso (a Japanese dollar store, or 100-yen store) and curious VooDoo Palace, Aberdeen Centre makes for an entirely unique shopping experience. A large food court offers many styles of Asian cooking at great value. Open daily.

where to eat

HK BBQ Master. 145-4651 No. 3 Rd., Richmond; (604) 272-6568. Tucked in an unlikely spot beneath a grocery store, head here for mouth-watering barbecue duck, pork, or free-range chicken. Order by the meal or by the bird. Cash only. $–$$.

Neptune Seafood Restaurant. 100-8171 Ackroyd Rd., Richmond; (604) 207-9888. Look for amazing chili prawns and other seafood treats on the menu. The dim sum draws regulars as does the polished, prompt service. Lots of family seating. $$–$$$.

day trip 05

north

>>> **olympic city:**
vancouver

vancouver

Having hosted the 2010 Winter Olympics, Vancouver has catapulted into the spotlight as a world-class city for its scenery and facilities. In summer the city's expansive parks welcome hikers and outdoorsy folk, while in winter it's time to head to the ski hills. Year-round cultural highlights include theaters, concerts, and art galleries.

Each neighborhood is practically a day trip in itself. Shop and people-watch at the beach in Kitsilano before heading to one of the local museums by transit ferry. The University of British Columbia campus gardens, the world-class Museum of Anthropology, and beaches create a lively community. In the downtown district excellent restaurants demonstrate Vancouver's culinary diversity and pair nicely with an amble through historic Gastown.

getting there

With the fate-decided blessings of a quick border crossing, I-5 followed by Hwy. 99 leads directly to Vancouver in a little over 2 hours (about 140 miles). From there, explore the city's many neighborhoods by ferry, foot, or transit.

Alternately, opt for a four-hour journey on the Amtrak Cascades train (800-872-7245; www.amtrak.com). The route proves easier than driving and is ideal for those spending a weekend in the city without worrying about parking.

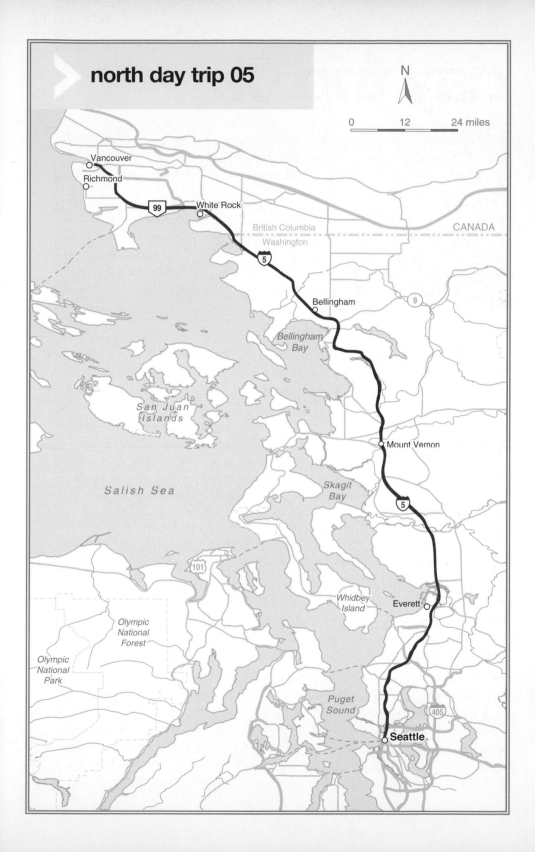

north day trip 05

N

0   12   24 miles

Vancouver
Richmond
99   White Rock
British Columbia
Washington
CANADA
5
9
Bellingham
Bellingham
Bay
San Juan
Islands
Mount Vernon
Salish Sea
Skagit
Bay
5
101
Whidbey
Island   Everett
Olympic
National
Forest
Olympic
National
Park
Puget
Sound   405
Seattle

where to go

Tourism Vancouver Visitor Centre. Plaza Level, 200 Burrard St., Vancouver; (604) 683-2000; www.tourismvancouver.com. With lots of staff members, the visitor center is able to assist in directing visitors to attractions, booking accommodations, and providing information. Look for the nearby Tickets Tonight booth that offers great deals on Vancouver-area performances. Open daily.

Granville Island. Beneath the Granville Street Bridge, Vancouver; (604) 666-5784; www.granvilleisland.com. This once-industrial district transformed into a center for independent merchants and fine-art studios during the 1970s. Although the cement plant still holds fast to the industrial days, a vibrant, year-round public market (open daily), theater district, public art, and marinas have revitalized the atmosphere. Take a ferry from downtown (False Creek Ferries and the rainbow-colored Aquabus both transit to the island) and then explore the alleys of artists, restaurant patios, and kid-friendly parks.

Kitsilano Beach. Arbutus Street at Cornwall Street, Vancouver; (604) 257-8400 (City of Vancouver); http://vancouver.ca/Parks/rec/beaches/kitsb.htm. *Forbes Traveler* named Kitsilano Beach one of North America's sexiest. But with a large outdoor saltwater pool and grassy areas perfect for playing bocce or spreading out a picnic, Kits is also a haven for those still in touch with the eternal, internal child of summer. The beach is also within walking distance of some of Vancouver's finest museums: Museum of Vancouver (1100 Chestnut St.; 604-736-4431; www.museumofvancouver.ca); HR MacMillan Space Centre (1100 Chestnut St.; 604-738-7827; www.hrmacmillanspacecentre.com); and Vancouver Maritime Museum (1905 Ogden Ave.; 604-257-8300; www.vancouvermaritimemuseum.com).

Museum of Anthropology. 6393 Northwest Marine Dr., Vancouver; (604) 822-5087; www.moa.ubc.ca. Totems stand like trees in a forest at this top-quality museum. Between the carvings, ceramics, and tapestries from around the world, and from the Northwest in particular, large walls of glass occasionally provide forest, mountain, or ocean views. Open daily during summer; closed Mon mid-Oct through mid-May. $$$.

Queen Elizabeth Park. West 33rd and Cambie Street, Vancouver; www.vancouver.ca/parks/parks/queenelizabeth. Attractions in Queen Elizabeth Park include fountains, walking trails, an arboretum, and the Bloedel Conservatory—which was threatened with closure as this book goes to press. In the conservatory, the humid tropical zone creates a vastly different ecosystem than the typical Pacific Northwest climate. Chattering parrots and cockatoos, opera performances by guest artists, and vibrant flowers all create a unique wonderland. Inside and out the conservatory makes a stunning photo opportunity thanks to the softly arcing triodetic dome of glass. Also in the neighborhood are the curling rinks at the Vancouver Olympic Centre, the baseball diamonds at Nat Bailey Stadium (4601 Ontario St.; 604-872-5232; www.canadiansbaseball.com), and more plants at VanDusen

Botanical Garden (5251 Oak St.; 604-257-8665; www.vancouver.ca/parks/parks). Open daily year-round. $.

Science World. 1455 Quebec St., Vancouver; (604) 443-7443; www.scienceworld.ca. This alien-looking sphere houses kid- and adult-friendly science exhibits that engage inquiring minds. Despite a hefty admission charge, head inside for many hours of exploring, IMAX films, and experiments. A message to adults: Just remember to let the kids have a turn. Occasionally that is. Open daily. $$$.

Stanley Park. West Georgia Street, Vancouver. www.vancouver.ca/parks/parks/stanley. A 5.5-mile seawall wraps the park, giving walkers, runners, bikers, and in-line skaters access to acres of forest, ocean, and mountain views as well as historic sites and Vancouver's best beaches. The Malkin Bowl hosts summer concerts, the rose garden is the sweetest in bloom, and the ecology society's Nature House, provides keen insight into the habitat of this urban park.

Vancouver Aquarium. 845 Avison Way, Vancouver; (604) 659-3474; www.vanaqua.org. Belugas, dolphins, sea lions, and otters are the main attractions at the aquarium, but the large tanks of fish, coral, and octopi equally mesmerize. Clownfish Cove play area offers great distractions for younger children to make the aquarium a day-long adventure. Located in Stanley Park, the aquarium pioneered the Ocean Wise program to highlight sustainable seafood options at local restaurants—ask for information before heading out to dinner. Open daily. $$$.

Vancouver Art Gallery. 750 Hornby St., Vancouver; (604) 662-4719; www.vanartgallery.bc .ca. Drawing from a strong permanent collection, the Vancouver Art Gallery hosts multiple exhibits each year. Arthur Erickson, one of Vancouver's preeminent architects, transformed the building from a courthouse into the present-day gallery. Open daily with family admission options. $$$.

Vancouver Police Museum. 240 East Cordova St., Vancouver; (604) 665-3346; www .vancouverpolicemuseum.ca. Displays that include confiscated weapons and counterfeit currency are set in a former morgue. The museum has a strangely wide appeal, drawing on a curiosity surrounding death and danger. Closed Sun. $$.

Wreck Beach. Northwest Marine Drive at University Boulevard, Vancouver. The infamous local nudist beach, Wreck Beach endures thanks to its community spirit. Open year-round.

where to shop

Robson Street. From Burrard Street through to Denman Street, window-shopping on Robson serves up storefront after storefront of style. From shoes and clothing to souvenirs, you'll find it all available daily in this top urban shopping district.

West Fourth Avenue. Drawing on the hip vibe of Kitsilano, stores such as the first Lululemon, organics-focused Capers, and innovative clothiers Skylar's and Gravitypope make this street one long but varied shopping excursion.

where to eat

The Gallery Café. 750 Hornby St., Vancouver; (604) 688-2233; www.thegallerycafe.ca. Strong elements of casual, fresh food complement the garden-gallery atmosphere. As sparrows hop below the tables, corporate and visiting diners serve themselves cafeteria style. Soups, sandwiches, salads, and quiches pair nicely with a latte or a glass of wine. Open for breakfast, lunch, and weekday dinners. $–$$.

Japadog. 530 Robson St., Vancouver; www.japadog.com. A new take on the hot dog, these wieners come topped with nori, mashed potatoes, wasabi, or miso—just to name a few of the eyebrow-raising ingredients employed in these Japanese-style hot dogs. The lines are long, but the prices are reasonable and the unique factor unbeatable. And, after years as a street-side vendor, Japadog opened its first restaurant in spring 2010. Cash only. $.

The Sandbar. 1535 Johnston St., Granville Island, Vancouver; (604) 669-9030; www.vancouverdine.com. The glass-walled dining room reveals beautiful views of Yaletown and False Creek. The menu is imbued with an international flair, whether it is the wok squid or seafood hot pot. Open daily for lunch and dinner as well as weekend brunch. $$–$$$$.

Tojo's Restaurant. 1133 West Broadway, Vancouver; (604) 872-8050; www.tojos.com. In Vancouver, you have the option of the $6 sushi special (which can be found in almost every city block) or fine-dining sashimi. At Tojo's—one of Vancouver's finest sushi restaurants—you'll find the latter. Opt for *omakase,* where the chef creates your dinner and you simply enjoy. Or choose a selection of sashimi, sushi rolls, and tempura. Open daily for dinner, except closed on Sun. $$$–$$$$.

Vij's. 1480 West 11th Ave., Vancouver; (604) 736-6664; www.vijs.ca. This no-reservations restaurant is famous for its lamb popsicles, spot-on service, and scrumptious wait-line appetizers. It's been lauded by the *New York Times* and featured on Anthony Bourdain's *No Reservations.* Open daily for dinner—visit the next door Rangoli for lunch items and lower prices. No reservations accepted. $$$.

where to stay

The Sylvia Hotel. 1154 Gilford St., Vancouver; (604) 681-9321; www.sylviahotel.com. Close to Stanley Park and English Bay, this historic hotel rates as one of Vancouver's best for personality and charm. Each room is different—some have kitchens while others are budget options. In any season the creeper on the brick-and-stone exterior creates a color sensation. A restaurant and lounge serves everything from breakfast through to evening

> ## vancouver olympics

In February and March 2010, Vancouver hosted the Winter Olympics and Para-lympics in conjunction with Whistler. The games showcased the amazing skiing and snowboarding opportunities in the area as well as the stunning panoramas of mountains and aqua-blue glacial lakes.

Today, Olympic venues have transformed into community facilities where you can ski or skate in the same tracks as world-record holders.

For a longer trip, head north along the Sea-to-Sky Highway to Whistler. End-less hiking trails, river rafting, wildlife watching, and wilderness cabins deliver the irresistible Pacific Northwest scenery at provincial parks like Garibaldi and Joffre Lakes. As a bonus, the traffic and trail use will be lighter than many Washington wil-derness areas.

cocktails. Kids will enjoy the tales of Mr. Got To Go—a stubborn cat who inspired a series of children's books that are available for reading in the lobby. $$–$$$$.

A TreeHouse Bed and Breakfast. 2490 West 49th Ave., Vancouver; (604) 266-2962 or (877) 266-2960; www.treehousebb.com. Rich colors and comfy furniture make the four rooms a haven from travel. Away from the traffic of downtown yet close to all the attrac-tions (by transit or car), the TreeHouse B&B has long been a favorite of visitors. An atypical B&B, it has an Asian-modern decor in the common areas, and glass walls create a bright space. The rooms offer privacy and a little more independence than is standard at most inns. $$–$$$.

northeast

>>>

day trip 01

>>> **wine country:**
woodinville, snohomish

Fine wines and aged antiques draw visitors to Woodinville and Snohomish. Wineries and tasting rooms seem to appear at an ever-quickening pace, with a count of more than forty as this book goes to print. Each has different hours and different varietals to taste. Venture into the expansive grounds of Chateau Ste. Michelle, a small family winery, or the lone beer brewery in town.

Heading north to Snohomish, hot air balloons rise above SR 9, and Mount Rainier lingers in view on a clear day. Known as the Antique Capital of the Northwest, Snohomish delivers as promised: a pretty town swept up in the finery of yesteryear.

woodinville

Arriving in the winery heartland of Woodinville, the road curves down to a wooded area and opens up into views of Mount Rainier behind expansive wineries. Chateau Ste. Michelle started the boom in the wine region when it opened its doors to a French-style chateau in 1976. With so many tasting rooms to explore, Woodinville endures as a regional favorite. Tasting fees can range from nothing to about $10 and are often waived with purchase.

From romantic escapes to brewery tours (yes, there's beer here too) and bicycle rides through the landscape, Woodinville is a spot to take things slowly.

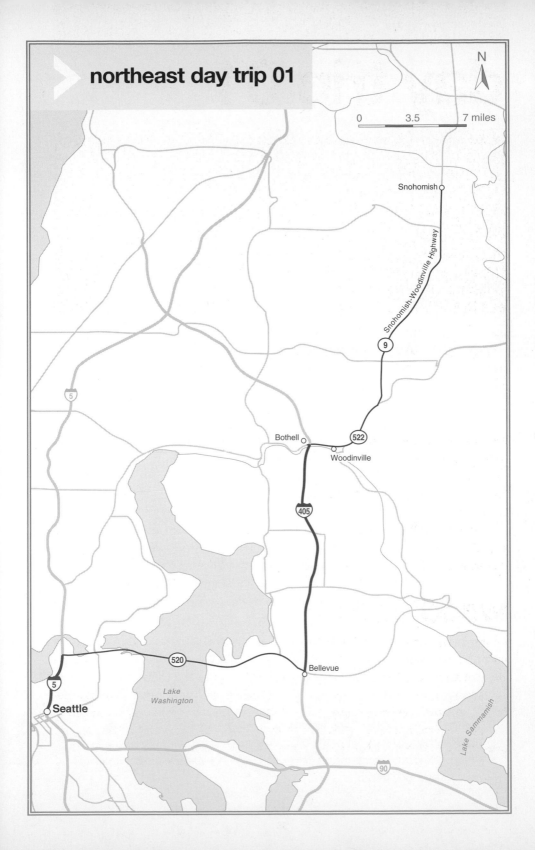

N

0   3.5   7 miles

Snohomish

Snohomish-Woodinville Highway

9

522

Bothell

Woodinville

405

I 5

520

Bellevue

5

Seattle

Lake
Washington

Lake Sammamish

90

getting there

To Woodinville, cross Lake Washington then head north on I-405 to the junction with SR 522 at exit 23. Head briefly east on SR 522 then take the exit for SR 202 leading into Woodinville.

   To reach Snohomish, the Snohomish-Woodinville Road connects with SR 9, providing a beeline route to Snohomish.

where to go

Hollywood Schoolhouse. 14810 Northeast 145th St., Woodinville; (425) 481-7925; www .hollywoodschoolhouse.com. This state historical monument is a handsome brick building that now operates as an event facility with wine tasting rooms.

Redhook Brewery Tours. 14300 Northeast 145th St., Woodinville; (425) 483-3232; www .redhook.com. Amidst one of the densest areas of Washington wine country, Redhook Brewery stands alone with its ales. Offering daily tours (usually in the afternoons) for a nominal price, the large brewery makes a nice taste addition to the local wines. $.

Woodinville Wineries. For the most up-to-date and comprehensive listings (without contacting each winery individually) check with **Woodinville Wine Country.** (425) 205-4394; www.woodinvillewinecountry.com.

   Woodinville is home to dozens of wineries. Here's a listing of some noteworthy Woodinville wineries that are *regularly open for public tastings.* You can find contact details on additional wineries on the Woodinville Wine Country Web site, mentioned above.

   Chateau Ste. Michelle. 14111 Northeast 145th St., Woodinville; (425) 415-3300; www.ste-michelle.com. The largest winery in Woodinville, and in fact the largest in the state, Chateau Ste. Michelle excels at entertaining its visitors. In addition to tasting, visitors can explore the expansive grounds, catch a summer concert, or indulge in a special dinner. At the same location you'll also find **Domain Ste. Michelle** (425-415-3657 or 866-701-3187; www.domaine-ste-michelle.com), which produces delightful champagne-style sparkling wines. Open daily.

   Columbia Winery. 14030 Northeast 145th St., Woodinville; (425) 482-7490; www .columbiawinery.com. The region's largest tasting room is also a slick, modern space that exudes charm and cool. A turret and ornate eaves of the tasting room building retain a touch of history to complement the wines. Open daily.

   Dusted Valley Vintners Tasting Gallery. 14465 Woodinville-Redmond Rd. Northeast, Woodinville; (425) 488-7373; www.dustedvalley.com. The casual, fun atmosphere complements the family-focused winery operations based in the Walla Walla Valley. Open daily.

Januik/Novelty Hill Winery. 14710 Woodinville-Redmond Rd. Northeast, Woodinville; (425) 481-5502; www.noveltyhilljanuik.com. Two wineries share an ultra-modern space. On weekends, order a brick oven pizza to complement the wine. Open daily.

Matthews Estate. 16116 140th Place Northeast, Woodinville; (425) 487-9810; www.matthewsestate.com. With cooking classes, music, and social evenings, the Matthews Estate cellar becomes a happening spot. The winery is centrally located, but there is also a warehouse tasting bar out of the fray (19495 144th Ave Northeast, A-120). Winery open daily; tasting bar open Sat and Sun.

Silver Lake Winery. 15029-A Woodinville-Redmond Rd., Woodinville; (425) 485-2437; www.silverlakewinery.com. Since releasing its first vintage in 1989, this winery has only grown as a favorite. Open daily.

Woodhouse Family Cellars. 15500 Woodinville-Redmond Rd., Suite C600, Woodinville; (425) 527-0608; www.woodhousefamilycellars.com. Woodhouse is better known as five separate labels: Maghee, Hudson • Shah, Dussek, Darighe, and Kennedy Shah. Open daily.

For more tasting, and less traveling, head north to 19501 144th Ave. Northeast. At this one address, you'll find more than a dozen wineries and tasting rooms including **Alexandria Nicole Cellars** (Suite C-900; 425-483-2968; www.alexandria nicolecellars.com), **Anton Ville Winery** (Suite D300; 206-683-3393; www.antonville winery.com), **Des Voigne Cellars** (Suite B500; 206-478-3231; www.desvoigne cellars.com), and **Patterson Cellars/Washington Wine Company** (Suite D600; 425-483-8600; www.pattersoncellars.com).

where to eat

Barking Frog Restaurant. 14580 Northeast 145th St., Woodinville; (425) 424-2999; www .willowslodge.com. Food with a casual Northwest flair complements the local wine offerings at the restaurant. An outdoor deck is open to diners in summer, while a fire pit keeps the restaurant cozy in winter. Prompt service and a creative, affordable menu make dining here a fun experience. Open daily for breakfast, lunch, and dinner. $$–$$$.

The Herbfarm. 14590 Northeast 145th St., Woodinville; (425) 485.5300; www.theherb farm.com. This pastel bungalow is a world-class destination restaurant. Offering set nine-course menus that are inspired by what's in season, the restaurant has received accolades from endless publications including *National Geographic, Zagat,* and top wine magazines. A local wine pairing accompanies each course, and all the menus draw on the fresh local produce and bounty from the restaurant's kitchen garden. Reservations are a must. $$$$.

where to stay

Willows Lodge. 14580 Northeast 145th St., Woodinville; (425) 424-3900 or (877) 424-3930; www.willowslodge.com. With more than eighty rooms, the lodge is perfectly positioned to facilitate a weekend in wine country. Rent bicycles, stroll to a neighboring winery, meet the lodge dog, relax at the spa, or cozy up around the outdoor fire pit. The staff takes great care to be welcoming to guests and their pets. $$$$.

washington wine countries

If Washington wine has captured your taste buds, there are a few other regions in the state to swill, taste, and spit the day away. The Washington wine region outside Yakima offers the bulk of winery tours in the state (Southeast Day Trip 03), and its rich agricultural lands are also a major source of grapes for wineries around the state. Or venture to Leavenworth (East Day Trip 03) where more wineries produce fine-quality wines in a Bavarian setting. You'll also find a small selection of wineries on Vashon Island (Southwest Day Trip 01).

snohomish

As the Antique Capital of the Northwest, Snohomish rates as a top place to search for rare china, hunt out a bargain, and discover treasures. But the small town also offers lovely park walks, dining on the riverbanks, and a well-maintained community museum.

where to go

Visitor Information Center. 1301 First St., Snohomish; (360) 862-9609; www.snohomish vic.com. An easy-to-find visitor center offers advice and antique guides on the way into town. Open daily.

Blackman House Museum. 118 Ave. B, Snohomish; (360) 568-5235; www.blackman house.org. Built in 1878, this historical-society-run museum displays furniture and household items belonging to the house's first owners—Hyrcanus and Ella Blackman—as well as other Snohomish settlers. Open weekends; Sun only Jan to Apr. A small donation covers tea, cookies, and a tour. $.

where to shop

Because Snohomish is nicknamed the Antique Capital of the Northwest, it's tough to turn around in town without fixing your gaze on an appealing antique treasure. A walk through downtown offers the greatest concentration of shops. **Legends Antiques and Clocks** (905 First St.; 360-568-1820) focuses on timepieces and is easy to find thanks to a gilt-and-green street clock outside. **Star Center Antique Mall** (829 Second St.; 360-568-2131) opens daily and features 200 dealers in its multiple levels. **Antique Warehouse** (1019 First St.; 360-568-7590) assembles an eclectic mix of antiques, all of which are clearly priced. No doubt you'll discover many other prized spots.

where to eat

Cabbage Patch Restaurant & Catering. 111 Ave. A, Snohomish; (360) 568-9091; www .cabbagepatchrestaurant.com. Set in a single-dwelling home, this restaurant serves all manner of eats. From lemon caper chicken and hand-cut filet mignon to the home-style turkey dinner, meat loaf, or pot roast, the fare is heart warming. Open daily for breakfast, lunch, and dinner. $$–$$$.

The Repp. 924 First St., Snohomish; (360) 568-3928; www.therepp.com. Exposed brick, cool-toned wood, and dark beams give an urban feel without losing the olden-times style of the town. Seafood and steaks are the prime picks, but booth seating at the Repp also makes it a casual spot for appetizers and a drink. Open daily for dinner, except closed Mon. $$–$$$.

Snohomish Bakery Cafe. 920 First St., Snohomish; (360) 568-1682; www.snohomish bakery.com. Hearth-oven pizzas are the headliner at the Snohomish Bakery Cafe. Serving from breakfast through an early dinner daily, the cozy cafe sits on the main street. Perfect for a quick morning bite or a fuel up before returning home. Open daily for breakfast and lunch, closing most days at 5 to 6 p.m. $–$$.

day trip 02

>>> **roos, rails, and rivers:**
arlington, sedro-woolley, concrete

From Arlington and Sedro-Woolley, not far from Seattle, to the unromantically named but quaint town of Concrete, which verges on the Cascades, this day trip explores the easy reaches of SR 20, also known as the North Cascades Highway and part of the Cascade Loop Scenic Highway. Logging, railroad, and pioneer history abound amidst the steam engines and stump houses. But just before the region becomes too industrial, you can extend the stay with an escape to a perfect forest location at River Rock Inn, with wine tasting, or with a locally brewed pint at the Birdsview Brewery.

It's not the most glamorous of day trips but the raw history, the few gems of attractions, and ever-friendly locals make a visit here a worthwhile trip.

arlington

The lumber town of Arlington serves as a commuter city that retains its history. The main street, Olympic Avenue, parallels railroad tracks, and Arlington serves as an excellent home base for exploring all points north- and eastward.

Within the area you'll find a kangaroo farm, a delightful B&B, and a preserved stump house—a small home fashioned from a giant hollowed-out tree stump.

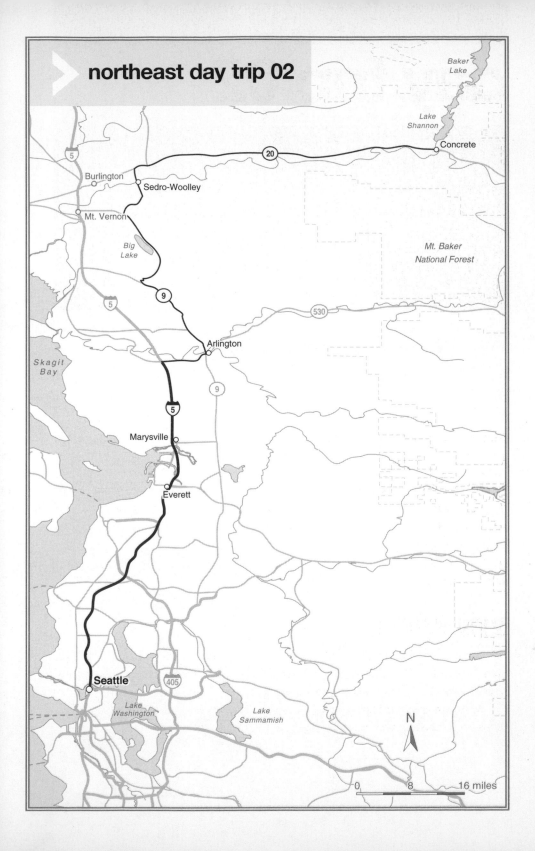

Baker
Lake

Lake
Shannon

5

20

Concrete

Burlington

Sedro-Woolley

Mt. Vernon

Big
Lake

Mt. Baker
National Forest

5

9

530

Skagit
Bay

Arlington

9

5

Marysville

Everett

Seattle

405

Lake
Washington

Lake
Sammamish

N

0   8   16 miles

getting there

I-5 north provides near-direct access to Arlington. After traveling 43 miles on I-5, take exit 206 and head east on 172nd Street Northeast, then north on 67th Avenue Northeast. Or take simply take exit 208 off I-5 and follow SR 530.

where to go

North Snohomish County Branch. 3710 168th St. Northeast, Suite C101, Arlington (I-5 exit 206); (360) 657-2326; www.snohomish.org. For details of local accommodations and attractions, head to this visitor information center. Open daily, although it is reliant on volunteers so hours are variable.

Outback Christmas Tree and Kangaroo Farm. 10030 SR 530 Northeast, Arlington; (360) 403-7474; www.christmastreesandroos.com. The farm is home to all manner of marsupials including wallabies, kangaroos, and wallaroos. Forty-minute tours of the farm also introduce you to the resident lemurs, llamas, donkeys, parrots, and other animals. Open for 'roo tours Wed to Sun, Mar through Oct; open daily after Thanksgiving for Christmas trees. Call ahead to check the schedule. $$.

Stillaguamish Valley Pioneer Museum. 20722 67th Ave. Northeast, Arlington; (360) 435-7289; www.stillymuseum.org. Looking out over its namesake river—nicknamed the Stilly—this pioneer museum harbors a treasure trove of old photos, animal mounts, and artifacts. From music to military items and histories of the dairy and logging industries, the museum captures the past in its displays. Outside, the museum gardens, a totem pole, and the waterways of Pioneer Park provide more to explore. A preserved stump house sits roadside. What's that, you ask? A stump house takes its foundation from a giant hollowed-out tree stump with a roof and perhaps windows added above the cut line. This particular stump was once used as a photography studio. The museum opens Wed, Sat, and Sun, although call ahead for hours as it closes Nov to Feb; small admission fee for adults and children. $$.

where to stay

River Rock Inn. 15425 133rd Ave. Northeast, Arlington; (360) 403-7014; www.riverrockin nbnb.com. This tranquil, hidden spot is situated amidst calling birds and grazing deer. The deluxe rooms and on-site couples spa may make this one of Washington's best B&Bs. The Great Room is truly that, with vaulted ceilings, a central fireplace, and garden views. Each room has a subtle, natural theme, while private dinners and a complimentary snack bar will easily turn one night into many. $$$–$$$$.

sedro-woolley

Proud of its logging heritage, Sedro-Woolley's main street is lined with amber-toned chain-saw carvings from its annual competitions. The local museum and a display steam engine reiterate the area's previous prosperity as a lumber center.

getting there

From Arlington, SR 9 leads north 27 miles to Sedro-Woolley. Although I-5 is an alternate route, SR 9 passes the shores of McMurray, Big, and Clear Lakes, which is far better than interstate exits.

where to go

Harry Osborne Park. SR 20 and Ferry Street, Sedro-Woolley. An old steam-train locomotive and Douglas fir log slice dating to a.d. 1102 are the centerpieces of this quick stop. Harry Osborne Park's visitor center has been closed for some time, so chances are you'll have the place to yourself. No admission or set hours, but visitors can explore anyway.

Mount Baker–Snoqualmie National Forest—Mount Baker Office. 810 SR 20, Sedro-Woolley; (360) 856-5700. Open weekdays, this office provides thorough and friendly hiking advice.

Sedro-Woolley Museum. 725 Murdock St., Sedro-Woolley; (360) 855-2390; www .sedrowoolleymuseum.org. The museum presents a minitown series of exhibits, including re-creations of businesses: a dentist, blacksmith, firehouse, and bank. A model-train layout and old autos add interest for rail and car enthusiasts. Open Wed, Thurs, Sat, and Sun. $.

the marriage of two towns

Sedro and Woolley originally stood apart as two independent, and even rival, lumber towns. Sedro is a variation on the Spanish word for cedar (cedra), while Woolley is named for town founder Philip Woolley.

Tough economic times forced the towns to consider merging, which they officially did in 1898. Unable to agree on one name, the towns opted to adopt a hyphenated version incorporating both: Sedro-Woolley.

where to eat

Hometown Cafe. 818 Metcalf St., Sedro-Woolley; (360) 855-5012. You'll get a genuine hometown welcome at this classic main-street diner. Pies, coffee refills, and friendly locals fit perfectly with the booths and diner menu. Open daily for breakfast and lunch; Mon to Sat for dinner. $–$$.

concrete

Concrete teases you with the Cascades while providing a snapshot of its industrial history. Named for its production of cement, the town is a capsule of the past. While the town itself offers limited attractions, the local area includes a top-quality winery, quiet state park, and local brewery.

getting there

From Sedro-Woolley, head east on SR 20 for 24 miles to reach Concrete.

where to go

Challenger Ridge Vineyard & Cellars. 43095 Challenger Rd., Concrete; (425) 422-6988; www.challengerridge.com. This beautiful winery is adjacent to SR 20, Skagit River, and acres of vines. The former farmhouse welcomes wine tasters, and Pinot Noir aficionados in particular. Open weekends for tasting.

Concrete Heritage Museum. 7380 Thompson Ave., Concrete; (360) 853-7042; www .stumpranchonline.com/concreteheritagemuseum. The museum runs summertime tours on its Sockeye Express—a train-bus on wheels. Head inside to discover the rich roots of the town, which include logging and, of course, cement. Call ahead for hours. $.

Rasar State Park. 38730 Cape Horn Rd., Concrete; www.parks.wa.gov. Alongside the Skagit River, Rasar State Park offers camping, fishing, and restrooms. Riverside, forest, and field trails provide about 4 miles of hiking in total. But the kid's play area and the picnic area make a nice complement of facilities for families. Open daily.

where to eat

Birdsview Brewing Company. 38302 SR 20, Concrete; (360) 826-3406; www.birdsview brewingco.com. Concrete itself offers little choice in terms of restaurants, but west of town Birdsview Brewing houses a deli with sandwiches and burgers. You'll find nine beers on tap and occasionally additional seasonal brews. The octagonal building is easy to spot with lots of parking. Open daily for lunch and dinner, except closed Mon. $–$$.

day trip 03

northeast

>>> **kerouac country:**
rockport, marblemount, newhalem,
diablo to north cascades national park

Over just 65 miles, this stretch of the North Cascades Highway (SR 20) climbs from barely above sea level to the heights of Washington Pass (5,477 feet). On the way, snowy peaks top evergreen forests surrounding farmlands and recreational lakes. Each season brings something special to this region: the opening of the highway in spring; wildflowers in summer; salmon runs in fall; and eagle watching in winter.

The core of North Cascades National Park is the trio of glacial lakes, each paired with a power-generating dam. Canoe the lakes, hike to the peaks, immerse yourself in an outdoor classroom, hear the hum of the power lines, or lodge at a floating cabin—all within the confines of one of the nation's least-visited national parks.

In these mountains, American writer Jack Kerouac spent sixty-thee days as a fire watcher. His experiences on the lookout atop Desolation Peak provided both material and the title for *Desolation Angels,* and he writes about the North Cascades in *The Dharma Bums,* describing the range as "unbelievable jags and twisted rock and snow-covered immensities, enough to make you gulp."

And gulp you will, and not just to pop your ears as the elevation increases. With the time-warped company towns of Newhalem and Diablo, the panoramas from countless overlooks, and the chilled glacial waters to explore, a visit to the North Cascades effortlessly extends to a weekend or longer. Welcome to the "American Alps."

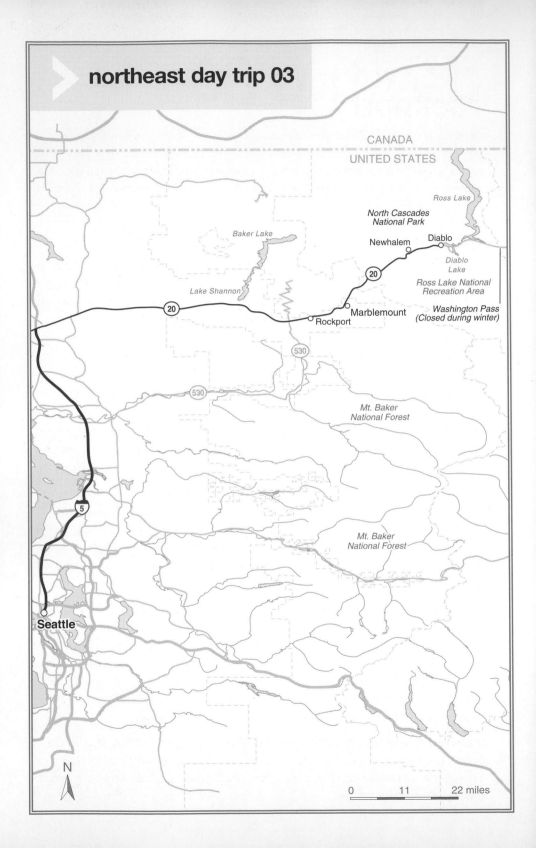

northeast day trip 03

CANADA

UNITED STATES

Ross Lake

North Cascades
National Park

Newhalem — Diablo

*Diablo
Lake*

Baker Lake

20

Ross Lake National
Recreation Area

Lake Shannon

Marblemount

*Washington Pass
(Closed during winter)*

20

Rockport

530

530

*Mt. Baker
National Forest*

5

*Mt. Baker
National Forest*

Seattle

N

0   11   22 miles

rockport

Rockport is not so much a destination as an address for some of the fantastic farms and parks in the area. The community is a crossroads of sorts: It was once the terminus for the railroad from Anacortes that was essential to constructing the Seattle City Light dams, and it now sits near the intersection of State Routes 20 and 530. The latter leads to Darrington and is an alternate route to Seattle.

getting there

From Seattle take I-5 north to exit 230 for Burlington/Anacortes. SR 20 heads east from the interstate—just follow the signs that lead you through the commercial outskirts of Burlington and Sedro-Woolley. Once you're steaming along the North Cascades Highway, the directions become simple: Head east through a 40-mile stretch of farmlands and foothills leading to Rockport, Marblemount, and the park beyond.

where to go

Glacier Peak Winery and Tasting Room. 58575 SR 20, Rockport; (360) 873-4073 or (360) 770-9811; www.glacierpeakwinery.com. Driving up to the tasting room you pass rows of Pinot Noir and Siegerrebe grapes that are beginning their journey to the glass. Friendly employees pour samples, answer questions, and offer suggestions in a simple, unpretentious tasting room. Call ahead for hours, although generally open daily June to Sept.

Rockport State Park. 51095 SR 20, Rockport; www.parks.wa.gov. This roadside park offers a wooded escape into an old-growth forest. Cross the highway from the parking area and follow the half-mile Sauk Springs Trail, which shelters the largest cedars and Douglas firs in the park. The short loop cuts into a mossy haven where garlands of greenery hang from every branch. Massive evergreens also surround the picnic area, where there are restrooms and showers. Open daily.

Sauk Mountain Lookoff. 7 miles on Sauk Mountain Road, Rockport; (360) 856-5700. A zigzag of switchbacks heads up the mountain to a hiking trailhead. Over a total hiking distance of four miles out-and-back, the hike gains nice elevation to provide views of the twisting Skagit River and the North Cascades. If you're lucky, there may be some hang gliders launching from the slopes. An important word of warning: While the views are worth the trip, a hunter accidentally shot a woman on this trail in 2008, mistaking her for a bear. Wear bright colors, preferably hunters' orange, when walking the trail.

Wildwood Chapel. 58468 Clark Cabin Rd., Rockport; (800) 273-2606. Part of Clark's Skagit River Resort (located across the highway), this tiny chapel has room for only a handful of people. But Wildwood Chapel still hosts weddings and provides a token of quiet for travelers. Generally open daily.

where to eat

Cascadian Farm. 55749 SR 20, Rockport; (360) 853-8173; www.cascadianfarm.com. Feasts of fresh or frozen blueberries and raspberries as well as homemade ice cream are the reward for stopping at this roadside fruit stand. Cascadian organic products and produce make a great choice for those planning to camp in the national park. Stock up on granola, jam, and the tantalizing berries, and then enjoy an espresso in the pretty gardenside seating area. There are restrooms and lots of parking. Open daily. $.

marblemount

Once a gold rush town, Marblemount now welcomes rushes of outdoor enthusiasts. Eight miles east of Rockport, the town offers the greatest concentration of services whether you're headed out on the Pacific Crest Trail, on a quest for Kerouac, or simply enjoying the views of the craggy mountains at Washington Pass. Stop in Marblemount to gas up, rest up, and feed up before heading east into the national park.

getting there

From Rockport drive east along the North Cascades Highway (SR 20) for 8 miles (about 10 minutes).

where to go

Blue Sky Outfitters. SR 20, Marblemount; (206) 938-4030 or (800) 228-7238; www .blueskyoutfitters.com. Floating serenely or running the rapids—you have the choice when rafting on the Skagit River. Although summer is the more popular white-water season, the wintertime concentration of bald eagles makes a winter float trip a popular excursion. Or pair your rafting journey with a wine tasting. Trips start at about $80 per adult. Call in advance for reservations. $$$.

North Cascades Visitor Information Center. 59831 SR 20, Marblemount; (360) 873-4150; www.marblemount.com. The visitor center provides the usual resources for attractions, restaurants, and lodging in the local area. Added bonuses include offers of free coffee and Internet access. For detailed park information, visit the Wilderness Information Center (see below) or the visitor center outside Newhalem.

Wilderness Information Center. Down Ranger Road (turn at MP 105.3 on SR 20), Marblemount; (360) 854-7245; www.nps.gov/noca. One of the six information centers for North Cascades National Park and surrounding forests, this visitor center is geared toward those headed into the backcountry. Registration services and parking passes are available here, as well as a few exhibits on the ecology of the park. A raised-relief map provides a hint of the dams, lakes, rivers, valleys, and mountains you'll see on your journey. Open daily May to Sept.

where to eat

Buffalo Run Restaurant. 60084 SR 20, Marblemount; (360) 873-2461; www.buffalorun inn.com. From farm to table is the emphasis here with elk, buffalo, and ostrich all featured on the hearty menu. The vegetarian options are out of the ordinary, making the restaurant a nice compromise for all diners. The buffalo hide on the wall, secluded garden patio, and friendly servers make the restaurant the best in town. Open daily for lunch and dinner with reduced hours in winter. $$–$$$$.

Marblemount Drive-In. 59924 SR 20, Marblemount; (360) 873-9309. For greasy good-ness, there's nothing quite like a drive-in. Burgers, fries, and sandwiches form the bulk of the menu, but with attentive service and a plant-trimmed deck at the back, this drive-in serves things up with an atypical flair. Open daily for lunch and dinner. $–$$.

where to stay

Buffalo Run Inn. 60117 SR 20, Marblemount; (360) 873-2103 or (877) 828-6652; www .buffaloruninn.com. Cozy rooms range from economical units to a well-equipped bunk-house. Hostel rooms share immaculately clean bathrooms and a comfy common area, while the regular rooms have private baths, coffeemakers, microwaves, and refrigerators. $–$$.

newhalem

There's a buzz about Newhalem—it's the humming electric wires that run overhead from the dams and power stations upstream to Seattle on the coast. Established as a Seattle City Light company town, Newhalem was built just below the first of the three dams. The community has seized on the appeal of the area, providing walking trails that abut the main street and superb services. A visitor center, restrooms, parking, public benches, and out-door sculptures all invite you to stop.

Seattle City Light's boat tours on Diablo Lake also depart from Newhalem.

getting there

Drive northeast from Marblemount to reach the small community of Newhalem. The journey covers 15 miles and takes 25 minutes.

where to go

North Cascades Visitor Center. MP 120, Newhalem; (206) 386-4495; www.nps.gov/ noca. A short distance west of Newhalem, a large visitor center offers exhibits revealing the park in many seasons. A large raised-relief map uses lightbulbs to identify park features. It's an excellent way to become familiar with the peaks of the park. Look, too, for a binder containing ranger trip reports for the season. You'll find great tips on worthwhile hikes and corners of the park. Open daily May to Oct.

Gorge Dam. MP 123, Newhalem. A short, accessible trail leads to an overlook above the first dam. The oldest of the three, Gorge Dam demanded some creative construction techniques. Because the glacial sediment beneath the river was so prone to slides, engineers used refrigeration tubes to stabilize the ground while building progressed. Nearby is Gorge Creek Falls, one of the many cascading streams of water for which the national park was named. Open year-round.

Ladder Creek Falls. MP 120, Gorge Dam Powerhouse, Newhalem. The falls rate as a favorite with many visitors. Follow the trail beside the powerhouse over a suspension bridge, up steps of wide paving stones, and past pretty gardens to the headliner—the tiered Ladder Creek Falls. Open during summer only.

Skagit Visitor Center. MP 120, Newhalem; (206) 684-3030; www.skagittours.com. The information center is the departure point for explorations with Skagit Tours, which are run by Seattle City Light. Daytime and dinner cruises set a course across the aqua waters of Diablo Lake. You'll also cross the impressive stretch of Diablo Dam, which was the world's highest dam when it was completed in 1930 (although it didn't generate power until 1936). Adult prices start at $25 for weekend cruises running June through Sept. Make advanced reservations to secure a spot. $$$.

Trail of the Cedars. South of the main street, MP 120, Newhalem. A swaying suspension bridge leads to the trail. First winding along the edge of the Skagit River, the trail then loops through the old-growth forest. A half-mile loop trail, the Trail of the Cedars makes a quick addition to a stop for restrooms and homemade fudge. Open year-round.

where to eat

Skagit General Store. 500 Newhalem St., Newhalem; (206) 386-4489. The general store is not so much a dinner option as a source for picnic supplies, but it's the lone option in Newhalem. Here you can grab a few sandwich items or hot soup and a coffee to enjoy on the store's veranda. For dessert, try a slice of homemade fudge—a Newhalem favorite. Open daily during summer, weekdays in the off-season. $.

diablo to north cascades national park

A quick drive into Diablo yields little to see beyond the shingled homes built for Seattle City Light employees. A few are boarded up, but most house current employees of the electric company. Instead continue on the North Cascades Highway, stopping in at each of the dams and lookouts. All are well signposted from the main route.

Feel the gusting winds over Diablo Lake, rent a canoe at the floating Ross Lake Resort, or photograph the big skies and big mountains at Washington Pass. En route forests, trails, and falls line either side of the road.

getting there

Reach Diablo in just 10 minutes from Newhalem. The much longer journey to Washington Pass adds another hour (one-way) to the road trip.

where to go

Diablo Dam. MP 127.5, Diablo. The second of the park's dams, Diablo Dam was once the world's largest. When traveling east, a left turn near MP 127.5 takes a steep, narrow route down across the dam. There's no stopping allowed, but continue to the far side and visit the environmental learning center or simply admire the scenery from the lakeshore.

Diablo Lake Overlook. MP 132. Far below lies the reservoir that is held in by Diablo Dam. From the roadside overlook, the lake's turquoise hue cuts against the evergreen slopes and pencil line of the dam. Easy and stunning photo opportunities abound.

North Cascades Environmental Learning Center. MP 127.5, north shore of Diablo Lake; (360) 856-5700; www.ncascades.org. A modern cedar-planked complex becomes the nerve center for adult and children's programs tackling everything from climate change to writing and relaxation. The center provides meals, lodging, and lessons to participants—review the list of seminars in advance. $$$.

Ross Dam and Overlook. MP 134 and MP 135, Ross Lake. In addition to the roadside overlook (MP 135) where the panoramas include Kerouac's Desolation Peak, there's a well-graded mile-long trail down to the reservoir from the parking area at MP 134. En route, gaps in the evergreens reveal frames of the lake, the floating Ross Lake Resort, and the largest of the dams: Ross Dam.

desolation peak

A fire-watching station on Desolation Peak has become a pilgrimage of sorts for modern followers of the Beat Generation. A fire lookout on the peak served as home to many writers over the years, including Jack Kerouac, who served as a fire watcher in 1956. The On the Road *author penned* Desolation Angels *and* The Dharma Bums *based on the experience.*

Beat Generation poets and figures in the San Francisco Renaissance Philip Whalen and Gary Snyder also served at the fire-watching post. A Pulitzer Prize winner, Snyder was Kerouac's inspiration for the character Japhy Ryder in The Dharma Bums.

where to stay

Colonial Creek Campground. MP 130. An arm of Diablo Lake provides a sheltered area for camping, picnics, and fishing in the national recreation area. Be cautious with watercraft: The levels of the lake rise and fall as water is held and released through the dams. Don't be left high and dry! $.

Ross Lake Resort. Ross Lake; (206) 386-4437; www.rosslakeresort.com. This floating lodge dating to the 1950s is accessible only by a short hike and boat ride, or a long hike. Floating cabins range from simple to deluxe, and families will be particularly entertained thanks to on-site boat rentals. Canoes and kayaks are also available to nonguests on a per-hour or daily basis. The resort is a truly hidden find, and its limited accessibility means it will remain so. $$–$$$$.

worth more time

Washington Pass. MP 162, 42 miles from Newhalem. At 5,477 feet, a rocky overlook provides panoramic views from the highest point of the highway. Look down and see the brake-light-burner road snake down the mountain face. Heading further east will take you to the Wild West town of Winthrop and Idaho farther beyond. This portion of the highway (from Ross Lake through to Silver Star at MP 171) is closed from November to April because of heavy snowfalls, but events such as a July 2009 mudslide can mean additional, unexpected closures. Check with the Washington State Department of Transportation for highway updates (www.wsdot.wa.gov).

east

day trip 01

east

fish ladders and waterfalls:
bellevue, issaquah, snoqualmie

This easy jaunt east is all about luxury. Well, with a few fishy bits thrown in for interest. From the gold-paved streets of Bellevue to the tranquility of the Salish Lodge spa at Sno-qualmie Falls, the attractions along the western portion of this nationwide highway (I-90) are diverse, popular, and engaging.

Cheer on the spawning salmon as they climb the fish ladder at the salmon hatchery in Issaquah, hear the white noise of the power-generating Snoqualmie Falls, and stare down the frozen-in-time dolls at the Rosalie Whyel Museum in Bellevue—all within a half-hour drive from downtown Seattle.

bellevue

Across Lake Washington, Bellevue is synonymous with money: Main offices pack the down-town district. But amidst the suits, you'll find a few gems to visit as well as some of the best high-end shopping in the state.

getting there

I-90 runs east from Seattle, providing access in minutes to Bellevue (10 miles, 15 minutes), Issaquah (17 miles, 20 minutes), and Snoqualmie (29 miles, 35 minutes). Allow plenty of extra time in traffic. Or follow SR 520 east and cross Lake Washington on the Evergreen Point Floating Bridge, the world's longest floating bridge, then head south on I-405 to the I-90.

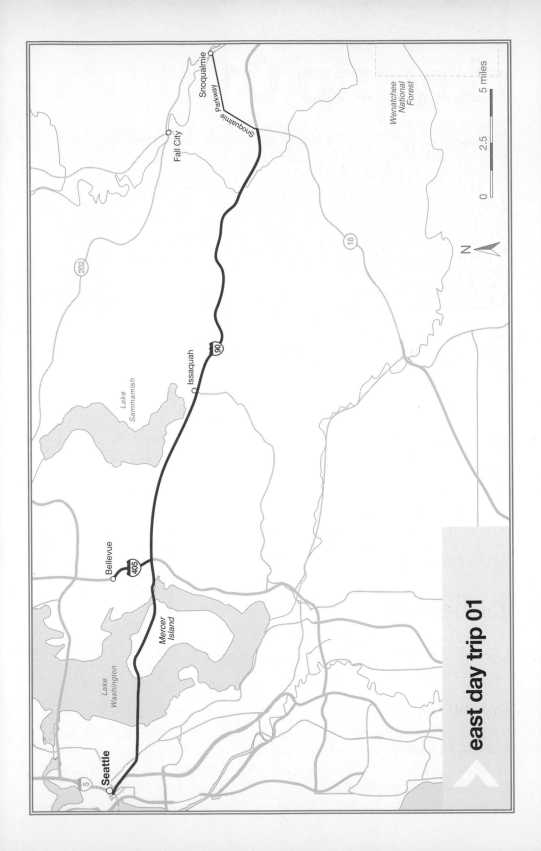

Snoqualmie

Snoqualmie Parkway

Fall City

202

18

Wenatchee
National
Forest

Lake
Sammamish

Issaquah

90

N

5 miles

2.5

0

Bellevue

405

Mercer
Island

Lake
Washington

Seattle

5

east day trip 01

where to go

Bellevue Arts Museum. 510 Bellevue Way Northeast, Bellevue; (425) 519-0770; www .bellevuearts.org. The beautiful vibrant brick-red building designed by Steven Holl provides a polished exterior for the museum's exhibits, which focus on craft and design. Past exhibits have ranged from quilts and tapestries to ceramics and glass. Open daily. $$.

Bellevue Botanical Garden. 12001 Main St., Bellevue; (425) 452-2750; www.bellevue botanical.org. This hilltop garden eschews the bustle and traffic of Bellevue to offer a green oasis of twisting paths, creative gardens, and educational exhibits. The Waterwise and Alpine Rock Gardens are particularly commendable for their Northwest elements, while the Rhododendron Glen celebrates the state flower, and the spring blooms of the Perennial Border inject intense color to the garden beds. Bellevue Botanical Garden lies alongside Wilburton Hill Park, a favorite spot for picnics. Open daily. $.

Rosalie Whyel Museum of Doll Art. 1116 108th Ave. Northeast, Bellevue; (425) 455- 1116; www.dollart.com. More than 1,500 dolls on display are part of a private collection that is accompanied by doll houses, teddy bears, and other antique toys. Many dolls date to the 1800s, but there are also recognizable contemporary favorites such as Barbie. Open daily. $$.

where to shop

The Shops at the Bravern. 11111 Northeast Eighth St., Bellevue; (425) 456-8795 (for the concierge); www.thebravern.com. With the Northwest's first Neiman Marcus, this shopping destination also boasts a Salvatore Ferragamo, Jimmy Choo, Hermès, and Anthropologie. Valet parking and a concierge service show that the Bravern is no regular shopping experi- ence. Open daily.

Three other favorite Bellevue shopping meccas cluster around Bellevue Way at North- east Eighth Street. The downtown properties include **Lincoln Square, Bellevue Place,** and the largest of the three, **Bellevue Square.** The latter features a Macy's, Nordstrom, and JCPenney plus two levels of smaller boutiques and shops. The Hyatt anchors Bellevue Place where you'll also find art galleries, restaurants, and services. Sharing a corner with the Bellevue Arts Museum, Lincoln Square includes dining favorites such as **Paddy Coynes Irish Pub** (425-453-8080), **Pearl Bar & Dining** (425-455-0181), and **Maggiano's Little Italy** (425-519-6476), plus a bowling alley, movie theater, and spa. All three properties are open to shoppers daily.

issaquah

Issaquah is where the wilderness of the east begins. Despite being just 20 minutes from Seattle, it retains its small town charm and connection to the outdoors. Cougar Mountain

Park, Squak Mountain State Park, West Tiger Mountain, and Lake Sammamish State Park edge the outskirts of the city.

Volunteers create wonders at the local salmon hatchery. The city's grand event is October's Salmon Days Festival, when thousands visit Issaquah to watch as volunteers capture the salmon from the river and harvest the roe. Other wild encounters include the cougar sanctuary and spontaneous wildlife encounters at the local parks.

getting there

Follow I-90 east from Seattle or Bellevue. From exit 13, a drive east along Newport Way directs you to Cougar Mountain Zoo, while exits 17 and 18 lead more directly into the downtown.

where to go

Cougar Mountain Zoo. 19525 Southeast 54th St., Issaquah; (425) 391-5508; www .cougarmountainzoo.org. Besides the cougars, the zoo is also home to macaws, reindeer, and tigers. Extra-fee "close encounters" experiences allow you to feed reindeer or come face-to-face with a tiger—through safety glass that is. Open Wed to Sun from Jan to Nov and daily in Dec for the Issaquah Reindeer Festival. $$$.

Gilman Town Hall Museum. 165 Southeast Andrews St., Issaquah; (425) 392-3500; www.issaquahhistory.org/townhall. Besides exhibits in the town hall that include a kitchen and a dynamite blaster, there's a 1914 jail in back with iron bars and thick concrete walls. Open Thurs to Sat. $.

Issaquah Depot Museum. 50 Rainier Blvd. North, Issaquah; (425) 392-3500; www .issaquahhistory.org/depot. All-aboard exhibits allow visitors to climb into a World War II army kitchen car or a caboose once used in the Weyerhaeuser logging railroad. The depot museum is one of the best in the state. Inside the restored Gilman train station, which dates to 1889, you'll discover a telegraph station and lots of interpretive displays. Open Fri to Sun. $.

Issaquah Salmon Hatchery. 125 West Sunset Way, Issaquah; (425) 427-0259 or (425) 392-8025; www.issaquahfish.org. Visit the hatchery to follow the life cycle of the salmon that return to Issaquah Creek each fall to spawn. Trace the salmon's journey from the weir that prevents the adult fish from heading further upsteam and directs them into the hatchery where volunteers collect the roe. Outside the salmon run, underwater holding tanks show salmon beneath the surface as they swim. A note for families: The spawning salmon are at the end of their life cycle and are killed before the eggs are harvested—it could be upsetting, but most kids tend to be intrigued. The non-profit Friends of the Issaquah Salmon Hatchery runs the volunteer programs and tours. Open daily with free admission, although donations are accepted at various collection points throughout the hatchery. $.

Village Theatre, Issaquah. Francis J. Gaudette Theatre, 303 Front St. North, Issaquah; (425) 392-2202 or (866) 688-8849; www.villagetheatre.org. Issaquah's Village Theatre specializes in musicals, particularly those they've commissioned or those that are new to the West Coast. Five shows each season. Full-price tickets start at about $40. $$$.

where to eat

The Front Street Cafe. 485 Front St. North, Issaquah; (425) 427-9886; www.thefront streetcafe.com. For a hearty breakfast or lunch sandwich, this downtown cafe exudes local charm. It's family friendly (with diapers and a large changing table in the bathroom), a treat for espresso fans (brewing Cafe D'arte coffee), and a spot to recharge on sweet morsels including cupcakes and cookies. Comfy chairs and home-style decor make the cafe the best spot in town for a post-adventure bite. Open daily for breakfast and lunch. Main courses $4–8.

snoqualmie

Meaning "moon" in Salish—the language spoken by the Native American people of the same name—Snoqualmie has endured and only grown as a popular destination. Mainly travelers flock to see the 270-foot waterfall, which is nearly 100-feet taller than Niagara Falls.

But besides the namesake falls, the town boasts a luxury lodge where spa treatments, intimate dinners, and hearty breakfasts make for a true escape. Railroad interests include a street-long depot featuring rail cars, cabooses, and engines from varying regions and eras.

getting there

Traveling from Seattle, I-90 provides quick access to the Snoqualmie (25 miles, 35 minutes). Taking exit 25, then head along Snoqualmie Parkway to the falls and downtown.

where to go

Northwest Railway Museum. 38625 Southeast King St., Snoqualmie; (425) 888-3030; www.trainmuseum.org. The Northwest Railway Museum is an added favorite with visitors who travel primarily to view the falls. A wonderfully restored Victorian depot reveals snapshots of the former grandeur of the rail age. The Snoqualmie Valley Railroad embarks on 5-mile journeys in antique coaches. The railroad runs on weekends during spring, summer, and fall, as well as special holiday-season trips. The depot is open daily with no admission charge. Train fares: $$$.

Snoqualmie Falls. Off Railroad Avenue Southeast, Snoqualmie; www.snoqualmiefalls .com. The 270-foot waterfall (although some sources note the height at 268 feet) serves many a purpose. It generates power for Puget Sound Energy, remains a spiritual place for the Snoqualmie tribe, and is a sight to behold for nearly two million annual visitors. There's a gift shop and a viewing platform providing vistas of the falls, which are 100-feet higher than Niagara Falls. A grand redesign of the site in late 2009 included plans to add gardens and improve public access. Open daily.

where to eat

The Attic at Salish Lodge. 6501 Railroad Ave., 4th Floor, Snoqualmie; (425) 888-2556 or (800) 272-5474; www.salishlodge.com/attic.php. Proximity to the falls, smaller plates, and a relaxed atmosphere are just a few reasons the Attic is my preferred yet lesser-discovered dining option at Salish Lodge. The halibut tacos, venison carpaccio, and salmon BLT keep the focus on fresh Northwest fare. Couches, chessboards, and a well-stocked bar provide excellent reasons to linger. Open weekends for lunch and daily for dinner. $$–$$$.

Woodman Lodge. 38601 Southeast King St., Snoqualmie; (425) 888-4441; www.wood manlodge.com. A classic steakhouse with an edge of modern Wild West and strong histori-cal roots, the Woodman Lodge bridges casual and fine polish. Steak options range from buffalo rib eye to pork chops and filet mignon, but the lighter fare is equally exceptional. A steak panzanella salad is elevated above its Italian tradition as a "leftover salad" with smat-terings of capers, herbs, and blue cheese. Burgers offer a more moderately priced option. Unfortunately for vegetarians, meat-free options are as rare as the steaks despite a great selection of seafood. Open daily for lunch and dinner; closed Mon in winter. $$$–$$$$.

where to stay

Salish Lodge. 6501 Railroad Ave., Snoqualmie; (425) 888-2556 or (800) 272-5474; www .salishlodge.com. A historical lodge dating back to 1916, the Salish Lodge underwent a room refurbishment in 2009. The open-concept bathroom windows, fireplaces, and Jacuzzi tubs still grace each of the rooms, but modern earth tones add a fresh, woodsy feel. It is arrestingly easy to slip away into an escape at the lodge. Great dining, an on-site spa, and being walking distance to Snoqualmie Falls mean there are few reasons to leave. But do at least make it to breakfast, where the traditional "honey from heaven" will christen a freshly baked biscuit, or to the fragrant spa, where soaking pools and saunas provide a silent retreat. $$$$.

worth more time

Spa at Salish Lodge. www.salishlodge.com/spa.php. Slip into a robe and slippers and sink into the spa. The soft, natural floral fragrances of the waiting room and treatments draw inspiration and fresh herbs from the lodge's own garden. Its hot river-stone massage endures as a signature. Treatments start at about $100 for massages and body therapies. If staying in the hotel, the spa's bath butler service is certainly an unbeatable in-room relax-ant. Spa attendants fill the soaking tub with the soft fragrances of rosemary and mint, a nourishing honey-and-milk mixture, or floral lavender.

day trip 02

east

>>> **chimps, cowboys, and northern exposure:**
roslyn, cle elum, ellensburg

Venturing from the Roslyn streets that formed the backdrop for the town of Cicely on television's *Northern Exposure* to the beautiful community museum and historic downtown in Ellensburg, this day trip rates as a personal favorite. Roslyn retains the spirit of Cicely, Alaska, with buildings such as the Brick and Roslyn Café that welcome patrons daily.

In Cle Elum, railroad history and a busy main street remind of travelers who once would have arrived in town on horseback or on the Burlington Northern Railroad.

Further east along I-90, Ellensburg delivers attraction after attraction. A chimp sanctuary where the primates use American Sign Language to communicate, art and historical museums, plus beautiful natural surroundings make the town an excellent getaway.

roslyn

Founded as a coal mining town in the 1880s, Roslyn produced two million tons of the black stuff annually in its peak. More recently Roslyn gained fame as the setting for television's favorite fictional Alaskan town—*Northern Exposure*'s Cicely. Fans of the television show regularly visit to sit in the bar, enjoy a coffee at the Cicely Cafe, or explore the town museum. You'll see many folks posing for photos in front of the Brick, relaxing at the Roslyn Cafe, or reading production sides and viewing props at the local museum. With Hollywood appeal, the television element outshines.

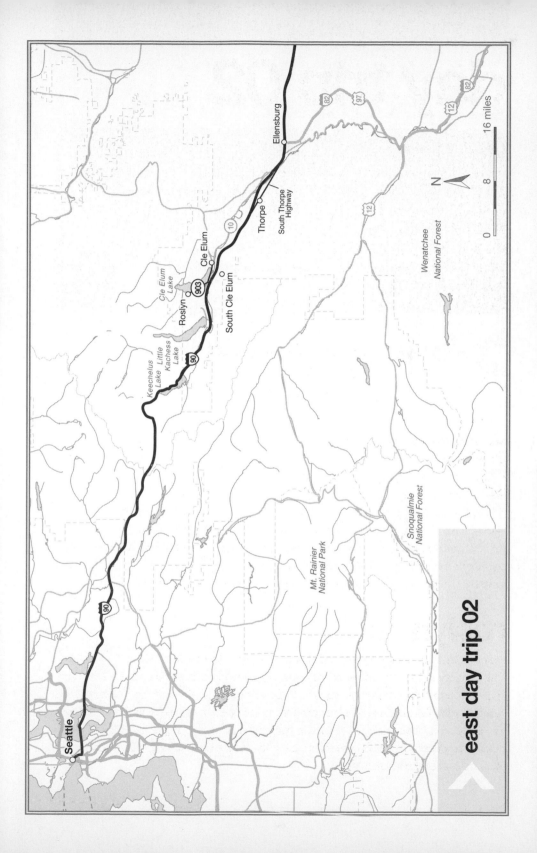

east day trip 02

The history of the coal-mining era lives on in museums, historical markers, and trails around town. It is remembered in the 25 cemeteries.

getting there

I-90 provides quick access to the area. Take exit 80 for Roslyn (83 miles, 90 minutes from Seattle) then follow Bullfrog Road past Suncadia to First Street, which leads into town.

where to go

The Brick Bar. 100 West Pennsylvania Ave., Roslyn; (509) 649-2643. A staple exterior shot in *Northern Exposure,* the Brick is a favorite place for fans of the show to visit. Add to that the bar is reputed to be one of the state's oldest saloons and that it has its own water-flowing trough for the olden-days delight of tobacco spitting, and it's a place you'll not find the likes of anywhere else. Open daily.

Roslyn Museum. 203 West Pennsylvania Ave., Roslyn; (509) 649-2355; www.roslyn museum.com. The strength of the coal industry once drew many new residents to this now-small city. In fact the population during the 1920s was greater than today. Exhibits touch on the coal-mining history, the roots of the diverse ethnic groups who came to work in the mines, and ever-present television series *Northern Exposure.* Most items have been donated by local community members, making the eclectic collection easier to appreciate as a collection that is about and from a community. This by-donation museum is open daily. $.

where to eat

Cafe Cicely. 107 West Pennsylvania Ave., Roslyn; (509) 649-2909. For breakfast and lunch Cafe Cicely makes a great option for a quick stop. The cafe keeps it simple with a selection of wraps, salads, and sandwiches. Fussy eaters on board? A classic PB&J is available

coal mines trail

A 4.7-mile trail connects Cle Elum to Roslyn and Ronald, near the shores of Cle Elum Lake. The route follows the bed of the now-dismantled Burlington Northern Railroad and is popular with bicyclists and walkers. Twenty points of interest are described in a locally produced tour guide. Although the scenery isn't exceptional, the exercise and excellent interpretive booklet make it a worthwhile journey. Check with **Roslyn Cyclery** *(105 North 2nd St.; 509-649-2863; www.roslyn cyclery.com) for maps and bike rentals.*

here. You'll also find brewed coffee made from fresh-roasted beans from Cle Elum's Pioneer Coffee Roasting Company. $.

Roslyn Cafe. 201 West Pennsylvania Ave., Roslyn; (509) 649-2763. Another familiar site to *Northern Exposure* fans, the cafe appeared in the TV series as the slightly rebranded Roslyn's Cafe. A sunny outdoor patio and cozy indoor dining area provide excellent options for breakfast through dinner. The menu features uncomplicated favorites such as fish-and-chips, hearty salads, and portobello burgers. $$–$$$.

cle elum

Although the heavily trafficked First Street means the town doesn't offer the best options for a weekend stroll, venture off the main drag to find an excellent museum, freshly made treats, and locally roasted coffee that do make the town worth including in a day trip.

getting there

From Roslyn, follow SR 903 east to Cle Elum (4 miles, 10 minutes from Roslyn).

where to go

Carpenter Museum. 301 West Third St. (at Billings Avenue), Cle Elum; (509) 674-9766; www.nkcmuseums.org. This may perhaps be Washington's best community-run museum for its simplicity and community spirit. It's a collective operation between Cle Elum artists, who staff the museum and will most likely be painting on-site when you visit, and the local historical society. The airy, regal rooms of the Carpenter family home are filled with antiques, intricate quilts, and local art. Hidden staircases and freedom to explore the home extend a warm welcome. Open Fri to Sun. $.

Cle Elum Historical Telephone Museum. 221 East First St., Cle Elum; (509) 674-9766; www.nkcmuseums.org. Although closed for renovations when I visited town, the museum localizes the effects of telephone technology. The museum sits in the old offices of the Pacific Northwest Bell Telephone Company. Call ahead for hours. $.

Cle Elum–Roslyn Chamber of Commerce. 401 West First St., Cle Elum; (509) 674-5958; www.cleelumroslyn.org. With details on the Coal Mines Trail, *Northern Exposure* sights in Roslyn, and local museums, the chamber is conveniently located in the west end of Cle Elum. Open daily.

South Cle Elum Depot. 801 Milwaukee Ave., South Cle Elum; (509) 674-2006; www.milw electric.org. The South Cle Elum Depot is a restored railroad station that in 2009 became the location for the local senior center with a small museum inside. Open most days with a small cafe on-site. $.

where to eat

Cle Elum Bakery. 501 East First St., Cle Elum; (509) 674-2233. This street-front bakery supplies the side-street Bakery House cafe with fresh loaves and treats. Fresh sandwiches are available at the cafe, or pick up some picnic items at the bakery. Bakery open daily; cafe closed Sun. $.

El Caporal. 105 West First St., Cle Elum; (509) 674-4284. Although some other franchises of this restaurant can tend towards a strip-mall vibe, the hanging flower baskets that surround this location in summer create a stronger appeal for those on a getaway. A spacious dining room and attentive waitstaff round out a usual Mexican food menu. Open daily for lunch and dinner. $$–$$$.

ellensburg

Ellensburg combines one of the state's most charming historical districts with the youthful energy of Central Washington University. An 1889 fire leveled the city, meaning much of the architecture dates to the same late Victorian period with a few newer Art Deco–style buildings as well.

Ellensburg is full of surprises: A vibrantly painted house with an art-filled yard and fence bedecked in reflectors, chimpanzees who use American Sign Language to communicate, a February cowboy festival, and a summertime rodeo. Go explore: You'll find character-filled restaurants beside century-old roadhouses and university pubs.

i-90 recreation corridors

Iron Horse State Park includes the John Wayne Pioneer Trail and stretches more than 100 miles along I-90 following old railroad beds that connect Cedar Falls to the Columbia River. One neat feature is that the trail route heads through railroad tunnels that cut through hillsides thereby safely traversing mountain passes. Mountain biking through the tunnels with good lights and rain gear makes for a popular and unique adventure. Check the state parks Web site (www.parks.wa.gov) for updates on tunnel closures or dangerous conditions before heading out.

On the opposite side of I-90 runs the **Mountains to Sound Greenway** (206-382-5565; www.mtsgreenway.org). Providing a recreation route over Snoqualmie Pass, the greenway includes many miles of trail that link up with the John Wayne Pioneer Trail. But the trails also extend into the dense urban areas of Seattle, Redmond, and Renton, increasing green-space access to the state's most populous regions.

getting there

Both SR 10 and I-90 provide a quick, roughly 25-mile journey (30 minutes) from Cle Elum to Ellensburg. The city lies at exit 106, 110 miles (or 1 hour and 45 minutes) east of Seattle.

where to go

Ellensburg Chamber of Commerce. 609 North Main St., Ellensburg; (509) 925-2002 or (888) 925-2204; www.visitellen.com. Centrally located, the chamber runs a visitor center that is open daily from Memorial Day to Labor Day; closed Sun the rest of the year.

Chimpanzee and Human Communication Institute. D Street and Dean Nicholson Boulevard, Ellensburg; (509) 963-2244; www.friendsofwashoe.org. Meet Tatu, Dar, and Loulis, the signing chimps living at the CHCI. During the hour-long tour, you'll find out about the DNA shared by chimps and humans, brush up on your chimpanzee manners, and even learn a few signs. The highlight is certainly meeting the trio of chimps at the sanctuary as they swing and play in the large outdoor area. Call for an updated schedule, but tours generally run weekends Mar through Nov. $$$.

Clymer Museum of Art. 416 North Pearl St., Ellensburg; (509) 962-6416; www.clymer museum.com. The work of John Ford Clymer, much of which was created for U.S. and Canadian magazines, forms the foundation of this museum. The subjects are diverse, but the spirit and humor of the Northwest persist throughout. Open daily; closed Sun during winter. $.

Dick and Jane's Spot. 101 North Pearl St., Ellensburg; (509) 925-3224; www.reflectorart .com/spot. Whether you visit in the night or day, this house is a treat to behold. A fence of reflectors wraps a house and yard filled with whimsical art. While the house is certainly a must-see, it is also the private home (of Jane and Dick), so sign the guest book and admire respectfully. Street viewing welcomed year-round.

Kittitas County Historical Museum. 114 East Third Ave., Ellensburg; (509) 925-3778; www.kchm.org. Extensive geology exhibits, including one of the state's official gemstone—petrified wood—create a nice departure from a pioneer focus. The Rollinger Rock Collection and Native American artifacts feature in the handsome Cadwell building, dating to 1889. Closed Sun. $.

where to eat

Rodeo City Bar-B-Q. 204 North Main St., Ellensburg; (509) 962-2727; www.rodeocity barbq.com. Not the best place for vegetarians, but for lovers of ribs and steak this restaurant is a Main Street institution. Open daily for lunch and dinner, except closed Mon. $$–$$$.

Yellow Church Café. 111 South Pearl St., Ellensburg; (509) 933-2233; www.yellow churchcafe.com. Intimate and cozy, the Yellow Church Café presents comfort food with a modern flair. Planked salmon, veggie burgers, pastas, and various cuts of steak create an eclectic yet simple menu. The old Lutheran church, dating to 1923, makes a romantic and historic background for a quiet dinner. Open for weekend breakfast and daily for lunch and dinner. $$–$$$.

where to stay

Ellensburg KOA. 32 Thorp Hwy. South, Ellensburg; (509) 925-9319 or (800) 562-7616; www.koa.com/where/wa/47129. As Ellensburg enjoys a much warmer and drier climate than Seattle, the camping season is a little more reliable here. Pitch a tent beside the Yakima River at this clean campground. Just a short drive from downtown, the campground may be too close to an overpass for light sleepers. $.

Rose Hill Farm. 16161 North Thorp Hwy., Thorp; (509) 964-2427 or (866) 279-0546; www .rosehillfarmbb.com. Clean and bright, this farm-style B&B offers spacious rooms in a quiet, out-of-town location. Farm animals, a nearby river, a horse paddock, and fresh breakfasts provide an easy escape. Rooms are spacious, and the hilltop setting creates a kingly feel. Although the B&B is for adults only, the studio is great for those seeking more privacy, and the cottage (which can sleep up to ten) is ideal for families. $$–$$$$.

columbia river gorge

Winding through much of the state, the grand Columbia River offers superb rec-reational activities. From windsurfing to fishing and hiking, the river is the main artery of the Pacific Northwest.

Music fans make annual pilgrimages to see performances at one of the world's most spectacular venues: the **Gorge Amphitheater.** *With the plum-meting gorge as the backdrop and the desert sunsets as lighting, the music just sounds better.*

Tickets to events can go quickly, despite the 150-mile journey from Seattle to the Gorge, located between Quincy and George. Live Nation runs the amphi-theater and tickets are generally available through Ticketmaster (www.ticket master.com).

day trip 03

east

>>> **bavaria and apple country:**
leavenworth, cashmere

These two rival high-school-sports towns pair to create an engaging getaway to Bavaria and apple country. Leavenworth rates as one of best places in the state to experience the outdoors, having received mentions for its top rock climbing, rafting, and hiking. In-town oddities include a nutcracker museum, morning alpenhorn serenade, and mountain goats grazing on a putting course. Add a world-class walk of outdoor sculptures that includes a piece by famed glass artist Dale Chihuly, local wineries, great beer, and lively festivals, and Leavenworth will soon be on your list of annual-tradition day trips.

Further east on US 2 (called Highway 2 locally), Cashmere offers a delicate charm. With a main thoroughfare called Cottage Avenue, the well-kept detached homes create an idyllic Pleasantville feel. Visiting the pioneer village, candy factory, or cider mill all rate as engaging and easy-to-enjoy family activities.

leavenworth

Best known as a Bavarian-themed town, Leavenworth also reveals itself as a haven for wineries, the arts, and the outdoors. A day trip will suffice for only a taste.

In the mid-1960s, the town underwent a transformation from a lumber town to a stylized Bavarian village. Holding strongly to the theme, even major corporations have redesigned their signs in preapproved scripts. Oh, and don't be surprised to see lederhosen and alpine hats about town.

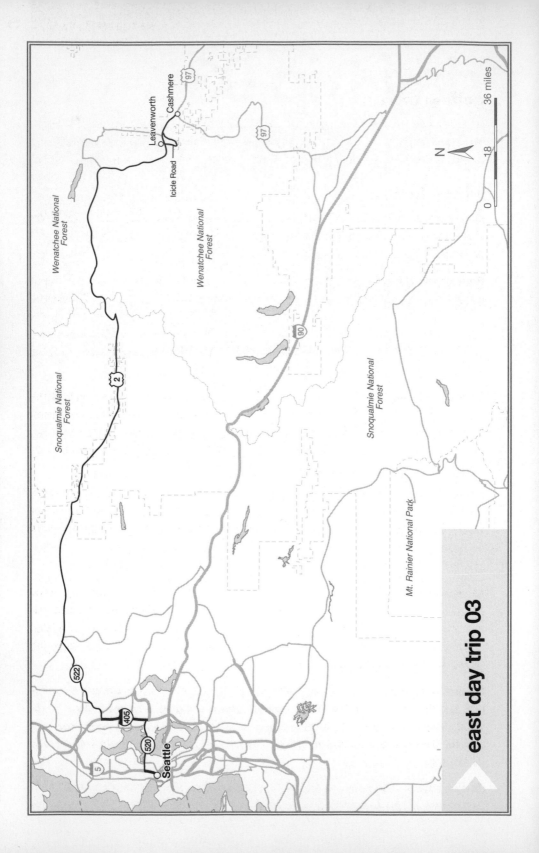

east day trip 03

getting there

Head north on I-405 to the junction with SR 522. The route leads northeast to US 2 (Highway 2) heading east. Winding through small towns and mountain passes, US 2 emerges on the sunny side of Washington and leads directly through downtown Leavenworth (2 hours).

where to go

Leavenworth Visitor Center. 940 Hwy. 2, Leavenworth; (509) 548-5807; www.leaven worth.org. Unable to snag that hard-to-find room? Head to this central visitor center for attentive assistance. Open daily, with later hours on Fri and Sat.

Barn Beach Reserve. 347 Division St., Leavenworth; (509) 548-0181; www.barnbeach reserve.org. The reserve houses the **Upper Valley Museum** (509-548-0728; www.upper valleymuseum.org) as well as local exhibits. Overlooking the Wenatchee River, the reserve ties the natural environment to the local culture. With most of the emphasis at the reserve being on the outdoors, most of Barn Beach is accessible daily; the museum is open Thurs to Sun. $.

Leavenworth National Fish Hatchery. 12790 Fish Hatchery Rd., Leavenworth; (509) 548-7641; www.fws.gov/leavenworth. This large hatchery welcomes those looking to learn about the Chinook salmon that return annually to the Icicle River. Large holding tanks, fish ladders, and the salmon life cycle will interest all ages. Informative brochures allow for self-guided tours. The government-run hatchery is open daily.

Leavenworth Nutcracker Museum. 735 Front St., Leavenworth; (509) 548-4573; www.nutcrackermuseum.com. It's all in how you crack it at the Leavenworth Nutcracker Museum. Thousands of nutcrackers on display demonstrate a real passion for the often-overlooked ornament, common symbol of the holidays, and kitchen implement. Open daily May to Oct, weekends Nov to Apr. $.

Leavenworth Ski Hill. Ski Hill Road, Leavenworth; (509) 548-5477 (winter only); www .skileavenworth.com. When a vesture of snow settles on Leavenworth, residents and visitors alike head out to enjoy it. Snowshoeing, Nordic (cross-country) skiing, snow tubing, ski jumping, and rope tow are all popular snow sports at this in-town ski area run by the Leavenworth Winter Sports Club. Open daily when the snow falls. $$$.

Silvara Vineyards. 77 Stage Rd., Peshastin; (509) 548-1000; www.silvarawine.com. A new tasting room with a clean-lined, polished design sits atop a hill overlooking Smallwood's (see next page) and the valley. Silvara is Leavenworth's newest winery, producing a lovely Riesling and easy-to-drink Cabernet Sauvignon amongst its varietals. Open daily for tastings.

Sleeping Lady Mountain. 7375 Icicle Rd., Leavenworth; (509) 548-6344 or (800) 574-2123; www.sleepinglady.com. A silent sanctuary for arts, fine cuisine, and nature, this retreat is a beautiful getaway—even if it's just for a quick stroll through the art walk. See the rare Dale Chihuly outdoor installation Icicles (which is made of more than 1,000 pieces of handblown glass), the fabulous riverside salmon sculptures, art glass hung as tree ornaments, and other spectacular outdoor artworks. The art walk is open daily, although it may be closed for special events. Especially during summer weekends it is best to call ahead. Behind the complex, the hills still show scars from the 1994 Leavenworth fires. From July 24 through December 24 of that year, fires destroyed fourteen homes and burned about 180,000 acres of land.

becoming bavaria

Faced with a slumping logging industry in the 1960s, town leaders brainstormed ways to draw in tourists to the picturesque community of Leavenworth. After settling on the adoption of a Bavarian theme, hours of self-funded work transformed the town into an alpine village. Woodwork, murals, and Gothic-script signage add authenticity to the town. Other Bavarian-themed experiences include the morning alpenhorn serenade at the Enzian Inn and the sausage and schnitzel served at the in-town German restaurants.

While you wouldn't have seen a pair of lederhosen in the town a half century ago, you just might today. The community pride over the adopted heritage has grown so much so that the census percentages of local residents claiming German ancestry has increased from zero to about 20 percent.

Smallwood's Harvest. 10461 Stemm Rd., Peshastin; (509) 548-4196; www.smallwoods harvest.com. This spot may just appeal to the whole group: There is a petting farm, corn maze, fresh farm produce, a wine-tasting room, and then the endless samples of the salsas, sauces, preserves, honeys, and other goodies produced under the Smallwood's label. Add to that overnight lodging and you may not depart until the next harvest season. Open daily. $.

where to eat

The Alley Cafe. 214 8th St., Leavenworth; (509) 548-6109; www.thealleycafe.com. Although the nearby Italian restaurant star Visconti's has received many accolades, the small, hidden Alley Cafe is a great alternative for an intimate dinner. Approaching on 8th Street, a sign directs diners, fittingly, to enter via the alley. Flower boxes in summer and a cozy warmth in winter greet diners. Expect hearty helpings and a full wine list. Open for weekend lunch and daily for dinner. $$–$$$.

Gustav's. 617 Hwy. 2, Leavenworth; (509) 548-4509; www.gustavsleavenworth.com. A little rough around the edges, Gustav's is a great destination for those who are retreating from the outdoors to warm up and relax over a beer. Dozens of brews on tap make the pub a favorite with hikers or during Oktoberfest. Although the menu tends toward the heavy-eating side (think burgers and German sausages), there is also a refreshing variety of salads. Open daily for lunch and dinner. $–$$.

Pavz. 833 Front St., Leavenworth; (509) 548-2103. Delicately crafted crepes served in a casual candlelit bistro make for a lighter dinner option. Tuck into a plate of seafood pasta followed by a chocolate gelato, baked cherry, or hazelnut nougat crepe. Or, make a crepe the main dish with filling options like roasted vegetables, spicy Italian sausage, or shrimp. The restaurant is open for lunch and dinner daily. $$–$$$.

where to stay

Enchanted River Inn. 9700 East Leavenworth Rd., Leavenworth; (509) 548-9797 or (877) 548-9797; www.enchantedriverinn.com. Supremely enchanting indeed, this B&B looks out over the Wenatchee River. Sandy beaches, rocky banks, and frequent wildlife sightings immediately draw visitors to the windows and river-view deck. Three rooms offer comfy beds, thoughtful and unique accent lighting, and either Jacuzzi tubs or deluxe showers. Visit in summertime and enjoy breakfast on the deck or relax by the fireplace in the colder months. $$$$.

The Enzian Inn. 590 Hwy. 2, Leavenworth; (509) 548-5269 or (800) 223-8511; www.enzianinn.com. With an amazingly palpable family personality and hospitality for a 105-room hotel, the Enzian also offers comforts that include down duvets, robes, and an open-air hot tub. The buffet breakfast spread and alpenhorn serenade make a lovely start to the morning. Putt a round on the eighteen-hole putting green as mountain goats mow the grass and the Enzian's own waterfall adds a gentle white noise. $$–$$$.

leavenworth festivals

One would expect Leavenworth's Oktoberfest to be the biggest party in town, but in fact it's the annual Christmas Lighting Festival that draws the largest crowds and leads to fully booked rooms. Started in 1969, the Christmas lighting sees Leavenworth flick the switch on countless twinkling lights, harkening crisply from under the Bavarian eaves and winter snows. The Christmas Lighting Festival generally runs the first three weekends of December.

cashmere

On the south banks of the Wenatchee River, Cashmere features antique shops, a twenty-building pioneer village, and the Aplets & Cotlets candy factory. It's also the gateway to the Wenatchee Valley, beyond which apple orchards, dams, and forests stretch east.

getting there

Travel east from Leavenworth on US 2 for 11 miles (about 15 minutes). Turn onto Division Street and cross the Wenatchee River to the tightly knit downtown of Cashmere.

where to go

Cashmere Cider Mill Tasting Room. 5420 Woodring Canyon Rd., Cashmere; (509) 782-3564; www.gourmetcider.com. Often a host for special music events, Cashmere Cider Mill offers tastings to visitors. The mill presses cider from local Wenatchee Valley apples. Open Thurs to Sun. $.

Cashmere Museum and Pioneer Village. 600 Cotlets Way, Cashmere; (509) 782-3230; www.cashmeremuseum.org. An assembly of relocated yet original pioneer buildings stands outside the Cashmere Museum. From a schoolhouse and barbershop to hotel and doctor's office, the village, could almost operate as its own community. The museum sheds light on life during the pioneer days with collections of Native American and pioneer artifacts and exhibits exploring the natural world. The village is open daily Mar to Oct. Call ahead to confirm hours. $$.

Liberty Orchards. 117 Mission Ave., Cashmere; (509) 782-2191 or (800) 231-3242; www.libertyorchards.com. Aplets & Cotlets, the sugar-coated fruit-and-nut candies, have been produced by Liberty Orchards since the 1940s. From the preparation to cooking to packing, every factory tour has a sweet ending: a sample of the candy. Free tours run daily every 20 minutes. Closed weekends Jan to Mar.

apple country

Fruit stands are a staple in this area of the state, mostly stocking the valley's favorite varieties of apples, such as Fuji, Gala, Granny Smith, Braeburn, and Golden or Red delicious. For more on the local apple scene head further east to the **Washington Apple Commission Visitor Center** *(2900 Euclid Ave., Wenatchee; 509-663-9600; www.bestapples.com).*

Peshastin Pinnacles State Park. Off North Dryden Road, Highway 2; www.parks.wa
.gov. Popular with rock climbers, sandstone slabs jut up to 200 feet into the air as mini
craggy peaks at Peshastin Pinnacles State Park. This day-use park offers restrooms and
picnic areas, plus excellent views. Open daily.

where to eat

Brian's Bulldog Pizza. 107 Cottage Ave., Cashmere; (509) 782-1505; www.briansbull
dogpizza.com. The local pride is infectious here, with orange and black (the colors of Cashmere High School) covering every surface. Pictures of recent sports teams fill the walls,
while locals chow down on pizza or bowl at one of the neighboring four lanes. Open daily
for lunch and dinner. $–$$.

Country Boys BBQ. 400 Aplets Way, Cashmere; (509) 782-7427; www.countryboysbbq
.com. The bronze pig outside sits blissfully unaware—Country Boys BBQ is legendary for
its ribs. Outdoor picnic tables offer a relaxed summer feel, while the whittled-wood chairs
keep the interior casual. Open Tues to Sat for lunch and dinner. $$–$$$.

worth more time

Wenatchee Valley. Another 20 minutes further east on US 2 leads to Wenatchee and
the banks of the Columbia River. The region is home to power-generating dams, such as
Rocky Reach Hydro Project (Hwy. 97-A, Wenatchee; 509-663-7522; www.chelanpud
.org). But there are also lots of good things growing thanks to the Columbia River, a source
for agricultural irrigation. Plan a tour highlighting the local produce by stopping in at the
Washington Apple Commission Visitor Center (2900 Euclid Ave., Wenatchee; 509-
663-9600; www.bestapples.com). Or, enjoy the trails, ponds, and evergreens at **Ohme
Gardens** (3327 Ohme Rd., Wenatchee; 509-662-5785; www.ohmegardens.com). The
gardens are open daily mid-Apr to mid-Oct.

southeast

day trip 01

southeast

>>>

hendrix and hydroplanes:
renton, kent, auburn

A horse-racing track, memorial to a guitar legend, and the area's only IKEA store blend to create a curious mix of tourism south of Seattle. These communities along I-405 are so quick to access and, because of their population density, are home to a unique complement of attractions. They are often overlooked.

The diversity spans the Jimi Hendrix memorial and a restaurant with 800 seats in Renton, fall pumpkin patches and a race-boat museum in Kent, and antiques and horse racing in Auburn.

renton

The city's busy downtown sits amidst local attractions: The polished granite of the Hendrix memorial, a downtown museum, and a working glass-art gallery. Leading to the shores of Lake Washington, the riverside trails of Cedar River Park end at a boathouse where canoe and kayak rentals are available. Excellent, quality restaurants (think handsome steaks to sea urchin dishes) and hands-on glassblowing workshops create an eclectic mix of urban tourism.

getting there

Either follow I-5 south to the junction with I-405, which heads east to Renton, or take I-90 east to the junction with I-405 and then follow the interstate south. Both Kent and Auburn are an easy distance from Renton along SR 167, also known as the Valley Freeway.

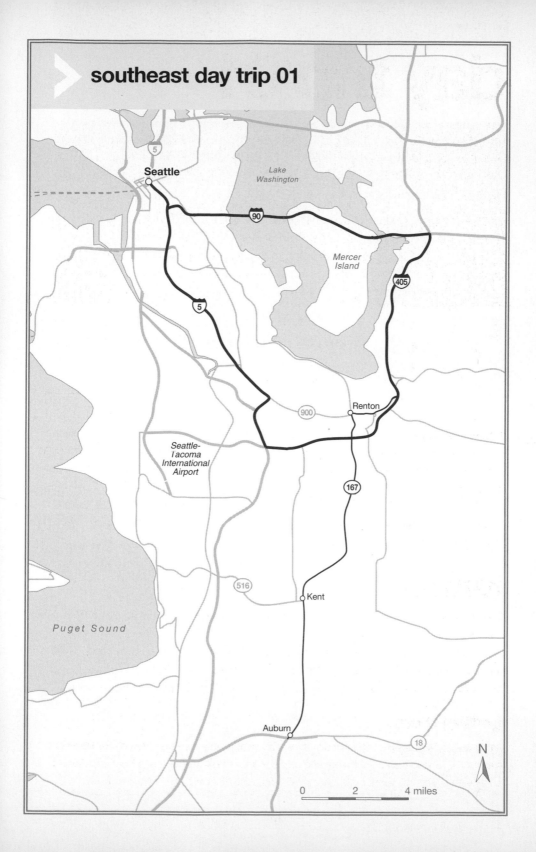

Seattle

Lake
Washington

5

90

Mercer
Island

405

900

Renton

Seattle-
Tacoma
International
Airport

167

516

Kent

Puget Sound

Auburn

18

N

0   2   4 miles

where to go

Cedar River Trail. Cedar River Park Dr. off Maple Valley Hwy., Renton. An in-town trail is great for walking, running, biking, and in-line skating. On-trail attractions include river views, a salmon weir, and canoe or kayak rentals at the **Cascade Canoe and Kayak Center** on Lake Washington (1060 Nishiwaki Lane; 425-430-0111; www.canoe-kayak.com). Rentals available by the hour or day: $–$$$.

Jimi Hendrix Memorial. Greenwood Memorial Park and Funeral Home, 350 Monroe Ave. Northeast, Renton; (425) 255-1511; www.jimihendrixmemorial.com. A large granite memorial is inscribed with lyrics and images familiar to Hendrix fans. In addition to being the resting place for Jimi Hendrix, the plot includes other Hendrix family members, including the guitar legend's parents and grandmother. Open daily during daylight hours.

Renton History Museum. 235 Mill Ave. South, Renton; (425) 255-2330; www.renton historymuseum.org. In a 1942 Art Deco–style fire station, the museum preserves photos and artifacts from local history, including Renton's days of coal mining, logging, and pioneers. The museum is close to the polished Veterans Memorial Park as well as the drinking fountain decorated with the portrait head of Chief Sealth. Open Tues to Sat. $.

where to shop

Fry's Electronic Store. 800 Garden Ave. North, Renton; (425) 525-0200; www.frys.com. A mecca for electronics, Fry's features specials on everything from laptops to housewares. Open daily.

IKEA. 601 Southwest 41st St., Renton; (425) 656-2980; www.ikea-usa.com. As the only IKEA location in the Seattle area, this megastore is an undeniably popular destination. You'll find the same products from this iconic Swedish manufacturer online, but the store has the amazingly cheap Swedish eats you can only snag in person and the always cutely designed display rooms. Open daily.

Uptown Glassworks. 230 Main Ave. South, Renton; (425) 228-1849; www.uptownglass works.com. This large downtown location presents the perfect spot for gift shopping. From functional to frivolous, the pieces vary greatly in size, style, and price. If you've been inspired by the works of Dale Chihuly in Tacoma (see South Day Trip 02), enroll in a glassblowing or glass-bead-making class and create a personalized treasure. This may not be the best spot for kids as every surface holds a breakable object. The glass shop in back provides a space where glass artists forge stunning and glowing pieces. Open daily.

where to eat

Blossom Asian Bistro. 305 Burnett Ave. South, Renton; (425) 430-1610; www.blossom asianbistro.com. From sushi to kimchee, menu items draw on the culinary creations of

Vietnam, Malaysia, Japan, Thailand, and Korea—just to name a few. Add in a French-trained chef and Blossom has quickly become a favorite spot in town. Open daily for dinner. $$–$$$.

Melrose Grill. 819 Houser Way South, Renton; (425) 254-0759; www.melrosegrill.com. Since 1901 this clapboard building has welcomed travelers and locals for merriment. The Melrose Grill survived Prohibition (1918), a fire that burned the top two floors (1928), a stint housing a sparring ring (1972), as well as many owners over the last century. But the historic building has endured and nowadays operates as an upscale and intimate steakhouse. Although the menu includes some chicken and fish, vegetarians will be happiest to head elsewhere. Open daily for dinner. $$$–$$$$.

Tea Palace. 2828 Sunset Lane Northeast, Renton; (425) 228-9393; www.teapalace restaurant.com. You may hear the crooning of Asian love songs as you visit here—the restaurant and banquet halls can accommodate, up to 800 people, and the Tea Palace is a popular spot for large wedding parties. But small parties can also visit for dinner or dim sum. A multipage menu covers specialties like sea urchin and shark fin soup as well as favorite seafood and vegetarian dishes. Open daily, 10 a.m. to 10 p.m. $$–$$$$.

kent

In addition to a pleasant main street, Kent offers unique museums (think hydroplanes or a creative take on local history). The city is an undemanding daytime destination with wonderful cafes, a polished shopping district, and tranquil downtown parks.

getting there

Travel south 6 miles on SR 167, also known as the Valley Freeway, then take Central Avenue into downtown. Not accounting for traffic, the journey takes under 10 minutes.

where to go

Centennial Center Gallery. City of Kent Campus, 400 West Gowe St., Kent; (253) 856-5050; www.ci.kent.wa.us/arts. Although small and located in a municipal building, the breezeway-style gallery features stunningly good examples of Pacific Northwest art. Unfortunately as the building is only open Mon to Fri, weekend day-trippers may be out of luck.

Hydroplane & Raceboat Museum. 5917 South 196th St., Kent; (206) 764-9453; www .thunderboats.org. Dedicated to the speedy sport of powerboat racing, the museum offers some incredibly unique events including open-mike nights, lectures, and an annual exhibition on Lake Chelan. Exhibits include full size hydroplanes (which look like floating UFOs), engines, race suits, and memorabilia. Open Tues to Sat. $$.

Kaibara and Yangzhou Parks. Railroad Avenue between Smith and Meeker Streets, Kent; www.ci.kent.wa.us/parks. The former is a Japanese garden with stepping stones, a pond, and beautiful foliage. The latter includes a Chinese pavilion. Both are easy to find near the shopping, railroad station, and dining district.

Kent Historical Museum. 855 East Smith St., Kent; (253) 854-4330; www.kenthistorical museum.org. Exhibits at the museum strike a unique chord that goes beyond the pioneers: Perhaps learn about the Japanese-American internment experience during World War II; hear recordings of the high school band during its 1920s glory days; or see the collection of cream pitchers that number in the dozens. Open Tues to Sat. $.

where to eat

Bittersweet Restaurant. 211 First Ave. South, Kent; (253) 854-0707; www.bittersweet restaurant.com. Local art hangs on the brick walls, creating a vibrant historical feel to the cafe. The biscuits are spectacularly fresh. Service can be a bit slow on a busy day, so relax and enjoy. Perhaps a fellow diner will start playing the in-restaurant piano. Open daily for breakfast and lunch. $–$$.

Wild Wheat Bakery Cafe and Restaurant. 202 First Ave. South, Kent; (253) 856-8919. The menu items are creative and superb versions of comfort food. Ocean-inspired twists like crab linguine, salmon tostadas, and a tempura platter complement the hearty soups, sandwiches, and bakery-fresh treats. Open daily for breakfast and lunch. $–$$.

where to stay

Victorian Garden Bed & Breakfast. 9621 South 200th St., Kent; (253) 850-1776 or (888) 850-1776; www.victoriangardensbandb.com. Well-loved gardens are the outdoor extension of this four-room B&B. There's an amphitheater, private sitting area, and lovely porch. Over three decades the owners have transformed a run-down 1888 farmhouse into a charming inn. A spiral staircase leads to one room, most have private balconies, and all have robes and in-room refrigerators. $$$.

auburn

Auburn is a family-oriented destination. Parks with disc-golf courses, festivals, and bocce ball courts add outdoor options that complement the museums and shops. A busy raceway— Emerald Downs—offers programming aimed at families making it a fun, activity-filled summer day-trip option.

The town originally went by the name Slaughter, but locals decided to rename the community given that the local hotel was called the Slaughter House. Some sources say the name *Auburn* comes from settlers who arrived from Auburn, NY. Others quote a line in an Oliver Goldsmith poem that begins "Sweet Auburn, loveliest village on the plain."

getting there

Auburn Way connects the downtowns of Kent and Auburn for a quick 6-mile trip. Or, take SR 167 from Kent and cut east on SR 18. Both routes take about 15 to 20 minutes in normal traffic.

where to go

Emerald Downs. 2300 Emerald Downs Dr., Auburn; (253) 288-7000 or (888) 931-8400; www.emeralddowns.com. From the "Call to Post" to the coming down the stretch, Emerald Downs provides a full day of race activities as well as dining options. Races run weekends and holidays starting in mid-Apr, then generally Thurs to Sun from late May through Sept. Admission charged for live racing events. $$.

Game Farm Wilderness Park. 2401 Stuck River Rd., Auburn; (253) 931-3043 or (253) 931-3095. Disc golf, camping sites, and festivals make the park a fabulous day-trip destination for families. Watch for s'mores signs posted around town roads: They advertise a minifestival in the park with a bonfire and live music. Open year-round.

Les Gove Park. 11th and Auburn Way South, Auburn. This downtown park is handy to the town museum and features bocce courts, horseshoes, and plenty of play areas. Open year-round.

White River Valley Museum. 918 H St. Southeast, Auburn; (253) 288-7433; www.wrv museum.org. The museum connects the region's history through unique and insightful temporary exhibits and permanent displays telling Native American, pioneer, and railroad stories. Family programs are a large focus. Open Wed to Sun. $.

where to shop

Comstock's Bindery & Bookshop. 257 East Main St., Auburn; (253) 939-8770. Endless shelves of quality (and well-organized!) secondhand books create a warm atmosphere. The bookshop cats are friendly and the staff helpful. Open Mon to Sat.

SuperMall of the Great Northwest. 1101 SuperMall Way, Auburn; (253) 833-4401 or (800) 729-8258; www.supermall.com. At the intersection of SR 167 and SR 18, the Super-Mall is a beacon of neon light. Shops include Levi's, Banana Republic, and Eddie Bauer discount outlets. Open daily.

where to eat

Marvel Ukrainian Food & Deli. 615 C St. Southwest, Auburn; (253) 887-8181, www.marvel foodanddeli.com. There's a small dining area where diners can enjoy grocery purchases or items from the hot-food counter. The family-run store stocks goods from Europe but also does much of the baking and cooking in-house. Open 9 a.m. to 9 p.m., Mon to Sat. $$.

worth more time

Flaming Geyser State Park. 23700 Southeast Flaming Geyser Rd., Auburn; www.parks .wa.gov. This park once featured a 20-foot flaming geyser and was privately run. Those days are no more. After stretched finances, the park was transferred to the state and now two small methane geysers still warrant the park's name. It is no Old Faithful, but it does make a nice day-trip destination. Park facilities include access to the Green River, hiking and biking trails, and fire pits; however, the park is currently undergoing upgrades and most of the park is closed to vehicle (but not pedestrian) traffic. Open year-round.

day trip 02

southeast

>>>

"the mountain"—mount rainier:
sunrise, paradise, longmire

One can truthfully say they've found Paradise in Mount Rainier National Park. It's not so much a village as a gathering of buildings (a ranger station, visitor center, and a timber-framed inn) set below the snowy slopes of "The Mountain" where hikers, climbers, and day visitors converge. The twisting roads, uncut timber, wind-blown vistas, creeping glaciers, and roaming wildlife all add immeasurable charm to a trip to the park.

Added as the fifth national park in 1899, Rainier—or *Tahoma,* its Native American name—features the mountain at its center. The 14,410-foot peak is the highest in the state and towers above the other volcanoes in the Cascade Range.

Mount Rainer's slopes are cloaked in twenty-six major glaciers, and its volcanic power has been quiet since an eruption 120–190 years ago. But steam vents hiss near the summit, and volcanologists anticipate the mountain will erupt again. Although it's difficult to predict just when, the mountain appears to trigger lahars—giant mudflows and signs of a large eruption—every of 500–1,000 years.

This day trip circles the mountain clockwise, starting at the freshly named Sunrise lookout. Visit the park in late summer for the wildflowers, when the lower slopes are dotted with asters, lupines, and red Indian paintbrush among countless varieties of blooms. In fall, the chill of winter begins to hint. Watch for forecasts of snow in late September and October. If you can stay longer than a day, the park pass (priced by the vehicle at $15) is valid for up to seven days. And with endless lodging options, making a day trip into a weekend getaway is all too easy.

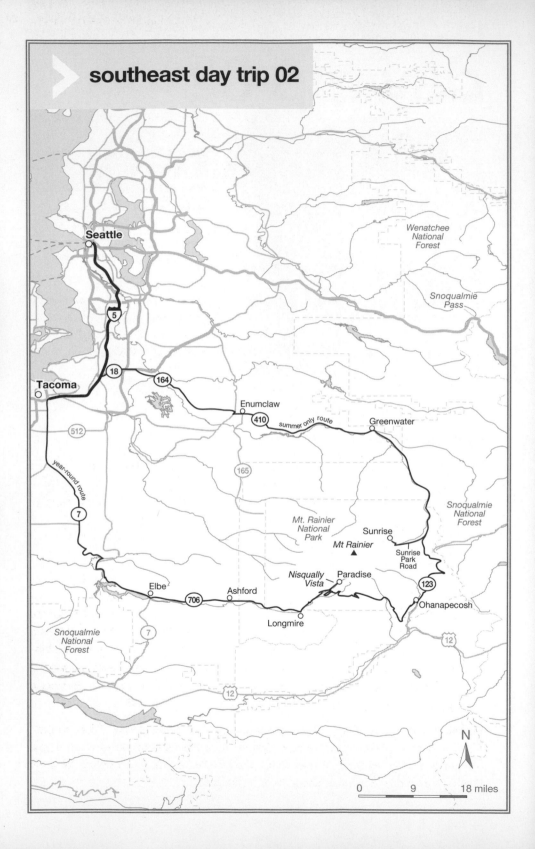

southeast day trip 02

getting there

Year-round, begin the journey at the Nisqually Entrance by taking I-5 south to exit 133 Tacoma, then following SR 7 to Elbe and heading east on SR 706.

The following route is a summer-only option since from November to May, SR 410 closes starting at the Crystal Mountain turnoff. Follow I-5 south of Federal Way to the junction with SR 18 at exit 142A. After heading east, follow SR 164 southeast. From here the directions get a lot simpler and traffic lighter: Take SR 410 from Enumclaw through Greenwater to Sunrise.

sunrise

Sitting at 6,400 feet on Sunrise Ridge, this is the highest point in the park reachable by car. Of course the vantage affords stunning views looking at the northeast flank of Mount Rainier's 14,410-foot peak, a mountain climbers' camp, and the Emmons Glacier—the largest on the mountain. From here lookouts and hiking trails lead to fantastic views and ever-higher elevations.

The few visitor services, including a visitor's center and restaurant, provide summer-only amenities and information.

getting there

Driving south on SR 410 through the Mount Baker–Snoqualmie National Forest, make a right turn onto Sunrise Park Road. Keep straight after 5 miles when there's a left-hand turnoff heading to the White River Campground. For 11 more miles the route climbs the ridge through a series of switchbacks.

The road to Sunrise is generally open from July to early October. Total travel time is 2 to 2.5 hours from Seattle.

where to go

Crystal Mountain Ski Area. 33914 Crystal Mountain Blvd. (5 miles before the Sunrise turnoff); (360) 663-3050; www.skicrystal.com. Like many ski hills, Crystal Mountain finds a new life in summer, welcoming visitors to lush hiking trails and stunning displays of wildflowers. Elk frequent the ski area, so watch and listen for them. In winter, eleven lifts provide access to the more than fifty runs that make the hill the largest in Washington. Ski season generally runs mid-Nov to mid-Apr. Day passes start at about $55. $$$.

Sunrise Point. MP 13, Sunrise Park Road, Mount Rainier National Park. Three-hundred feet lower than your eventual destination, Sunrise Point offers sensational views. The panorama includes five volcanoes: Rainier, Baker, Glacier Peak, Adams, and Hood are all within sight on a clear day. Accessible under the $15 park pass.

Sunrise Visitor Center. MP 16, Sunrise Park Road, Mount Rainier National Park. Exhibits and information on hiking trails are available at the visitor center at the end of the road. A historic building, the visitor center and adjacent ranger accommodations were built in a blockhouse style yet are still dwarfed by the peak of Mount Rainier behind. Head to the left of the visitor center where there's a telescope that looks out to the glaciers of the volcano. Look, too, for climbers at Camp Schurman—a climbing camp that sits at 9,510 feet. For a short walk, take the trail to Emmons lookout. The stone balcony sits on the side of the hill and is ideal for group shots with Mount Rainier in the back row. Sunrise makes an easy departure point for day hikes with multiple trails fanning out from the visitor area. Open July to Sept. Accessible under the $15 park pass.

where to eat

Summit House Restaurant. Crystal Mountain Ski Area. During summer this restaurant, sitting at a 6,872-foot elevation, serves sunset dinners and weekend brunch. All winter long it's open to skiers and snowboarders. As with Sunrise Point, you get views of the region's ever-impressive volcanoes on clear days. Dinner prices include the lift ticket, without which it'd be a very long hike! Call ahead for hours and reservations. $$$$.

where to stay

Crystal Mountain Lodging. 33000 Crystal Mountain Blvd., Crystal Mountain Ski Area; (360) 663-2558 or (888) 668-4368; www.crystalmountainlodging.com. Since there are so few available quality choices for dining on this side of Mount Rainier, bringing a few groceries and cooking in may be the best option. The kitchens at the condos are supremely stocked with everything you'd expect at home. Each has its own personality, depending on the owner, but generally the accommodations are cozy with clean linens and a friendly welcome. As an added bonus, the summer rates can be half the winter rates. $$–$$$$.

paradise

A one-way-in destination, Paradise is popular with all manner of visitors. Whether your style is sipping a glass of wine to the sounds of a live pianist or strapping on a helmet and crampons to climb a mountain, there's a version of Paradise for you.

Paradise sits on the southern flank on Mount Rainier at about 5,400 feet in elevation.

getting there

From Sunrise, take SR 410 then SR 123 south towards Ohanapecosh, before cutting west on Stevens Canyon Road. Driving between Sunrise and Paradise takes about an hour.

Direct from Seattle, enter the park through the Nisqually Entrance by taking I-5 south to exit 133 Tacoma, then following SR 7 to Elbe and heading east on SR 706 through Longmire to Paradise.

where to go

Grove of the Patriarchs. SR 706 (east of Paradise, west of the junction with SR 123), Mount Rainier National Park. About halfway between Sunrise and Paradise lies one of the shortest and most lovely hikes in the park. A well-worn trail leads to a suspension bridge spanning the Ohanapecosh River, taking visitors to a river island. There sandy paths skirt some of the largest trees in the park, including swollen trunks of cedar and Douglas fir. These trees seeded after a fire that roared through the area a millennium ago. Now river nutrients from seasonal flooding and the continual source of water keep these trees reaching upward. Accessible under the $15 park pass.

Henry M. Jackson Visitor Center. Paradise, Mount Rainier National Park; (360) 569-2211 (general park information line). Exhibits on ice climbing provide a new perspective on the park. The new visitor center was completed in 2008. Generally open May to Sept. Accessible under the $15 park pass.

Narada Falls Viewpoint. SR 706 (west of Paradise), Mount Rainier National Park. A short but at times steep trail leads to an excellent spot for admiring the 168-foot Narada Falls that is sourced from the Paradise River. Cascading down from below the road, the falls sometimes create a rainbow halo and remain a favorite photo stop. Accessible under the $15 park pass.

where to eat & stay

Paradise Inn. Paradise, Mount Rainier National Park; (360) 569-2275; www.mtrainier guestservices.com. The timber skeleton of the lodge tents a large social area with restaurants, gifts shops, and sitting areas. The 1916 inn includes 121 units on the doorstep of the mountain. A large main-level area filled with couches and fireplaces creates a lively atmosphere for planning hikes, swapping wildlife encounter stories, and sharing photos with fellow visitors. Rooms available with and without bathrooms. In addition to a Sunday

names of mount rainier

The towering peak of Mount Rainier goes by many names. The Native Americans call this volcano Tahoma, Takhoma, and Ta-co-bet—names meaning "snowy peak" and "big mountain." But in 1792 Captain George Vancouver spied the mountain and named it after his superior, Rear Admiral Peter Rainier.

Locally, however, you'll find Mount Rainier is most often simply referred to as "The Mountain."

brunch, the restaurant serves breakfast, lunch, and dinner. Creative and hearty dishes include buffalo meatloaf, rosemary prime rib, and crab macaroni and cheese. Restaurant: $$–$$$. Rooms: $$–$$$$.

longmire

Less of a destination than Paradise, Longmire features the park's lone museum and a second historic lodge. This is also the location of the original park headquarters, and it makes a convenient spot to gather information or stop for a meal.

getting there

From Paradise travel west on SR 706 for 11 miles (20 minutes) to Longmire.

Direct from Seattle, enter the park through the Nisqually Entrance by taking I-5 south to exit 133 Tacoma, then following SR 7 to Elbe and heading east on SR 706 to Longmire.

where to go

Longmire Museum. Longmire, Mount Rainier National Park; (360) 569-2211 ext. 3314. Telling the natural history as well as the history of the park from its 1899 establishment as the country's fifth national park, the Longmire Museum is part of a National Historic Landmark District. The building once housed the headquarters for the park but the log-and-stone building is now a museum. Next door, the Wilderness Information Center provides summertime information on trails and the backcountry. The museum is open 9 a.m. to 4:30 p.m. year-round. Free with $15 park pass.

where to eat & stay

National Park Inn. Longmire, Mount Rainier National Park; (360) 569-2275; www.mtrainier guestservices.com. The smaller of the two national park inns, the Longmire lodge has the longest history in the park, stretching back to 1884. About six miles from the Nisqually entrance, the year-round inn offers just twenty-five rooms, available with or without bath. An on-site restaurant serves breakfast, lunch, and dinner. Warming entrees include baked trout, a maple-glazed salmon, or pesto pasta. Restaurant: $$–$$$. Rooms: $$–$$$$.

worth more time

Outside the Nisqually Park entrance, take a relaxing trip through the scenery with **Mount Rainier Scenic Railroad** (349 Mineral Creek Rd., Mineral or 54124 Mountain Hwy. East, Elbe; 360-492-5588 or 888-783-2611; www.mrsr.com). The tiny village of Mineral is the departure point for the Mount Rainier Scenic Railroad. The tracks cut out a journey into the foothills below Mount Rainier. Tickets are about $20 per person, less for children, seniors, or military. $$$.

day trip 03

southeast

fruit bowl of the nation:
yakima

yakima

Arriving on the outskirts of Yakima via I-82, you'll not mistake the glaciered slopes of Mount Rainier and the dark hulk of Mount Adams on the western horizon. But after the initial wows, it's the foreground that draws your attention: the starkness of the desert, the subtleties of the millennia-old hills, and the alien-looking lushness of the agricultural lands.

Although the wide downtown streets are lined with opulent buildings, there's something missing in the grandeur. But look hard and you'll find a stunning concert venue and wine-tasting rooms. A large sector of life in the town surrounds Mexican heritage. One-third of the population is of Mexican descent, and there are plenty of roadside taquerias and upscale Mexican restaurants to feed hungry travelers. Add in the burgeoning wine industry and endless orchards of fresh fruit and the prospects for this middle-of-the-desert city look good.

Receiving a mere 6–8 inches in annual rainfall, the city feels a world away from the dampness of the state's west coast. Canyon Road leading north out of town provides access to recreation sites, where tubing is a popular and relaxing summer sport.

Between the local museums, quirky shopping experiences, winery tasting rooms, and a busy military base on the outskirts, Yakima pours out a unique taste of Washington.

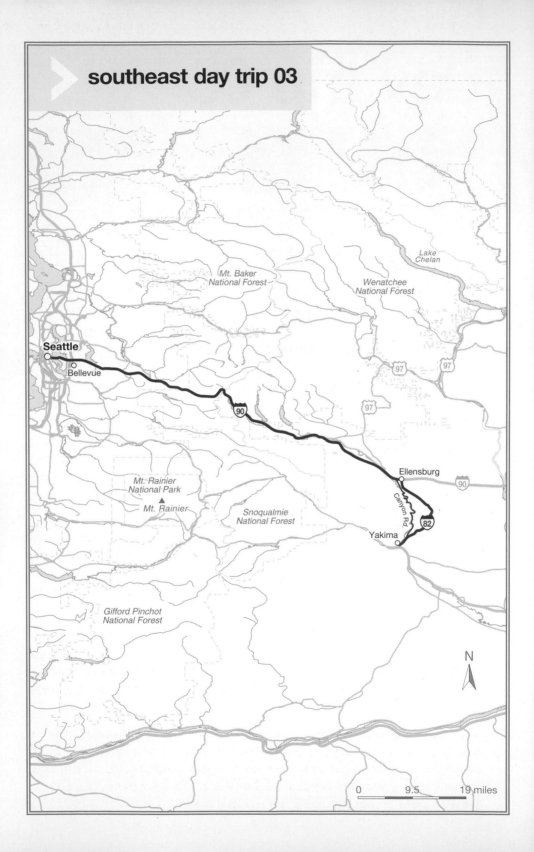

Lake
Chelan

Mt. Baker
National Forest

Wenatchee
National Forest

Seattle

Bellevue

97

97

90

97

Mt. Rainier
National Park

▲
Mt. Rainier

Snoqualmie
National Forest

Ellensburg

90

Canyon Rd.

82

Yakima

Gifford Pinchot
National Forest

N

0   9.5   19 miles

canyon road

My preferred route to Yakima is Canyon Road. In Ellensburg, South Main Street becomes Canyon Road, officially known as SR 821. The route follows the river through desert hills and columned basalt formations. Just north of Yakima the route meets I-82 for a short final stretch.

getting there

Head east on I-90 for about 110 miles, just past Ellensburg. Merge onto I-82, journeying 32 miles south to Yakima. The route climbs and descends hill after hill, with a few scenic lookouts en route. The journey, without heavy traffic, takes a little over 2 hours.

where to go

Yakima Valley Visitor Information Center. 101 North Fair Ave., Yakima; (509) 573-3388 or (800) 221-0751; www.visityakimavalley.org. With dozens of wineries in the Yakima Valley, some planning is required to select the highlights (see Worth More Time at the end of this chapter for some suggestions). At the information center, get a head start by picking up the winery guides and even stocking up on a few bottles. The information center's hours change with the seasons, but it's generally open daily with longer hours on tasting weekends and in summer.

Seasons Church. 101 North Naches Ave., Yakima; (509) 453-1888 or (888) 723-7660; www.theseasonsyakima.com. Built in 1902, the stained glass, domed ceiling, and heavenly acoustics of this church make it an excellent music venue. And the concerts and festivals held here do the venue justice: spring and fall music festivals bring world-class jazz musicians to play the Seasons. Performances year-round. Tickets prices vary, but are generally $10–20. $$$.

The Tasting Room. 250 Ehler Rd., Yakima; (509) 966-0686; www.winesofwashington .com. Atop a hill, this tasting room and art gallery teases the senses. Visitors can taste wines from three vineyards here, coming together under the branding Wines of Washington: Naches Heights Vineyards, Harlequin Wine Cellars, and Wilridge Winery. Open Thurs to Mon.

Yakima Area Arboretum. 1401 Arboretum Dr. (I-82 and Nob Hill Boulevard), Yakima; (509) 248-7337; www.ahtrees.org. Amidst the desert-like surroundings of Yakima, the arboretum is a calm, cool, and green destination to explore. Japanese-style gardens, winding paths, and exhibits at the Jewett Visitor Center all call for a longer-than-planned stop. The visitor center is open Tues to Sat; grounds open daily.

Yakima Valley Museum. 2105 Tieton Dr., Yakima; (509) 248-0747; www.yakimavalley museum.org. This modern museum edges the beautiful Franklin Park. Exhibits inside trace the Native American and farming roots of the area and even provide a glimpse of the valley 25 million years in the past through the Time Tunnel. Explore a pioneer home, dote on a collection of more than 500 valentines, or count the rings on 15-million-year-old trees as part of the Miocene Forest exhibit. Open daily. $$.

Yakima Valley Trolleys. South Third Avenue at West Pine Street, Yakima; (509) 249-5962; www.yakimavalleytrolleys.org. An old rail yard serves as home to the city's trolley routes. The tracks make a straightaway along Pine Street, and the trolleys draw power from the single overhead wire. Tours run on summer weekends, but calling ahead is a must. $.

where to eat

Essencia Artisan Bakery. 4 North Third St., Yakima; (509) 575-5570; www.essencia artisanbakery.com. Off the main drag, Essencia serves light lunches and freshly baked goodies. The artisan bakery is open daily for breakfast, coffee, and lunch. $–$$.

Santiago's Gourmet Mexican Restaurant. 111 East Yakima Ave., Yakima; (509) 453-1644; www.santiagos.org. One of Yakima's most acclaimed restaurants, Santiago's serves Mexican favorites. Tacos, burritos, enchiladas, tamales, and chile rellenos are all on the menu, but so are a local-inspired Yakima-apple pork mole and the spicy Chicano steak. Open Mon to Fri for lunch, Mon to Sat for dinner. $$–$$$.

Tim's Downtown Tasting Room. 312 East Yakima Ave., Yakima; (509) 248-5251. Board games, comfortable seating, live music, and fresh pizzas create a laid-back atmosphere for tasting the local Yakima Valley wines. Open for lunch and dinner, Tues to Sun; Thurs to Sun in off-peak season. $$.

Yakima Valley Museum Soda Fountain. 2105 Tieton Dr., Yakima; (509) 457-9810; www .yakimavalleymuseum.org/soda. Harkening back to the 1930s, this restored soda fountain is attached to the modern Yakima Valley Museum. Ice cream, hot dogs, and soda don't exactly make for the healthiest of lunches, but head here after a day in the park or as a treat (or perhaps bribery?) for the family after enjoying the museum exhibits. The menu also includes salads, soups, and sandwiches as more substantial options. Open Mon to Sat during summer only. $–$$.

where to stay

Ledgestone Hotel. 107 North Fair Ave., Yakima; (509) 453-3151; www.yakimawahotel .com. One of the newest hotels in town with 110 suites, the Ledgestone was built primarily for those on an extended stay. As such the modern decor complements excellent amenities including fully equipped kitchens and comfy sitting areas. The major downside is its highway-adjacent location. Ask for a room away from the highway. $$.

Orchard Inn Bed & Breakfast. 1207 Pecks Canyon Rd., Yakima; (509) 966-1283 or (866) 966-1283; www.orchardinnbb.com. At this B&B hidden amidst cherry orchards, each room delivers a different air, ranging from the vibrancy of the Orchard Room, the cool calm of the Riesling, or the privacy of the Northwest room with its separate entrance. Private baths and expansive breakfasts enhance the comfort of the stay. $$–$$$.

worth more time

Yakima Valley Wine Country. Rattlesnake Hills Tourist Trail; www.rhtt.org. Close to Yakima, the route connects the dots of wineries from Wapato to Sunnyside via Granger and Zillah. The route is also near the Yakama Nation with its casino, restaurant, and **Yakama Nation Museum and Cultural Center** (100 Spiel-yi Loop, Toppenish; 509-865-2800; www.yakamamuseum.com).

south

day trip 0i

>>> **oregon trail and animal treks:**
federal way, puyallup, eatonville

This day trip bridges city civilization and the wilderness that lies not far beyond. Walk through gardens of rhodies—the state's official flower—in Federal Way, then head south to hear about Ezra Meeker's days as hop king, mayor, and pioneer advocate in Puyallup. Finally venture into the forest to encounter the wolves, cougars, and bears at Northwest Trek Wildlife Park.

Nature parks, animals, water slides, and pioneer villages prove family friendly, while the endless tales of Meeker's cross-nation treks, his bizarre construction projects, and the decor of Victorian hair sculptures will interest even the most reluctant historians.

federal way

Federal Way doesn't boast a historic or quaint downtown that may provoke the description of "strollable," but world-class gardens and fun family attractions make the city a worthwhile exit from I-5. Close to the interstate the absorbing theme park Wild Waves (a destination to flag for a summer heat wave) promises roller coasters, waterslides, and pools, while the state flower gets full billing at the Rhododendron Species Botanical Garden. Fun restaurants lighten the spirit in town.

Established when smaller lumber towns amalgamated under the same school district, Federal Way first connected to Seattle and Tacoma by SR 99 (also called the Pacific Highway) in the late 1920s. Now you don't leave one city before entering another, and the boundaries of Federal Way abut Washington's largest urban districts.

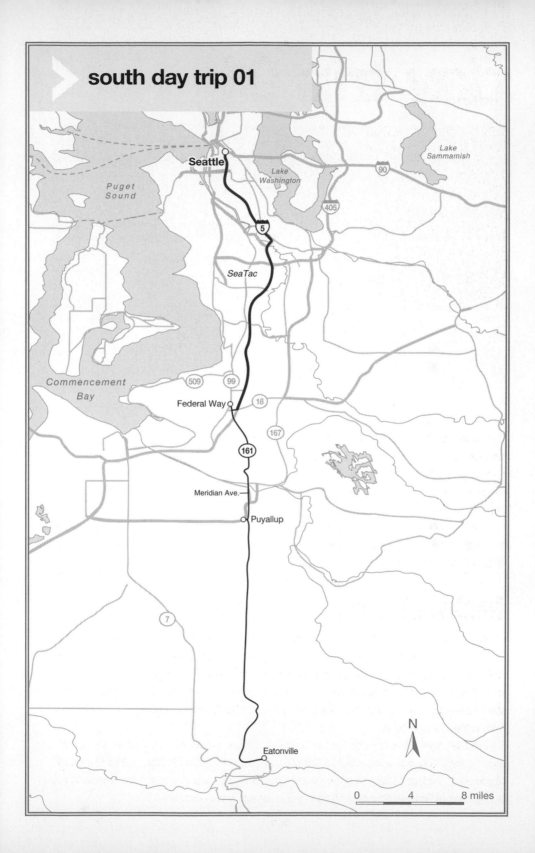

south day trip 01

getting there

With little traffic, travel at a mile-a-minute to Federal Way on I-5 south (22 miles, 22 minutes). Exit 143 leads to the commercial center while exits 142A and B lead to Wild Waves and the rhododendron garden. For a more leisurely drive take SR 99 south. Remember, though, that leisurely also means stopping for miles of traffic lights.

where to go

Dash Point State Park. 5700 Southwest Dash Point Rd., Federal Way; www.parks.wa .gov. Perched on the western edge of Federal Way, this state park provides a secluded slice of Puget Sound recreation. Beachcombing and bird watching on the shore are favorite park activities along with camping and hiking the 11 miles of forest trails. Open daily.

Rhododendron Species Botanical Garden. 2525 South 336th St., Federal Way; (253) 661-9377; www.rhodygarden.org. The rhododendrons number more than 10,000, and the soft shades of pink, yellow, and orange peak from March through May. Washington's state flower has a heritage that spans the globe, and the gardens include hundreds of species from dwarf rhodies to bushy blooms. The garden is located near the impressive Weyerhaeuser head offices and the former Pacific Rim Bonsai Collection, which closed in 2009 due to financial reasons. For an update on the bonsai collection, call (253) 924-5206. The rhododendron garden opens Fri to Wed from Mar to Sept; open Sat to Wed from Oct to Feb. $$.

West Hylebos Wetlands Park. 411 South 348th St., Federal Way; (253) 874-2005; www .hylebos.org. Close to the core of Federal Way, a one-mile trail leads visitors on an interpretive route through the wetlands. Birds, including pileated woodpeckers and black-headed grosbeaks, feature as the bog's most active main residents, but look a little closer to see the frogs, salmon, and perhaps even a weasel. Two historic cabins—the Denny and Barker Cabins, both of which the Historical Society of Federal Way is restoring—sit adjacent to the parking area. Open daily.

Wild Waves Theme Park. 36201 Enchanted Pkwy South, Federal Way; (253) 661-8000; www.wildwaves.com. With water slides, amusement rides, rafting routes, and dining, this water-and-land theme park fills a day. Hours and open dates change with the weather and seasons, but the park is generally open daily from early June through August. While admission is pricey, a season-pass option provides summer-long access to the park for about the price of two-day passes. $$$.

where to eat

Blue Island Sushi & Roll. 35002 Pacific Hwy. South, Suite 101, Federal Way; (253) 838-5500. This is sushi for tire kickers. Diners face a conveyor belt loaded with small plates ranging from *gyoza* to edamame and California rolls. Color-coded plates denote the price, and diners are free to self-serve whatever catches their eye. Whether ultra hungry (and not looking to wait) or ultra cautious, Blue Island Sushi provides an engaging meal. Ordering directly from the menu is an option too. Open daily for lunch and dinner. $$.

Jimmy Mac's Roadhouse. 34902 Pacific Hwy. South, Federal Way; (253) 874-6000; www.jimmymacsroadhouse.com. Drop your peanut shells on the floor, eat your fill of fresh rolls, and order your steak just as you like it. The menu encompasses big portions of seafood, steak, and chicken delivered with cheeky humor by friendly staff. Open daily for lunch and dinner. $$–$$$.

puyallup

Named for the long-resident Native Americans whose name means "generous people," Puyallup is the closest small town to the big city. In 1877 infamous resident Ezra Meeker platted the community, and the community's prosperity grew based on hops and agriculture.

Even though Meeker's pioneer days are long gone, it is his influence that still draws visitors to Puyallup. A pioneer himself, the spry seventy-five-year-old Meeker rejourneyed the Oregon Trail in 1906, wrote books, and lobbied politicians to raise awareness of its importance. While the pioneer spirit lives on, Puyallup has also settled into a more modern mix of family festivals, superb bakeries, and the late-summer Puyallup Fair.

getting there

From Federal Way, follow Enchanted Parkway south past Wild Waves. The route (also called SR 161) becomes Meridian Avenue and leads directly into downtown Puyallup (10 miles, 20 minutes).

where to go

Meeker Mansion. 312 Spring St., Puyallup; (253) 848-1770; www.meekermansion.org. Although best-known as the home of Ezra Meeker, this ornate Victorian mansion was actually built at the direction and expense of his wife, Eliza Jane. Ezra was happy living in a log cabin, but after a trip to England Eliza Jane desired a more elaborate abode. Sure, said Ezra (or so I paraphrase), if you pay for it. The house was built, and Eliza Jane retained the title. But this is not the only quirky twist in the tale of the Meekers. From Ezra's cross-nation treks to revive the Oregon Trail to the city-block-long building he constructed to prevent access to a church (with whom he'd had a falling out), a visit to the Meeker home is illuminating and entertaining. Some original Meeker pieces furnish the house as well as the eerie but undeniably well-crafted Victorian-era sculptures made from locks of hair. The historical society is lovingly restoring ornate ceiling murals and preserving the home of the city's founder. Open Wed to Sun. $.

Pioneer Park. 324 South Meridian, Puyallup; www.cityofpuyallup.org/services/parks-recreation/city-puyallup-parks/pioneer-park. This park becomes a converging point for the city on weekends. An indoor farmers' market (running, weekends May to August; Sat only September to October), the town library, and cafes border the public space. In addition to a statue of Ezra Meeker, view the ancient-looking ivy planted by Eliza Jane Meeker. Having grown thick like a tree with a heavy wood trunk in the 150 years or so since being planted, the Baltic ivy leans heavily on a concrete arbor. Open daily.

ezra meeker and the oregon trail

Prior to championing the history of the Oregon Trail, Meeker made a good living as a hop grower and served as the first mayor of Puyallup. But an infestation of hop lice ruined crops and financially strained Meeker. After trips to the Klondike and various business ventures, Ezra Meeker journeyed from his Puyallup home to Washington D.C., in 1906 at the age of seventy-five.

His mission was to memorialize the Oregon Trail—a route blazed by the pioneers that he too had traveled as a young man. With a wagon and two oxen named Dave and Dandy, Meeker made the journey, giving speeches and enlisting support en route.

He traveled the Oregon Trail again by cart in 1910, by automobile in 1915, and by airplane in 1924. He was planning a second journey by car, but died in 1928, aged ninety-seven.

where to eat

Comfort Food Cafe. 210 West Pioneer, #103, Puyallup; (253) 770-6147; www.comfort foodcafe.org. Mac and cheese, meat-loaf sandwiches, spaghetti pie, and freshly baked cookies: Food here has a way of warming up a cold day. Friendly service, a central location, and lots of caffeinated drinks all add to the appeal. Open Mon to Sat for breakfast and lunch. $–$$.

Pioneer Bakery. 120 South Meridian St., Puyallup; (253) 845-8336; www.thepioneer bakery.com. For more than eighty years this bakery has crafted fresh treats and breads for the community. Select from a range of sandwiches or indulge in a monstrous yet delicious Danish. The prices are cheap and the downtown location perfect en route to the Meeker Mansion, Pioneer Park, or to the downtown antique shops. Open Tues to Sat for breakfast and lunch. $–$$.

Powerhouse Restaurant & Brewery. 454 East Main, Puyallup; (253) 845-1370; www .powerhousebrewpub.com. The modern dining room, house-brewed beers, and historic red-brick architecture of the 1907 Puyallup substation create a lively destination for a meal. The menu spans pub dishes (fish tacos, burgers, and fish-and-chips) and plates with an international, healthful flair (vegan curry, Indonesian chicken salad, or a black-bean burger). Open daily for lunch and dinner. $$–$$$.

eatonville

Although offering only a half-handful of things to do on the outskirts of town, the attractions are superb, whether it's silently watching wolves and listening to elks snort in the wilds of Northwest Trek Wildlife Park or dodging chickens amidst the aged timbers of a pioneer village.

Eatonville's proximity to Mount Rainier National Park (see Southeast Day Trip 02) also provides ever-stunning vantages of the mountain on a clear day.

getting there

To reach Eatonville, again head south on SR 161 passing Northwest Trek before reaching Washington Avenue and the town center (25 miles, 45 minutes from Puyallup).

where to go

Eatonville Visitor Information Center. 136 Washington Ave. North, Eatonville; (360) 832-4000; www.eatonvillechamber.com. Located on the main route, the small visitor center is open by chance.

Northwest Trek. 11610 Trek Dr. East, Eatonville; (360) 832-6117; www.nwtrek.org. With cougar habitats, bear dens, eagle perches, and wolf lairs, the park offers so much to observe on the self-guided walking tours. See animals from the Pacific Northwest in forest settings. An hour-long tram tour travels into a restricted-access portion of the park where herds of animals are within sight of the roadway. Elk, deer, swans, and buffalo all amble past the naturalist-guided tram. Cafes, lots of parking, and interpretive signage make the park an easy trip to plan and fun experience for all. Open daily Mar to Sept; Fri to Sun from Oct to Dec. $$$.

Pioneer Farm Museum & Ohop Indian Village. 7716 Ohop Valley Rd. East, Eatonville; (360) 832-6300; www.pioneerfarmmuseum.org. An 1880s homestead provides an enclave of pioneer life. Chickens, goats, and horses all add to the farm feel. Or head to the Native American village to discover life in the Northwest before Europeans arrived. Open daily between Father's Day and Labor Day; weekends only mid-Mar to Father's Day and mid-Sept to Nov. Separate admission pricing and hours for the village and the farm museum. $$.

where to eat

Bruno's. 204 Center St. East, Eatonville; (360) 832-7866; www.eatbrunos.com. From burgers to clams to steaks, this downtown restaurant is a popular local choice. The large, easy feel to the dining room and ample parking complement a straightforward menu. Open daily for breakfast, lunch, and dinner. $$–$$$.

Tall Timber Restaurant. 121 Mashell Ave. North, Eatonville; (360) 832-3535. Burgers are the specialty here and are prepared with unique tastes, whether it's the spike burger with jalapeño, the Mount Rainier with ham and cheese, or the two ⅓-pound patties of the logger burger. Open daily for breakfast, lunch, and dinner. $$–$$$.

day trip 02

south

>>> **museum city:**
tacoma

tacoma

Let's not even touch on Tacoma's past. Instead, explore the city's revitalized downtown—a combination of the timeless museums, polished dining, gorgeous city parks, palpable history, and elevated architecture that create a striking vibe.

At the center of downtown lies the museum district. The worthy feature presentations include the Museum of Glass with its working hot shop, the Northwest-focused Tacoma Art Museum, and the tongue-in-cheek Washington History Museum. The luminescent Chihuly Bridge of Glass connects these core attractions.

But around the city you'll find more excellent museums: A museum of treasured manuscripts lies near a lush park, and in Point Defiance the fur traders' Fort Nisqually rates as a local favorite. Plus there are plans for an aerodynamic-looking new LeMay Car Museum in the Dome District.

Whether it's catching a show in the tightly knit theater district or venturing west to the 702-acre woodland Point Defiance Park with its zoo and aquarium, a raft of attractions eclipse the reputation of the old Tacoma.

getting there

From Seattle, head south on I-5 to exit 133. The short stretch of I-705 leads into town (35 miles, 35 minutes without traffic).

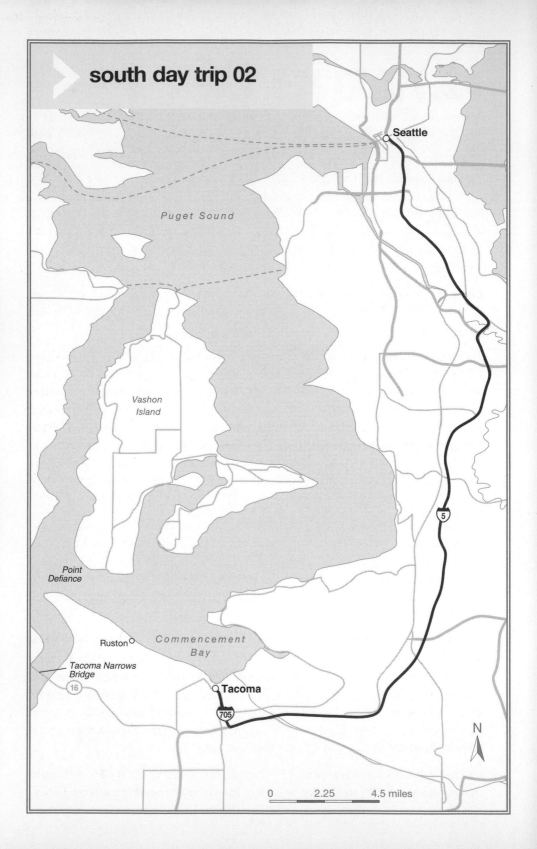

Puget Sound

Vashon
Island

Point
Defiance

Ruston

Tacoma Narrows
Bridge

16

Commencement
Bay

Seattle

5

Tacoma

705

N

| 0 | 2.25 | 4.5 miles |

where to go

Tacoma Visitor Information Center. 1516 Pacific Ave., Tacoma; (253) 627-2836 or (800) 272-2662; www.traveltacoma.com. Located in the Courtyard by Marriott and within a short distance of the downtown museums and dining, the information center is open daily.

Broadway Center for the Performing Arts. 901 Broadway Ave., Tacoma; (253) 591-5894 or (800) 291-7593; www.broadwaycenter.org. With a smattering of NYC Broadway, the theater district pops to life in the evening. The district centers on the three performance venues of the Broadway Center for the Performing Arts: Pantages, Rialto, and Theatre on the Square. From opera and comedy to youth performances and symphonies, the venues stage works from Tacoma's foremost performers. $$$.

Children's Museum of Tacoma. 936 Broadway Ave., Tacoma; (253) 627-6031; www .childrensmuseumoftacoma.org. Focusing on hands-on exhibits, the Children's Museum lets kids explore the food chain, banking, and art. Open daily. $$.

Fort Nisqually Living History Museum. 5400 North Pearl St., #11, Tacoma; (253) 591-5339; www.fortnisqually.org. This Hudson's Bay Company outpost has defensive block-house-style towers, a granary, blacksmith shop, and many actors who reenact history and bring the year 1855 to life. Although not originally at this location, Fort Nisqually recalls Puget Sound's first European settlement, which sat aside Nisqually River in present-day DuPont. The visitor center is generally open daily in summer and Wed to Sun from September to May. The Living History Museum is open the same hours, although the number of costumed interpreters can range from one (on weekdays) to dozens (for special events). Call ahead to confirm hours to ensure you catch the very worthwhile living-history interpreters. $$.

Job Carr Cabin Museum. 2350 North 30th St., Tacoma; (253) 627-5405; www.jobcarr museum.org. This pioneer cabin is known as the birthplace of Tacoma. Hands-on kids' activities comprise the majority of the exhibits inside the cabin. Located just one block from the cabin's original site, the building is an authentic reconstruction and sits affront the grassy Old Town Park. Regardless, it is worth pulling over for the views of Commencement Bay alone. Open Wed to Sat; closed during Jan. $.

Karpeles Manuscript Museum. 407 South G St., Tacoma; (253) 383-2575; www .karpeles.org. Heard of Einstein's Theory of Relativity, the Bill of Rights, or the Wedding March? Seen them? Likely not. The Karpeles Manuscript Museums around the country hold such paper treasures. The Tacoma location is no exception: It features ancient Egyptian tablets, treaties that abolished the slave trade, letters by novelist Gaston Leroux (author of *The Phantom of the Opera*), and Florence Nightingale's documents. Exhibits rotate so call ahead to confirm the current showings. Open Tues to Fri.

LeMay America's Car Museum. 325 152nd St. East, Tacoma; (253) 536-2885; www .lemaymuseum.org. With plans in the works for a speedy new museum in the Dome District, this museum's hundreds of automobiles will be on display for all to see. Until then, visit this location south of downtown. Open Tues to Sun from Apr through Sept; Fri to Sun from Oct to Mar. $$$.

Museum of Glass. 1801 Dock St., Tacoma; (253) 284-4750 or (866) 468-7386; www .museumofglass.org. Indoors and out, the Museum of Glass twinkles with lightness and transparency. Whether it's crossing Dale Chihuly's Bridge of Glass with the Venetian Wall and undersea-like flowers of the Seaform Pavilion, or pausing at the reflecting pool to admire Martin Blank's *Fluent Steps,* the outside exhibits absorb attention. Inside the museum visitors feel the heat in the hot shop and admire the rotating exhibits. Open daily from Memorial Day to Labor Day; Wed to Sun year-round. $$$.

glass artist dale chihuly

Looking at the Venetian Wall on the Tacoma's Bridge of Glass, the word "prolific" immediately springs to mind: The 80-foot span wows with 109 glass sculptures— all intricate, elaborate, and unique pieces.

Chihuly's process of creation involves numerous glass artists working together to create multielemental sculptures. The Tacoma native is credited with pushing glass art towards this collaborative work method. In Tacoma, you can see works produced at his Lake Union studio at the Museum of Glass, Tacoma Art Museum, Union Station, and Hotel Murano.

Point Defiance Park. 5400 North Pearl St., Tacoma; (253) 305-1000; www.metroparks tacoma.org. Hiking trails, a waterfront promenade, landscaped gardens, and historical museums, as well as the separately introduced Point Defiance Zoo & Aquarium and Fort Nisqually Living History Museum, all make Point Defiance a local favorite. The 5-mile drive guides visitors through a full loop of the park. Wildlife sightings are practically guaranteed—particularly of raccoons that clamor towards vehicles because (against warnings not to by park officials) many visitors stop to feed the critters. With road-crossing wildlife and distracted drivers, it is best to drive slowly. Open daily.

Point Defiance Zoo & Aquarium. 5400 North Pearl St., Tacoma; (253) 591-5337; www .pdza.org. These animal houses explore above and below the ocean. Tigers, red wolves, and Asian elephants highlight the world's diminishing on-ground species, while shark, octopi, and eels rule the underwater aquariums. Family programs and a friendly approach to engaging visitors make the zoo and aquarium a top destination. Open daily, except closed Tue and Wed from Nov to Feb. $$$.

Tacoma Art Museum. 1701 Pacific Ave., Tacoma; (253) 272-4258; www.tacomaart museum.org. Since its 1935 establishment the Tacoma Art Museum has compiled a world-class collection. A large exhibit of Dale Chihuly glass art makes a fitting complement to a Tacoma day trip, while Northwest art exhibits explore Native American culture, Mexican heritage, and nature. Open Wed to Sun. $$.

Tacoma Nature Center. 1919 South Tyler St., Tacoma; (253) 591-6439; www.metroparks tacoma.org/page.php?id=20. Seventy acres of parkland lie adjacent to Snake Lake. The Nature Center focuses on families and introducing kids to the plants and animals that make a home in the park. While the grounds open daily, the visitor center provides information Tues to Sat.

Union Station. 1717 Pacific Ave., Tacoma; www.unionstationrotunda.org. In the heart of Tacoma's museum district, Union Station stands out as a beautiful and historic destination. Although now operating as a courthouse and rental facility for functions, its first and former life was as the Pacific-coast terminus of the Northern Pacific Railroad. Look for glass works by Dale Chihuly. Open weekdays 8 a.m. to 5 p.m.

W. W. Seymour Botanical Conservatory. 316 South G St., Tacoma; (253) 591-5330; www.metroparkstacoma.org/page.php?id=21. The glass dome insulates a tropical para-dise of plants. Each month brings a vibrant new bloom from the February tulips and hyacinth to chili peppers in September and holiday displays of poinsettias in December. Located on the east side of Wright Park, the conservatory is surrounded by old-growth trees and grassy hills. Open Tues to Sun. $.

Washington State History Museum. 1911 Pacific Ave., Tacoma; (253) 272-3500 or (888) 238-4373; www.wshs.org. This state history museum documents the past with attitude. The slogan "History is not for wimps" sums this up, and the museum's history-exposing exhibits are not for the faint hearted, be it the trip through a coal mine or searching for the mysterious sasquatch. The Great Hall of Washington History retraces the peoples and places, sounds and sights of Washington history. Open Wed to Sun. $$.

where to eat

Indochine. 1924 Pacific Ave., Tacoma; (253) 272-8200; www.indochinedowntown.com. With curtained partitions, warm-toned wood, and a candle-lit atmosphere, this museum-district restaurant creates a subdued feel while still drawing vibrancy from the nearby University of Washington. The satay with a salad option is perfect for a light meal, while Thai favorites like drunken beef noodles and panang curry are more hearty options. Sesame ahi and honey walnut prawns deliver decadence that befits the restaurant. Open for lunch and dinner Mon to Sat. $$–$$$.

Tatanka. 4915 North Pearl St., Ruston; (253) 752-8778. Buffalo is the main ingredient of a quick, healthy menu at this restaurant that is located close to Point Defiance Park. Chili, tacos, burritos, melts, and burgers are available with bison meat, chicken, beans, or tofu. While you wait, admire the buffalo-themed kitsch in the dining room. Open daily 11 a.m. to 7 p.m. $–$$.

Twokoi. 1552 Commerce St., Tacoma; (253) 274-8999; www.twokoi.com. A spacious dining room and full bar give this sushi restaurant a more formal feel. The bento boxes and sushi combos are expected, but a few unique items are hidden in the large Japanese-fusion menu. Order the carpaccio tuna or salmon served with onion and citrus, or Japanese-style *wafu* steak. Open for weekday lunch, and daily for dinner. $$–$$$.

Woody's on the Water. 1715 Dock St., Tacoma; (253) 272-1433; www.woodystacoma .com. On Tacoma's burgeoning waterfront, Woody's serves seafood and steak with a casual feel. A blueberry salad teases with tastes of summer, while the rosemary-garlic or cognac shrimp allure with aromas. Open daily for lunch and dinner. $$–$$$.

where to stay

Courtyard by Marriott. 1515 Commerce St., Tacoma; (253) 591-9100; www.marriott .com. Most Marriott guest rooms follow a predictable standard, but the wing that incorpo- rates a historic building rates as truly special. Three floors of unique and historic suites merge modern comfort with classic architecture. The location (closest to the museum district) and European spa-escape, Club Biella, create a stand-out accommodation. $$$–$$$$.

Hampton Inn. 8203 South Hosmer, Tacoma; (253) 539-2288; www.hamptoninntacoma .com. Despite its proximity to I-5, the rooms are quiet. Add the out-of-downtown discounts, beds of heavenly comfort, friendly greetings, and spacious facilities (that include a pool, fit- ness center, and breakfast) and this location provides a convenient base location if exploring further south. $$–$$$.

Hotel Murano. 1320 Broadway Plaza, Tacoma; (253) 238-8000; www.hotelmurano tacoma.com. A modern design befitting a newly modern city, Hotel Murano features more than 300 guest rooms as well as fine art of the caliber that you'll also see in the local muse- ums. The hotel seizes on Tacoma's glass-art pride and plays with glass forms in the decor, such as the bedside lamps, to more prominent pieces, like the lobby chandelier. Amenities include iPod docks, a fitness room, and organic coffee in each suite. Top-level suites include espresso machines and unbeatable views. $$$–$$$$.

day trip 03

south

mount st. helens:
mount st. helens, longview and
kelso

On May 18, 1980, Mount St. Helens erupted, sending a massive landslide and ripping explosion into the valley and a globe-circling cloud of ash into the sky. More than three decades later, the destruction is still evident with blast-felled trees, replanted forests, and a gaping mouth in the side of the mountain—which was once a snowy peak not unlike Mount Baker or Mount Rainier.

This day trip climbs along Spirit Lake Highway, which is metered by visitor centers. Be sure to check the weather before heading up the highway to Johnston Ridge—low clouds can obscure the crater and lava dome, making the trip a disappointment without the awesome views. Either call the visitor center (360-274-2140), or view the mountain via the observatory's Web cams at www.fs.fed.us/gpnf/volcanocams/msh.

After admiring the mountain, great food and accommodation options are just 15 minutes south on I-5 in Longview and Kelso.

mount st. helens

Since Mount St. Helens erupted on May 18, 1980, this area has transformed. Mud-swamped buildings have been shoveled out to show the extent of the landslide, trees have rerooted, polished visitor centers sit as sentries watching the volcano, and a smoothly paved highway makes the area easily accessible. But amidst this transformation, signs of the destruction still remain: the blast-zone of toppled trees, the moonscape of the Toutle River, and the active lava dome in the mountain's immense crater.

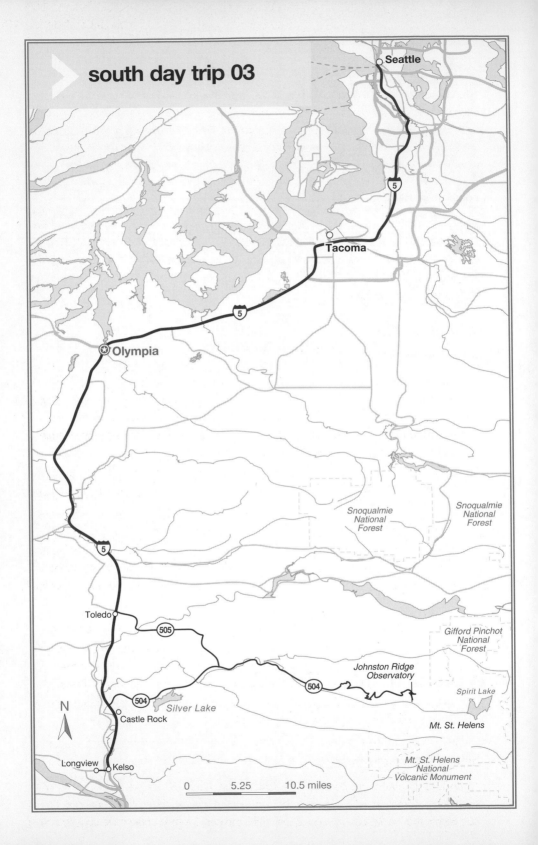

south day trip 03

Seattle

5

Tacoma

5

Olympia

Snoqualmie
National
Forest

Snoqualmie
National
Forest

Gifford Pinchot
National
Forest

Toledo

505

Johnston Ridge
Observatory

Spirit Lake

504

504

Silver Lake

Mt. St. Helens

Castle Rock

N

Longview   Kelso

Mt. St. Helens
National
Volcanic Monument

0   5.25   10.5 miles

Welcoming more than a half-million visitors annually, the national monument is a place of education and remembrance. While there are a few communities within easy reach of the monument, including Toledo, Kid Valley, Silver Lake, and Castle Rock, the services remain rather scarce. With so many visitor centers, budget your time to allow for a long visit at the main attraction— viewing the blasted crater of Mount St. Helens from the Johnston Ridge Observatory.

getting there

Follow I-5 south for about 100 miles. Take exit 63 and pick up SR 505 that leads through Toledo before coming to a T-junction with SR 504—Spirit Lake Highway. Climb this memorial highway to the Johnston Ridge Observatory. The one-way trip to the ridge summit is a 3-hour straight drive from Seattle, but visitor centers and viewpoints make the journey a leisurely trip with lots to see en route.

where to go

At the National Monument:

Forest Learning Center. MP 33, Spirit Lake Memorial Highway; (360) 414-3439. On a good day, you'll be rewarded with views of elk herds in the Toutle River Valley. If not, head inside to explore the timber exhibits. Along the highway blast-felled trees and replanted forests show the effects of the eruption on the forest industry—the learning center puts this into perspective. Open daily May to Oct.

Hoffstadt Bluffs Visitor Center. 15000 Spirit Lake Memorial Hwy., Toutle; (360) 274-5200; www.hoffstadtbluffs.com. The first of the visitor centers, Hoffstadt Bluffs is the departure point for helicopter tours that soar above the Toutle River and over the mountain crater. In addition, a few exhibits memorialize local characters such as Harry Truman, who refused to evacuate his home and later died in the eruption. See photos and video from Spirit Lake's tranquil days as a Boy Scout camp. A restaurant (one of the few spots to eat on the mountain), a gift shop, and a large viewing deck round out the facilities. Open daily May to Nov; call ahead for winter hours.

Johnston Ridge Observatory. MP 52, Spirit Lake Memorial Highway; (360) 274-2140. The jewel of the visitor centers, the Johnston Ridge Observatory connects the events of May 1980 to what you see today. Track the seismic activity on the mountain's new lava dome, measure your own seismic force, and watch the short film that dramatically reveals what happened beneath Mount St. Helens to create such an intense explosion. Open daily May to Oct. $$.

surrounding towns

7Wonders Creation Museum. 4749 Spirit Lake Hwy., Silver Lake; (360) 274-5737; 7wonders.nwcreation.net. Seizing on the sequence of events during the eruption at Mount St. Helens, the 7Wonders museum questions if the same forces could have sculpted other

> ## "vancouver! vancouver! this is it!"

Two months before the explosive day, Mount St. Helens started to show serious signs of unrest. In mid-March 1980, scientists measured increasing numbers of earthquakes that in turn triggered worrisome avalanches, ash, smoke, and cracks in the crater.

The world watched intently with extensive television coverage, tracking the mountain as it rumbled. Information centers and roads closed, and throughout the month of April 1980 more steam and ash emerged from the depths of the mountain. As the crater grew steadily wider, the north flank also began to bulge. The bulge continued to grow as the mountain quieted for a period—some wondered if it was a false alarm.

Then, on May 18, 1980, at 8:32 a.m., an earthquake rumbled one mile below the volcano. The earthquake caused the mountain's swollen north flank to collapse, falling away from the mountain in a massive landslide. The mountain— its tightly bottled pressure now uncorked—erupted with a force that flattened the valley and everything within a 15-mile radius.

It was amid this devestation that USGS volcanologist David Johnston radioed his last message: "Vancouver! Vancouver! This is it!"

Hot ash and the blast killed fifty-seven people, and mudflows (or lahars) measuring dozens of feet deep—like a tsunami of mud—coursed through the Toutle River Valley, overtaking homes. As you'll see, the valley is still recovering.

Even though the blast reduced the height of the mountain by more than 1,300 feet, smaller eruptions have formed a new lava dome in the crater. On a visit to the Johnston Ridge Observatory, look for the seismographs tracking the on-going rumblings at the lava dome.

ancient natural monuments, such as the Grand Canyon. The theories do require a bit of explaining and patience, but dedicated volunteers staff the site and are keen to present the creationist take. Open daily during summer and most days year-round; call ahead for exact hours.

Mount St. Helens Visitor Center. 3029 Spirit Lake Hwy., MP 5, Castle Rock; (360) 274-0962; www.parks.wa.gov/interp/mountsthelens. Run by Washington State Parks and Recreation Commission, the exhibits in the interpretive center span the natural world and geology. A trail leads to Silver Lake and a wetlands boardwalk. Traveling from Seattle, visiting this center first adds about 10 minutes in travel time to venture the extra distance down I-5, or it can be visited in conjunction with dinner in Longview and Kelso. Open daily. $.

where to eat

Back Woods Cafe. 14000 Spirit Lake Hwy., Toutle; (360) 274-7007 or (877) 255-1980; www.ecoparkresort.com. "Logger" is synonymous with hefty portions at this cafe, which is part of Eco Park Resort. Breakfast, lunch, and dinner all come in large portions, served in a camp-style dining room that's bright but simple. Logger stew is a lunch favorite, and the logger dinner with steak, vegetables, beans, salad, and toast is a full load of a meal. The Notta Carnivore plate serves beans with salad and vegetables. Open daily June to Sept; weekends only during May. $$–$$$$.

Fire Mountain Grill. 15000 Spirit Lake Memorial Hwy. (at the Hoffstadt Bluffs Visitor Center), Toutle; www.hoffstadtbluffs.com. Eat here if only for the views: A large outdoor deck overlooks the Toutle River and Mount St. Helens beyond. Watch elk herds traipse through the valley while you enjoy a selection of burgers, sandwiches, and entrees. Open daily for lunch and early dinner from May to Oct. $$–$$$.

longview and kelso

Longview offers the best services close to Mount St. Helens. If extending your trip to an overnight, the town will provide the most comfortable choices for dining and accommodation as well as some fun nightlife options, such as a theater-pub in Kelso where you can sip a local brew while taking in a first-run movie. Add to that a historic mansion and a bridge built for squirrels in the town center and this town beside the Columbia River serves up a few surprises.

getting there

Reach Longview-Kelso by returning along Spirit Lake Highway to I-5. Exit 39 leads to the dining and accommodation options in Kelso and Longview. One way, it's 2 hours from Seattle.

where to go

Kelso Visitor and Volcano Information Center. 105 Minor Rd., Kelso (close to I-5); (360) 577-8058. Open daily, information on both the local area and the main attraction, Mount St. Helens, are available here. Check out the view of the volcano from the "volcano cam"—some days Mount St. Helens is vestured in clouds and not visible.

Civic Center. Washington Way and Olympia Way, Longview. Public buildings border a grassy square in the middle of town where benches, shady trees, and monuments create a pleasant spot to relax. Look for the "Nutty Narrows Bridge"—a span built in 1963 for the resident squirrels. Open daily.

Cowlitz County Historical Museum. 405 Allen St., Kelso; Tel: (360) 577-3119; www.co
.cowlitz.wa.us/museum. Just before the Allen Street Bridge, the Cowlitz County Historical
Museum draws on the logging history that flourished alongside the Columbia River. From
the Cowlitz Indian tribes to the pioneer days and the eruption that shook the Northwest, the
museum presents photographs and artifacts retelling the stories. Open Tues to Sat.

Kelso Theater Pub. 214 South Pacific Ave., Kelso; (360) 414-9451; www.ktpub.com.
Pizza (by the slice or a made-to-order pie), sandwiches, salads, and beer are available to
theatergoers who want to combine dinner and a movie. A friendly staff provides a welcoming spot to escape for an evening. If dining in front of the big screen isn't your style, arrive
early and take a table at the Backstage Café next door, where candlelit tables make for a
cozy evening. The theater is open 30 minutes before movies start. $$.

where to eat

Backstage Café. 216 South Pacific Ave., Kelso; (360) 414-9451. Located next to the
Kelso Theater Pub (and serving from the same kitchen), the cafe offers a more dinner-like
atmosphere to enjoy freshly made pizzas and pastas. Service is excellent and the historical-
feel of the building adds to the charm. Open for breakfast and dinner Mon; breakfast, lunch,
and dinner Tues to Fri; dinner only Sat; closed Sun. $–$$.

Monticello Hotel and Restaurant. 1405 17th Ave., Longview; (360) 425-9900; www
.themonticello.net. The hotel has now been turned into suites, apartments, and offices, but
the opulent lobby still displays the grandeur of the days when railroad travelers and lumber
barons built the city. A pretty terrace overlooks Civic Center, and the restaurant features
live music on occasion. Sunday brunch is particularly popular, but the clientele tends to be
slightly older. Open daily for breakfast, lunch, and dinner. $$$.

Rutherglen Mansion. 420 Rutherglen Rd., Longview; (360) 425-5816; www.rutherglen
mansion.com. Built by lumberman John Tennant for his family in the late 1920s, Rutherglen
Mansion evokes a Southern spirit as well as the wealth that the Long-Bell Lumber Company
planned to bring to Longview. After many reincarnations, the property is now a bed-and-
breakfast, but it also serves Sunday brunch, special wine tastings, and dinner from Tues to
Sat. Spend a sunny weekend afternoon on the deck where you'll take in the views of the
Columbia River and the riverside lumber mills. $$$.

where to stay

Red Lion. 510 Kelso Dr., Kelso; (360) 636-4400; www.redlion.com. The only full-service
hotel in the area, the rooms are large and relaxing—perfect when returning from a day of
exploring Mount St. Helens. Rooms at the back of the hotel front the Coweeman River. A
pool, coffee shop, and restaurant all complement the clean, bright, and comfortable suites.
$$–$$$.

southwest

day trip 01

southwest

the independent state:
vashon island, maury island

The ideas are liberal and the locals friendly on Vashon Island, where most attractions and restaurants harbor an independent spirit. Request an island map when at the ferry ticket window, and take the 20-minute ferry from Fauntleroy to the north end of the island.

From end to end Vashon Island is a mere half-hour drive. Instead work your way slowly south through the local wineries, community museums, boutique shops, and welcoming restaurants. Add to the relaxed exploration with a trip across the portage to Maury Island— an even smaller and quieter spot than Vashon.

While driving on the island you'll likely encounter lots of cyclists and dogs. Vashon is a friendly spot with plenty of terrain to explore on two wheels or with four-legged friends.

vashon island

Vashon is the bigger island of the two. As such, it has the majority of attractions, restaurants, and accommodations. That's not to say the attractions are numerous, but the lavender farms, plant nurseries, gardens tours, and roadside llamas add life and color to this agricultural island. It's just big enough to get lost in the mazes of roads yet quiet enough to stand on a beach alone. Easy explorations here don't require traveling long distances.

First a home for Coast Salish people, settlers came to Vashon Island in the late 1800s to log and then to establish farms. The island culture has developed as a curious independence despite its proximity to the dense urban areas of Tacoma and Seattle.

120

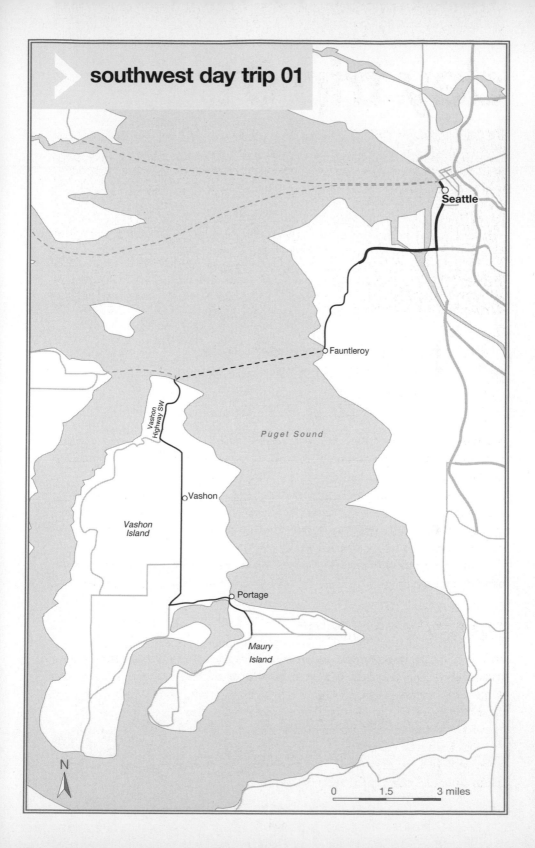

Seattle

Fauntleroy

Puget Sound

Vashon Highway SW

Vashon

Vashon Island

Portage

Maury Island

N

0   1.5   3 miles

getting there

Ferries make dozens of journeys daily from Fauntleroy to Vashon. The south end of Vashon Island is also accessible from Tacoma, where a ferry runs about twenty trips each day from Point Defiance to Tahlequah. A passenger-only ferry runs from Pier 50 in Seattle to Vashon.

where to go

Burton Acres Park and Jensen Point. Southwest Burton Drive, Vashon Island. The park looks out to Maury Island from a sandy beach with a nearby rental hall. The beach is an easy spot for launching kayaks and is also dog friendly. Open daily.

Palouse Winery. 12431 Vashon Hwy., Vashon Island; (206) 567-4994; www.palouse winery.com. This small island winery draws its name from the rolling hills in eastern Washington. Producing a delicate Riesling, an unusual Viognier, and a powerful Cabernet Franc amongst other varietals, the winery is easy to find alongside the island's main route. Open by chance or appointment, but call to confirm tasting times. Or just look for the tasting-room sign as you drive up the hill after arriving on the Fauntleroy-Vashon ferry.

Vashon Maury Island Heritage Museum. 10105 Southwest Bank Rd, Vashon; (206) 463-7808; www.vashonheritage.org. An old Lutheran church houses informative displays on the various epochs of Vashon history. From the Native American communities to the logging and agriculture industries, the bright museum lovingly presents the island's tales. The stories of water transportation to the island are also pivotal—even now ferries and boats are Vashon's only link to the rest of Puget Sound. Open Wed, Sat, and Sun, although hours can change; call ahead to confirm. $.

where to shop

The island's agricultural heritage is still growing with commercial nurseries and gardening shops to visit.

The Country Store and Gardens. 20211 Vashon Hwy. Southwest, Vashon Island; (206) 463-3655; www.countrystoreandgardens.com. For more than four decades the store has stocked varieties of local jams, clothing (especially gardening gear), and gifts. Ten acres of gardens at the Country Store feature summer blooms and fall foliage, making the grounds an excellent garden-themed destination. Open daily.

Dig Floral and Garden. 19028 Vashon Hwy. Southwest, Vashon Island; (206) 463-5096; www.dignursery.com. Splicing a muddy pastime with an urban vibe, Dig injects a modern feel into gardening. Stocking plants for big and small garden spaces, the nursery provides friendly, knowledgeable assistance. Open daily during planting season; Wed to Sun in fall and winter; closed Christmas through Jan.

Lavender Hill Farm. 10425 Southwest 238th St., Vashon Island; (206) 463-2322 (summer); www.lavenderhillvashon.com. From July to mid-August there is a distinct shade of pale purple and an ever-relaxing aroma around the farm—it's the fragrant lavender that roots here. Summer farm tours highlight the many uses of this aromatic herb. Or stop in for the u-pick. Open daily July to mid-Aug.

where to eat

Cafe Luna. 9924 Southwest Bank Rd., Vashon; (206) 463-0777; www.cafelunavashon .com. Vashon is a creative community and Cafe Luna provides a venue for local songwriters and poets. Excellent coffee, homemade soups, and hot grilled sandwiches make for a great lunch stop. The vegan salad is a hearty meal with cranberries, artichokes, olives, and vegetables, while the house soups prove satisfyingly good with beans, lentils, and bread. Open from breakfast through to evening coffee. $.

The Hardware Store. 17601 Vashon Hwy., Vashon; (206) 463-1800; www.thsrestaurant .com. The ever-social booth seating and a warming menu create a welcoming feel at the Hardware Store. This restaurant, on the main Vashon road, was indeed once a hardware store and is the island's oldest commercial building. Now instead of nails and appliances, Vashoners come here for plates like buttermilk fried chicken, a blue-cheese-and-bacon burger, and dinner salad with hazelnuts and green apples. Open daily for breakfast, lunch, and dinner. $$–$$$.

Vashon Island Coffee Roasterie. 19529 Vashon Hwy., Vashon; (206) 463-9800; www .tvicr.com. The copious teas and fresh allure of coffee act as temptress. With a small selection of eats and lots of seating on the outdoor veranda, it's tough not to take a few minutes to sit and relax over a hot brew as you adjust to island time. Open daily with breakfast and lunch hours. $.

where to stay

AYH Ranch Hostel. 12119 Southwest Cove Rd., Vashon; (206) 463-2592; www.vashon hostel.com. Get a feel for the old West with options to sleep in a tepee or a covered wagon. For the nonpioneers, however, there is also plenty of comfort with indoor dormitories and private rooms. The grounds offer lots to explore, plus there are free bike rentals. $.

Belle Baldwin House. 11408 Southwest Cedarhurst Rd., Fern Cove Nature Preserve, Vashon; (206) 463-9602; www.vashonparkdistrict.org. This secluded house offers three bedrooms and a waterside setting. Rubber boots, a full kitchen, and a fireplace create a fully equipped retreat. Admire the views of Puget Sound from an Adirondack chair on the deck. A prominent physician lived here in the late 1800s, and his daughter, Belle Baldwin, became the first female physician in the state in 1912. Three bedrooms can sleep up to six. There is a one-week minimum during the summer, two-night minimum during the off-season. $$$$.

Quartermaster Inn. 24007 Vashon Hwy. Southwest, Vashon; (206) 463-5355; www.quarter masterinn.com. Four second-floor rooms echo the cozy feel of the downstairs restaurant. Fresh decor, a quiet setting, and on-site dining set this inn apart as the best of the larger accommodation options on the island. Yes, with four rooms the Quartermaster is one of the largest overnight destinations on Vashon (where there are no hotels or motels). $$$.

maury island

Vashon Island's little brother makes a complementary side trip to an island tour. Cross between the islands at the military-constructed community of Portage and head off the trav- eled path to the Point Robinson Lighthouse. From the rocky beach appreciate the views of Tacoma and Mount Rainier on a clear day.

where to go

Point Robinson Park. Southwest Point Robinson Road, Maury Island; (206) 463-9602; www.vashonparkdistrict.org. Since 1885 this lighthouse has stood as a beacon for vessels navigating in fog and rough conditions. Automated in 1978, the building that once housed the lighthouse-keepers' quarters now serves as a vacation rental property through the Vashon Park District.

where to stay

Maury Cottage. 5313 Southwest Point Robinson Rd., Maury Island; (206) 463-4558; www .maurycottage.com. The deep-soaking tub provides an insulated escape. As the cottage is the only guest accommodation on the property, it provides an independent, restful lodg- ing option complete with star-studded skies, quiet nights, and coffee on the garden patio. Welcoming hosts help keep the secret. No credit cards. $$.

day trip 02

southwest

> **state capital:**
> olympia, tumwater, chehalis

Olympia offers the grandeur of a state capital—including palatial buildings and palpable history—but with an independent undercurrent. Beneath the marble surface the Washington state capital does things a little differently with a lively waterfront district, large farmers' market, and the alternative influence of Evergreen State College. Tour the grand state capitol campus, step up to an espresso bar at Batdorf & Bronson for a coffee tasting, or select ripe produce at the weekend market.

Just south of Olympia, and barely distinguishable as city borders go, lies Tumwater and its historical attractions. Two preserved historic buildings include a home built by Bing Crosby's pioneer grandfather and one built by an Olympia Brewing Company brewmaster. Nearby, visitors can enjoy a meal overlooking the tumult of Tumwater Falls on the Deschutes River. This day trip ends in Chehalis where museums, railroads, and quaint cafes provide a nice small town to explore.

olympia

Just as Washington is no ordinary state, Olympia is no ordinary state capital. Beyond the ornate domes and facades of the capitol buildings, visitors will uncover a diverse community, university-fueled nightlife, and urban market district. In fact, the local farmers' market, coffee tasting room, and waterfront parks embody the Washingtonian spirit (think good food, coffee, and the outdoors) far better than the grandiose architecture.

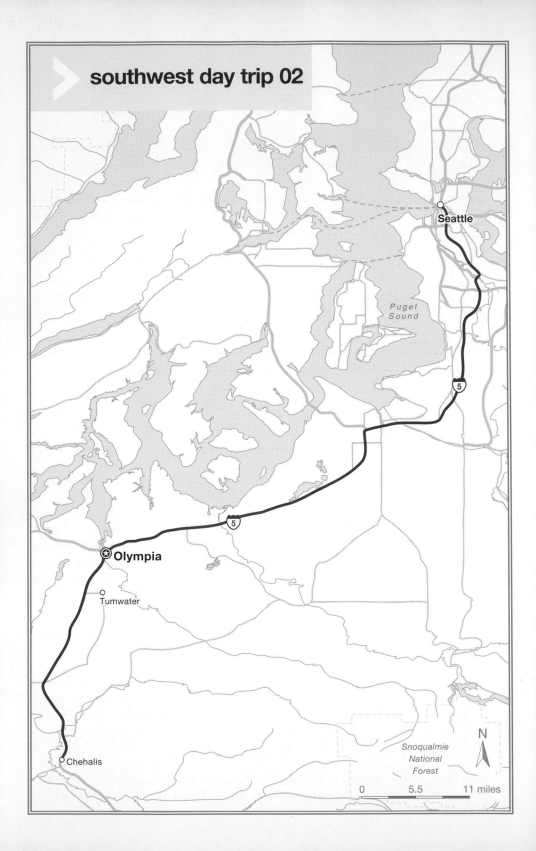

Seattle

Puget Sound

5

5

Olympia

Tumwater

Chehalis

Snoqualmie National Forest

N

0   5.5   11 miles

getting there

Head south on I-5 from Seattle (60 miles, 1 hour). Exit 105 leads to downtown Olympia and the State Capitol Campus.

where to go

Olympia-Lacey-Tumwater Visitor and Convention Bureau. 103 Sid Snyder Ave. Southwest, Olympia; (360) 704-7544 or (877) 704-7500; www.visitolympia.com. This source for visitor information is open Mon to Fri; closed weekends.

Batdorf & Bronson Tasting Room. 200 Market St. Northeast, Olympia; (360) 753-4057; www.batdorf.com. Yes, Washingtonians do take their coffee this seriously: This tasting room is certainly not to be mistaken for a coffee bar. You won't find cozy seating or sugary syrups here. Instead the "brewmasters" illuminate the subtle flavors and roasts of the beans. For a more coffee-cozy atmosphere visit the cafe location of **Batdorf & Bronson Coffeehouse** (516 South Capitol Way) or the **Dancing Goats Espresso Bar** (111 Market St. Northeast), which is across the street from the tasting room. The cafes are open daily, while you'll find coffee brewing in the tasting room Wed to Sun.

Nisqually National Wildlife Refuge. 100 Brown Farm Rd., Olympia; (360) 753-9467; www.fws.gov/nisqually. Migratory birds find sanctuary in this protected section of the Nisqually River Delta. The 3,000-acre refuge (which could see a future expansion to more than 6,000 acres) includes boardwalks, trails, and a visitor center plus bird-friendly natural habitat. The visitor center is open Wed to Sun while the refuge is open daily during daylight hours.

Old State Capitol and Sylvester Park. 600 Washington St. Southeast, Olympia; (360) 725-6000; www.k12.wa.us/aboutus/oldcapitolbldg.aspx. Originally built from Chuckanut-area stone as a courthouse, this 1892 building across from Sylvester Park became the legislature building in the early 1900s. Fires, renovations, and earthquakes have changed its appearance over the years, but a major 1980s restoration saw the building revitalize its public function: It is now the Office of Superintendent of Public Instruction. Visitors can admire the storied building, the 8-foot round glass window depicting George Washington, and the fountain from Sylvester Park.

Olympia Farmers' Market. 700 Capitol Way North, Olympia; (360) 352-9096; www .olympiafarmersmarket.com. Live entertainment and local producers create a vibrant market atmosphere that is one of the largest open-air markets in the state. Seafood, produce, flowers, desserts, and cheeses are all available at the covered but breezy market. Goods are on sale Thurs to Sun from Apr to Oct; weekends only Nov and Dec.

Percival Landing Park. 217 Thurston Ave. Northwest, Olympia; www.ci.olympia.wa.us/ city-services/parks/percival-landing.aspx. A small slice of park connects with a waterfront stroll past great dinner restaurants and marinas. Moored at the docks is the tugboat *Sandman*—a national historic vessel that has been restored as a floating museum (www .tugsandman.org). The park is open daily.

State Capital Museum & Outreach Center. 211 Southwest 21st Ave., Olympia; (360) 753-2580; www.washingtonhistory.org/scmoc. A Spanish-colonial-style mansion houses collections on Native American history, Washington government, and pioneer settlement. The former home of city mayor Clarence Lord has a thirty-two-room floor plan plus gardens that are open to the public. Open Sat. $.

Washington State Capitol Campus. 14th Avenue Southeast and Capitol Way, Olympia; (360) 902-8880 (tours); www.ga.wa.gov/visitor. Arriving in Olympia via I-5, the legislature building—the largest on the State Capitol Campus—forms a majestic opening frame. The largest brick-and-concrete dome in North America is crowned with a cupola and the dome rises well-above Olympia's tree-lined streets. Climb the forty-two steps to the entrance and explore the campus buildings on a variety of tours. The most popular tour (running daily with departures between 10 a.m. and 3 p.m.) explores the legislative building and its marble halls, legislative assembly, pioneer statutes, and a Tiffany chandelier. Tours on Wed visit the Governor's mansion, and education-focused tours are offered to groups.

where to eat

The Budd Bay Cafe. 525 Columbia St. Northwest, Olympia; (360) 357-6963; www.budd baycafe.com. Cedar-planked or blackened salmon, tiger prawns, and sea scallops comple-ment the waterfront views of Budd Bay. Arrive early for dinner and snag the well-priced sunset dinner specials that include soup or salad, an entree, and dessert. Open daily for breakfast, lunch, and dinner. $$$–$$$$.

The Lemon Grass Restaurant. 212 Fourth Ave. West, Olympia; (360) 705-1832. This modern dining room is divided into an upscale dining spot and bar in one half and a more casual spot to grab a quick meal in the other. Fresh and flavorful Thai and Vietnamese dishes span noodles, curries, and rice dishes. The mango salad combines ripe fruit with crunchy vegetables and a unique fennel flavor, while the apple curry with tofu makes a great vegetarian dish. Open Mon to Sat for lunch and dinner; closed Sun. $$–$$$.

where to stay

Swantown Inn Bed-and-Breakfast. 1431 11th Ave. Southeast, Olympia; (360) 753-9123; www.swantowninn.com. This historic, family-run inn provides classic rooms decorated with regal textiles, deluxe king-size beds, and private baths. A Victorian garden enhances the spacious house (which once included a ballroom on its third floor), while the one-mile walk to downtown allows visitors to indulge in the excellent local restaurants. $$–$$$.

tumwater

At the end of the pioneer Oregon Trail, Tumwater sits at the southernmost end of Puget Sound. Positioned to harness the power of Tumwater Falls on the Deschutes River, the community—then known as New Market—was one of the first non-Native settlements in the state. Now historical attractions and views of the power-generating falls highlight a quick tour of the city.

getting there

From Olympia follow Capitol Way south as it crosses I-5 and become Capitol Boulevard. Turn onto C Street Southwest to access the historical attractions along Deschutes Way.

where to go

Crosby House Museum. 703 Deschutes Way Southwest, Tumwater; (360) 943-9884; www.ci.tumwater.wa.us/historicalcrosbyhouse.htm. Built by Nathaniel Crosby III for his new bride, Cordelia Jane Smith, the Crosby House dates to the 1860s. Beyond the pioneer-period furnishing, the house draws interest because the Crosbys were the grandparents of famous actor and singer Bing Crosby. Open Fri and Sun; closed Nov to Mar.

Henderson House Museum. 602 Deschutes Way, Tumwater; (360) 754-4217; www.ci .tumwater.wa.us/historicalhendersonhouse.htm. A brewmaster at the Olympia Brewery commissioned this then-modern home in 1905. The house had hot water and was wired for electricity, with the power drawn from the Olympia Power and Light Company's power-house at the lower falls. Open Thurs and Fri.

Tumwater Falls Park. C Street and Deschutes Way, Tumwater; (360) 943-2550; www .olytumfoundation.org. The drop of the falls presented a powerful opportunity to the pio-neers who first settled nearby, and it later provided power for an Olympia Power and Light Company powerhouse and the Olympic Brewing Company. There are three sections to the falls, with the lower falls being the largest. A riverside trail connects them. Open daily.

where to eat

Falls Terrace Restaurant. 106 Deschutes Way Southwest, Tumwater; (360) 943-7830; www.fallsterrace.com. A large dining area with lots of windows provides views of Tumwater Falls on the Deschutes River. Enjoy signature dishes such as halibut with crab and shrimp, prime rib, or steak and salmon. After a meal, stroll along the river to the lower falls and the historic park where the river meets Puget Sound at its most southerly point. Open daily for lunch and dinner. $$–$$$$.

chehalis

Railroads and Ezra Meeker's historic travel along the Oregon Trail feature most prominently in the town, along with its main street of cafes and museums. From vintage motorcycles to old train stations, the town preserves its heritage with a passion. But it wasn't always so: Chehalis was one of just three towns that broke its promise to Meeker by not erecting an Oregon Trail marker. In 2006 the town finally fulfilled that promise.

getting there

Follow I-5 south, taking exit 79 or 77 for Chehalis.

where to go

Chehalis-Centralia Railroad. 1101 Sylvenus St., Chehalis; (360) 748-9593; www.steam trainride.com. Another example of Washington's great love of railroads, this train steams out of a station on the outskirts of Chehalis alongside the Chehalis River. The 1916 Baldwin generally makes two journeys a day on weekends: one 13-mile roundtrip to Milburn and an 18-mile roundtrip ticket to Ruth. Full-price tickets start at about $11, with additional options for seasonal train rides and dinner on the rails. $$$.

Lewis County Historical Museum. 599 Northwest Front Way, Chehalis; (360) 748-0831; www.lewiscountymuseum.org. A finely restored train station houses Lewis County Historical Museum. Exhibits of course include train history but also the histories of Native Americans and the Oregon Trail—for which there is a belatedly erected marker in town. Coffee and pastries are available as well as brochures on local attractions. Open Tues to Sat year-round; Tues to Sun in summer. $.

Veterans Memorial Museum. 100 Southwest Veterans Way, Chehalis; (360) 740-8875; www.veteransmuseum.org. The 9,000-square-foot museum opened its new doors in 2005. A September 11 display includes fragments of the fallen World Trade Center, and a Korean War exhibit recalls America's "forgotten war." Open Tues to Sun from June through Sept; Tues to Sat from Oct through May. $$.

Vintage Motorcycle Museum. 545 North Market Blvd., Chehalis; (360) 748-3472; www .antiquemotorcycles.net. The museum collection specializes in pre-1916 motorcycles, including some wooden bikes. With more than forty bikes in total, the unusual side of the collection features an amphibious car and a pedal-powered Harley-Davidson bicycle. Open weekday mornings. $$.

where to eat

Mary McCrank's Restaurant. 2923 Jackson Hwy., Chehalis (south of town); (360) 748-3662; www.marymccranks.com. An institution for road-weary travelers, Mary McCrank's delivers only smiles. A hearty menu offers no surprises, only classic dishes: steaks, chicken, and liver and onions. Open for weekend breakfast; Tues to Sun for lunch and dinner; closed Mon. $$–$$$$.

Sweet Inspirations. 514 North Market Blvd., Chehalis; (360) 748-7102. Be treated as a local at this cafe, where the historic building adds charm to the menu offerings of fresh, hot comfort food. The dishes are diner style with well-done classics such as tuna melts and turkey soup. Open daily for breakfast and lunch; Fri and Sat for dinner. $$–$$$.

day trip 03

southwest

walking on the ocean shore:
aberdeen and hoquiam, ocean
shores, westport and grayland

Grays Harbor is a Seattle seaside getaway. Drive directly on the sandy beaches at Ocean Shores, admire burgundy fields of cranberry harvests near Westport, or recall the grunge scene at Kurt Cobain's home in Aberdeen.

Grays Harbor features unique birdlife and distinct geography. Aberdeen and Hoquiam (both industry towns) sit at the head of the harbor, while Westport and Ocean Shores face each other across the harbor mouth. Life beside the ocean is rich, filled with razor-clam dinners, trips to the casino, strolling the boardwalk, buying fresh fish direct from the marina, surfing waves at state parks, and embarking on whale-watching excursions.

This day trip also offers perhaps the largest concentration of state parks. Most front the ocean and make serene destinations for clamming, camping, or watching the surf roll in. Add historical museums, interpretive centers, and opportunities to boat, fish, hike, and build sand castles and this day trip so easily becomes either a longer getaway or the first of many.

aberdeen and hoquiam

Despite the industrial face of Aberdeen and Hoquiam—separate towns although I include them together here because their downtowns sit a mere 5 minutes apart—there's a hidden glamour to the town. Visit the former homes of lumber barons at Hoquiam Castle and the Polson Museum. Both ornate properties recall the prosperity of the lumber age.

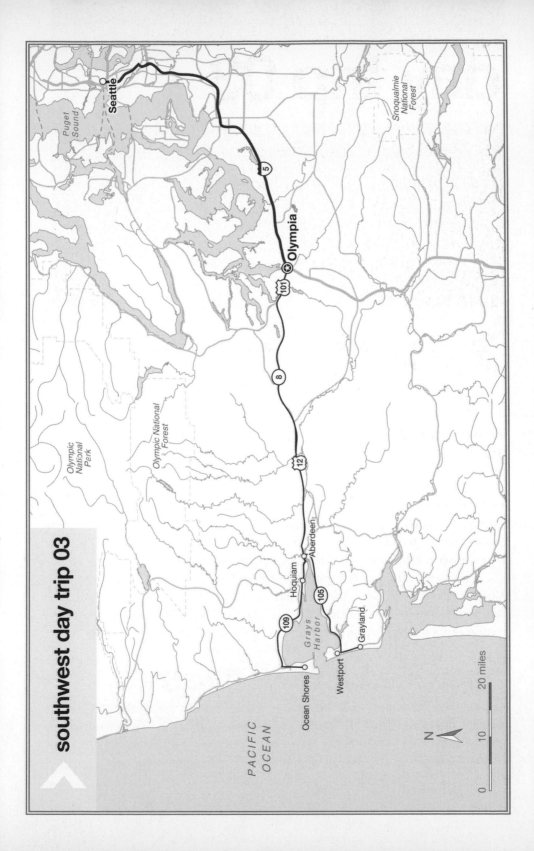

southwest day trip 03

Seattle

Puget
Sound

Snoqualmie
National
Forest

5

Olympia

101

8

Olympic
National
Park

Olympic
National
Forest

12

Hoquiam

Aberdeen

109

105

Grays
Harbor

Ocean Shores

Westport

Grayland

PACIFIC
OCEAN

N

0   10   20 miles

At the head of Grays Harbor where the Chehalis River meets the ocean, the towns also provide access to protected wildlife areas. Consider too the famous former residents—who include Nirvana singer and guitarist Kurt Cobain and the founder of Boeing, William Boeing—and the towns prove surprisingly worth exploring.

getting there

From Seattle, take I-5 south to exit 104, just south of Olympia, and the junction with the US 101. Head west first on US 101, then continue on SR 8. SR 8 becomes US 12 at Elma and takes the final stretch to Aberdeen (2 hours, 110 miles). From this lumber town, SR 109 heads to Ocean Shores (25 miles, 40 minutes) while SR 105 cuts a route along the opposite shore of Grays Harbor to Westport (20 miles, 35 minutes).

Previously, a passenger ferry—*El Matador*—ran between the mirrored towns of Ocean Shores and Westport during summer months, but service was discontinued in 2008. At press time, the ferry faced a questionable future.

kurt cobain and seattle grunge

Born in Aberdeen, Kurt Cobain lived in Hoquiam for a year before his family returned to Aberdeen—a lumber town. When his parents divorced, Cobain's life changed greatly. He moved between parents, towns, and family friends throughout his teenage years before moving out on his own and dropping out of school.

Cobain started playing music early. He began as a drummer in the school band and then picked up guitar at age fourteen. The Aberdeen punk band the Melvins held a strong influence over the young musician and artist.

Nirvana took form when Cobain convinced fellow Aberdeen resident Krist Novoselic to start a band—the beginnings of Nirvana. They recorded their first album with Chad Channing on drums and later changed drummers to Dave Grohl. With their 1991 album Nevermind, *Nirvana brought attention to the Seattle grunge scene and became the biggest band of the early 1990s.*

Despite this success, Cobain was found dead with a shotgun pointed at his chin on April 8, 1994. Much speculation has emerged over his death, and many books have since been published rehashing his heavy drug use, marriage to Courtney Love, and Aberdeen childhood.

where to go

Grays Harbor Visitor Information Center. 506 Duffy St., Aberdeen; (360) 532-1924 or (800) 321-1924; www.graysharbor.org. Pick up a guide to the rain forest and coast at the chamber and visitor center. Closed Sat and Sun.

Aberdeen History Museum. 111 East Third St., Aberdeen; (360) 533-1976. Amidst the pioneer and historic exhibits, the museum's most modern and unique information includes a self-guided Kurt Cobain tour. The walking tour introduces visitors to the places in Aberdeen where Cobain lived, worked, slept, and went to school. From his first house in Aberdeen at 1210 East First St. to the Young Street Bridge, the museum traces the life of Cobain in the town. Open Tues to Sun. $.

Grays Harbor National Wildlife Refuge. Airport Way off Paulson Road, Hoquiam; www .fws.gov/graysharbor. Tidal flats are a haven for shorebirds. Each spring on their return migration, shorebirds flock to the marshes and grasses that comprise this 1,500-acre refuge. And these birds certainly need the rest stop—some are stopping en route between Argentina and the Arctic, a 7,000-mile journey. Open daily.

Hoquiam's Castle. 515 Chenault Ave., Hoquiam; www.hoquiamcastle.com. While this former bed-and-breakfast would normally appear in the Where to Stay section of this guide, Hoquiam's Castle was on the selling block and not accepting B&B guests at press time. Still, the elegant three-story wooden structure with towers and an arched veranda makes a beautiful historic site to admire—even just from the roadside. If tours of the twenty-room mansion built by lumber baron Robert Lytle in 1897 are running, you'll see the antique furnishings and lovingly collected china, glassware, and art.

The Polson Museum. 1611 Riverside Ave., Hoquiam; (360) 533-5862; www.polson museum.org. Spacious grounds include railroad displays, artifacts from the lumber industry, and the large Polson mansion. The twenty-six-room mansion, built by another lumber-rich family, was a wedding gift to Arnold Polson from his uncle Robert Polson. The museum includes two acres of grounds with gardens, the riverbanks of the Hoquiam River, and a blacksmith shop. Historical maps, photos of the Polson family's time in the house, and preserved furnishings make the museum an excellent stop year-round. Open Wed to Sun. $.

where to eat

Anne Marie's Cafe. 110 South I St., Aberdeen; (360) 538-0141. A classic diner-style joint, greasy breakfasts and friendly service are a requisite here. Open for breakfast and lunch daily. $–$$.

satsop nuclear power plant

South of US 12, you may spot the two massive, eerie-looking towers of the Sat-sop Nuclear Power Plant—or what was intended to be a plant at least. In the 1970s plans were forged to build two nuclear power plants here, but by the mid-1980s costs and safety concerns had mushroomed.

With more than $2 billion invested in the Washington Public Power Supply System (WPPSS) project but funds gone, the site was transferred to the county. Now the project has been revitalized as a business park, and the WPPSS project has earned the unfortunate moniker of "Whoops." For more details on the development park visit www.satsop.com.

ocean shores

The picture windows for homes in Ocean Shores seem to begin on the second level—all to maximize the views of the Pacific Ocean that reach to the horizon from the sandy beaches.

Drive on the sand, visit a hands-on wildlife interpretive center, or test chance at the oceanside casino. Accommodations, most offering easy access to the beach, line the roads and are a summertime city for those seeking a beach getaway from Seattle.

getting there

From Aberdeen, SR 109 heads to Ocean Shores (25 miles, 40 minutes).

where to go

Damon Point State Park. Off Discovery Avenue Southeast, Ocean Shores; www.parks .wa.gov. A one-mile strip of dune grass and sand leads to Damon Point. Go for a short hike that contrasts views of the protected harbor and the wild ocean. The park is close to the 683-acre Oyhut Wildlife Area, which provides one of the rare nesting grounds in the state for the snowy plover. Open daily.

Ocean City State Park. 148 SR 115; www.parks.wa.gov. The area's rich sea life meant that Native Americans long visited this spot because of its abundant food sources. Many cooking and hunting artifacts have been found in the area. Nowadays clamming, fishing, driving on the sands, and camping are popular state park activities. Open daily.

Ocean Shores Interpretive Center. 1033 Catala Ave. Southeast, Ocean Shores; (360) 289-4617; www.oceanshoresinterpretivecenter.com. Large and dynamic, the interpretive center displays exhibits on natural history with plenty of hands-on appeal—touch everything from sea critters to the inner ear of a whale. The center illuminates the natural environment of Grays Harbor, and helpful, friendly docents are available to answer questions. Open daily Apr through Sept; weekends only from Oct through Mar.

where to eat

Emily's. 78 SR 115, Ocean Shores; (360) 289-6038; www.quinaultbeachresort.com. With a hearty buffet or made-to-order items such as razor-clam steaks, scallops, or steak and lobster, Emily's offers the most diverse local menu. A handsome dining room reveals snap-shots of the ocean and beach views. The restaurant is named for a respected elder in the Quinault Nation, and around Quinault Beach Resort and Casino you'll see beautiful pho-tography revealing the Native history and heritage. Hours are variable, but generally open daily for dinner and weekends for breakfast and lunch; more hours during peak season. $$$–$$$$.

where to stay

The Judith Ann Inn. 855 Ocean Shores Blvd. Northwest, Ocean Shores; (360) 289-0222 or (888) 826-6466; www.judithanninn.com. With the appearance of a Cape Cod mansion but the hardy vinyl siding required to withstand the Pacific storms, these vacation rentals offer a fun getaway. Jetted tubs stand out as the perfect spot from which to watch the ocean, while the gas fireplaces make the inn a cozy spot for the winter-storm-watching season. All the suites have separate bedrooms with king-size beds and full kitchens. While the decor in most suites is a tad dated, the spacious 900-square-foot layouts are ideal for longer stays. $$$.

westport and grayland

Westport retains its old-fashioned seaside charm while still offering all the accommodations, dining, and tour options of a resort. It's not just the harbor boardwalk, large marina, and seafood restaurants you'll savor, but also the fresh catch available from the town marina, the local surf culture, oceanside parks, viewing towers, scenic lighthouses, and beaches prepped for sand-castle building.

Along with the pastoral charm of nearby Grayland, where cranberry farmers harvest the tart berries each fall, this destination rates as a personal favorite.

getting there

From Aberdeen, SR 105 cuts a route along the southern shore of Grays Harbor to Westport (20 miles, 35 minutes). Grayland is just south of Westport.

where to go

Grayland Beach State Park. Off Cranberry Beach Road, SR 105 Spur, Grayland; www .parks.wa.gov. Beach day: That's what the nearly 1.5 miles of beachfront at this state park warrants. Camping, clamming, crabbing, and watching the ocean are all top activities for parkgoers. Open daily.

Twin Harbors State Park. 3120 SR 105, Westport; www.parks.wa.gov. Once a military training ground, Twin Harbors now welcomes the area's beachgoers. As with other local state parks along this stretch, camping, clamming, and bird watching are popular thanks to the dunes, sands, and park facilities. Open daily.

Westport Aquarium. 321 East Harbor St., Westport; (360) 268-7070. The aquarium is a tiny spot with display tanks and a touch tank. The facilities are basic, but there's lots to learn about the underwater world at the town's doorstep. Open daily during summer; call ahead for winter hours. $$.

Westport Light State Park. Off Ocean Avenue, Westport; www.parks.wa.gov. Walk the dunes from Westhaven Park near the marina and south jetty to Westport Light, which is further south and close to the downtown district. Surfable breaks, car-free beaches, and more bird and ocean watching are additional attractions at the park. Built in 1898, the lighthouse is also called Grays Harbor Lighthouse and is run by the Westport Maritime Museum. The park is open daily.

Westport Maritime Museum. 2201 Westhaven Dr., Westport; (360) 268-0078; www .westportwa.com/museum. You'll find a unique set of local-focused exhibits here, ranging from cranberries to the coast guard. Skeletons of minke and gray whales along with other sea mammals draw curiosity in the outdoor display buildings. The museum building once housed the coast guard lifeboat station. Open daily Apr to Sept; Fri to Mon from Oct to Nov and Feb to Mar. Closed Dec and Jan. $.

Westport Scenic Boardwalk. End of Neddie Rose Drive, Westport. The boardwalk circles the large marina, which helps protect the fishing fleets that find a safe harbor at Westport. View the ocean juxtaposed against the boats hunkered down in port. On a day with swell, surfers catch waves at a break called the Groynes. Stroll along the boardwalk and indulge in dinner and dessert at the nearby Half Moon Bay Restaurant. Open daily.

Westport Winery. 1 South Arbor Rd., Aberdeen; (360) 648-2224; www.westportwines .com. You can't, miss Westport Winery's lighthouse that is constructed miles from the heaving Pacific. This fairly new winery produces many varietals and fruit wines for sampling in the large tasting room. Names like Surfer's Last Syrah draw on local inspiration, while a sparkling cranberry wine also sources locally. Open daily. $.

> ## westport surfing
>
> *Westport thrives with a small, local community of surfers. Two surf shops in town offer advice, sales, and rentals.* **Surf Shop** *(207 North Montesano St.; 360-268-0992; www.westportsurfshop.com) and* **Steepwater Surf Shop** *(1200 North Montesano St.; 360-268-5527; www.steepwatersurfshop.com) both provide rentals starting at about $40. For beginners, enquire about summer surf clinics.*
>
> *As the Pacific stays cold year-round, be sure to rent booties and gloves with your board and wet suit.*

where to eat

Bennett's Restaurant. 1800 SR 105, Grayland; (360) 267-2350. The signature dish is the Cranberry Coast chicken salad with local berries, but the restaurant also serves a selection of seafood and steak. It's a local favorite and worth the drive. Open daily for lunch and dinner during summer; Thurs to Sun in winter. $$–$$$.

Fog Cutter Cafe. 1155 Ocean Ave. West, Westport; (360) 268-6097. Serving classic diner breakfasts and lunches with a cozy country-kitchen feel, the Fog Cutter is a welcoming spot to fuel up. The cafe sits across from the Grays Harbor Lighthouse and also goes well with an early morning walk on the beach. Open daily for breakfast and lunch. $–$$$.

Half Moon Bay Bar and Grill. 421 Neddie Rose Dr., Westport; (360) 268-9166; www.half moonbaybarandgrill.com. This is the local hangout where visitors and residents converge. With a full bar, a kitchen that is open late, and friendly service, come here for daily specials and a wide range of entrees. Alongside the many seafood options (from fresh fish tacos and oysters to shrimp and crab dishes), the menu also provides some vegetarian dishes. Open daily for lunch and dinner. $$–$$$.

where to stay

Chateau Westport. 710 West Hancock Ave., Westport; (360) 268-9101; www.chateau westport.com. Just minutes from the beach, Chateau Westport is the local resort with an indoor pool, restaurant, and secluded location. Basic guest rooms offer simple, clean accommodations from which to explore the area. Things are more upscale in the suites that include fireplaces, kitchens, and saunas. $$–$$$.

Ocean Spray Beach Resort. 1757 SR 105, Grayland; (360) 267-2205; www.oceanspray motel.com. Having recently undergone renovations and new ownership, each self-contained cottage is painted and decorated with an individual style. Some cottages were built as army barracks during World War II. Spacious interiors, full kitchens, and large sitting areas nicely complement the fresh linens and friendly hosts. $–$$.

grayland cranberries

You'll only need two hints as to what you'll find down Cranberry Road—it's red and tart. In Grayland boggy acres of the berries line the miles of road. Farmers harvest in mid-fall, coinciding with the mid-October Cranberry Harvest Festival. The wet harvest method is the most fun to watch as farmers flood the fields and the ripe cranberries float to the surface.

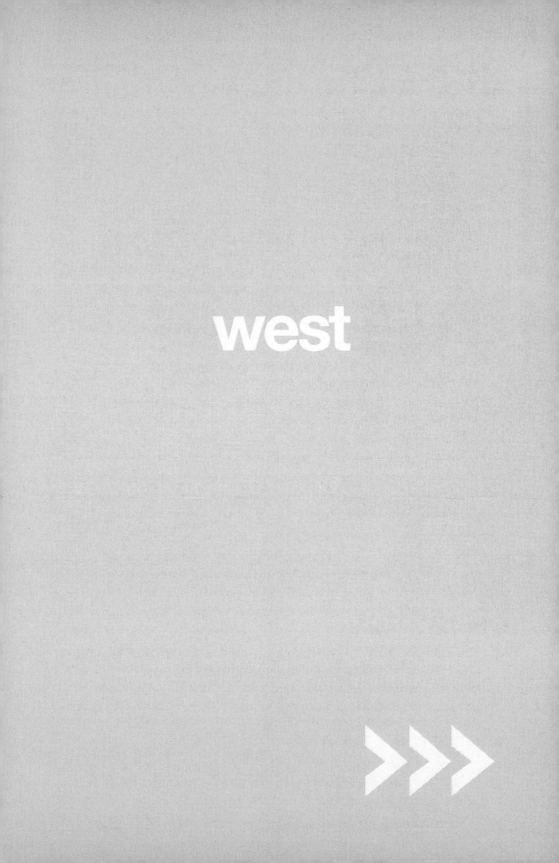
west

>>>

day trip 0 i

west

>>> **in the navy:**
bremerton, port orchard, gig
harbor

A day trip into the heart of Kitsap explores cities tied to the ocean whether it's through the naval base, boat building, or fishing heritage. Venture to the naval heartland of Bremerton, where revitalization projects are creating an ever-changing city to explore. Museums, parks dotted with synchronized fountains, and restaurant patios cluster around the ferry dock and overlook the transportation hub.

On the opposite side of Sinclair Inlet, Port Orchard preserves the history of the lumber industry and pairs it with the community's present-day artists. Further south in the ever-quaint Gig Harbor, parks and marinas line the waterfront and draw on a strong sailing heritage.

bremerton

A strong naval presence and a dubious reputation persist a bit in Bremerton, Kitsap's largest city. But stroll by the ferry dock watching the synchronized, lighted fountains perform a dance of water in Harborside Fountain Park and those ideas quickly fade. Naval and puppet museums as well as public art create a vibrant and varied city so close to Seattle via ferry.

getting there

Take the Seattle-Bremerton ferry, which runs about a dozen times daily. From Bremerton, Port Orchard sits 9 miles away by road on the other side of Sinclair Inlet.

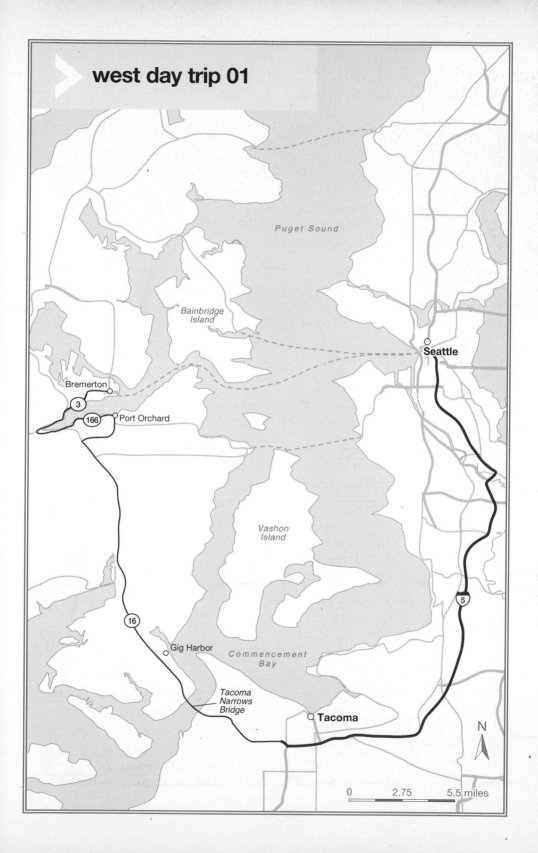

Puget Sound

Bainbridge
Island

Seattle

Bremerton

③

⑯⑥ Port Orchard

Vashon
Island

⑯

Gig Harbor

Commencement
Bay

Tacoma
Narrows
Bridge

Tacoma

⑤

N

0   2.75   5.5 miles

SR 16 connects to Gig Harbor, which can also be reached via Tacoma and the Tacoma Narrows Bridge (45 miles, 45 minutes from Seattle).

where to go

Aurora Valentinetti Puppet Museum and Evergreen Children's Theatre. 257 Fourth St., Bremerton; (360) 373-2992; www.ectandpuppets.com. Enter the world of puppetry at this unique museum where ventriloquist dummies, Thai puppets, and miniature theater sets show the diversity of the art. Keep watch for special puppet performances featuring kid-friendly stories such as *Rumpelstiltskin* or *Charlotte's Web*. Open Wed to Sat. $.

Elandan Gardens. 3050 West SR 16, Bremerton; (360) 373-8260; www.elandangardens .com. With the closure of the Pacific Bonsai Collection in Federal Way, Elandan Gardens offers a rare glimpse of the special art of bonsai. The trees have a distinctly Pacific North-west appeal: ponderosa pine, Douglas fir, and Rocky Mountain juniper. Acres of gardens snake between paths, ponds, and stone boulders. Open Tues to Sun from Apr to Oct; Fri to Sun Nov to Mar. $$.

Kitsap Historical Museum. 280 Fourth St., Bremerton; (360) 479-6226; www.kitsaphis-tory.org. From farm, cottage, and pioneer life to the shipbuilding and forestry industries, this museum covers the region's past with a passion. Open Tues to Sat. $.

Puget Sound Navy Museum. 251 First St., Bremerton; (360) 479-7447; www.history.navy .mil/museums/psnm/psnm.htm. In a historic building near the ferry terminal, exhibits display collections of naval artifacts and documents. Close to Puget Sound Naval Shipyard, the museum delves into the history of the navy in Bremerton. Open daily June to Sept; Wed to Mon from Oct to May.

USS *Turner Joy*. 300 Washington Beach Ave., Bremerton; (360) 792-2457; www.uss turnerjoy.org. The ship, which was launched in 1958, is restored to recall its days of Vietnam action. A ship tour explores the destroyer, heading below decks to the crew cabins, engine room, and galley. Open daily May through Sept; Fri to Sun from Oct through Apr. $$$.

where to eat

Anthony's. 20 Washington Ave., Bremerton; (360) 377-5004; www.anthonys.com. Few reliable choices for restaurants feature in downtown Bremerton, but from Anthony's you can watch the ferries dock and depart and admire the waterfront fountains. Seafood and steaks from this multilocation restaurant create an upscale menu that matches the panorama. Open daily for lunch and dinner. $$–$$$.

bremers of bremerton

In 1891 William Bremer platted the community on the shores on Sinclair Inlet and later secured the building of Puget Sound Naval Shipyard in Bremerton. By the 1970s the Bremer family still owned a large portion of the commercial buildings in the downtown core, and ownership had fallen to sole heir Edward, one of William and Sophia Bremer's three children.

A condition of the inheritance was that the heir could never marry. Sounds a bit like a fabricated tale, but in reality it had a devastating effect on the downtown. Under Edward's ownership, buildings deteriorated and the downtown district crumbled. Reports say the ferry terminal closed when a floor caved in under someone's foot. Edward fought legal battles to keep malls out of the downtown, and by the mid-1980s many brand-name tenants had left the waterfront, opting for lower taxes in Silverdale.

Today revitalization projects are in progress, and waterfront fountains, public museums, and outdoor art flag the city as a solidly rebounding district.

Source: Seattle Post-Intelligencer *article "Remaking downtown Bremerton City now has chance to get ball rolling" by Gil Bailey. Published October 28, 1987.*

port orchard

This small community on Puget Sound looks out on the bright lights of Bremerton on the opposite side of Sinclair Inlet. Yet Port Orchard shines in its own right with museums, waterfront dining, and a busy main street. In addition to a waterfront boardwalk and marina, historical museums and an art gallery attract visitors to the small but entertaining downtown district.

The town, once called Sidney, thrived with the lumber industry. It is the seat of Kitsap County.

getting there

From Bremerton follow SR 3 south and merge shortly thereafter onto SR 166. Southwest Bay Street follows the shore, leading to downtown Port Orchard.

where to go

Log Cabin Museum. 416 Sidney Ave., Port Orchard; www.sidneymuseumandarts.com. Look for the lone log house on busy Sidney Avenue. Constructed by a Civil War veteran in 1914, the cabin recreates the daily life of yesteryear. Open Sat and Sun in summer.

Sidney Art Gallery and Museum. 202 Sidney Ave., Port Orchard; (360) 876-3693; www
.sidneymuseumandarts.com. The first-floor gallery and second-floor museum fascinate visitors with a diverse look at the community in the past and present. Shops, a school, and a
doctor's office envision snippets of Kitsap history, while the gallery livens the ground level
with local art and monthly exhibitions. Open Tues to Sun.

where to eat

Amy's on the Bay. 100 Harrison Ave., Port Orchard; (360) 876-1445; www.amysonthebay
.com. Amidst the classic burgers and seafood, a few internationally infused dishes brighten
the menu. Seared tuna *poki* is served with rice and a soy-sesame salad, the trout is sourced
from the Columbia River, and mussels zing with Tom Yum curry. Open daily for lunch and
dinner. $$–$$$.

Gino's at Port Orchard. 429 Bay St., Port Orchard; (360) 874-2075; www.ginos
restaurants.com. After years as the restaurant Tweten's Lighthouse, this iconic building
is refashioned as a bayside, Italian-style restaurant. Hospitable service, water views, and
comforting dishes work well together. Open for Sunday breakfast and daily for lunch and
dinner. $$–$$$.

gig harbor

Once a mecca for boat building, Gig Harbor now features more as a pretty bedroom community with a vibrant waterfront life. The Harbor History Museum and interpretive signs
preserve the boatbuilding heritage, while shops and restaurants create a modern small-
town feel. Dine on the waterfront then stroll past luxury marinas—it's all part of exploring
this safe harbor.

getting there

SR 16 connects Port Orchard to Gig Harbor (18 miles, 25 minutes). You can also arrive via
Tacoma and the Tacoma Narrows Bridge (45 miles, 45 minutes from Seattle).

where to go

Gig Harbor Visitor Information Center. 3125 Judson St., Gig Harbor; (253) 857-4842;
www.gigharborguide.com. It's easy to drop in to the information center on the way into
town from SR 16. The friendly help is exceptional. Open daily during summer; closed Sun
and Tues during off-peak season.

Harbor History Museum. 4121 Harborview Dr., Gig Harbor; (253) 858-6722; www.harbor
historymuseum.org. A new museum styled as a boat shed harbors exhibits on the area's

> ## galloping gertie

It's best to read about the history of the Tacoma Narrows Bridge after a safe crossing. In 1940 the first Tacoma Narrows Bridge opened and soon earned the nickname Galloping Gertie—called such because of the way the bridge swayed and shook in the wind. Just months after opening, the bridge collapsed, killing a dog that was trapped in an abandoned car. Amazingly the collapse and the bridge's buckling twists are caught on camera; they are worth searching for online.

The replacement bridge, which was completed in 1950 and an expansion added in 2007, has earned a far more reassuring moniker: Sturdy Gertie.

boatbuilding culture and was preparing to open as this book goes to print. Call ahead for hours. $.

where to eat

Brix 25°. 7707 Pioneer Way, Gig Harbor; (253) 858-6626; www.harborbrix.com. Hailed for its polish with an edge of casual cool, Brix 25° boasts a clean-cut menu and an impressive wine list with some delicate ice wines. Simple menu selections like peppercorn steak, wild salmon, and lamb put the focus on quality. Open daily for dinner and Sat lunch in summer. $$$–$$$$.

where to stay

The Maritime Inn. 3212 Harborview Dr., Gig Harbor; (253) 858-1818; www.maritimeinn .com. Without sacrificing their intimate quality, the guest rooms at the Maritime Inn are fresh and clean with excellent amenities. Queen- or king-size beds, waterfront views, and fireplaces add comfort and elegance to the classic decor. $$$.

day trip 02

west

>>> **chief sealth, swans, and vikings:**
bainbridge island, suquamish,
poulsbo

From within sight of Seattle to the grave of the city's namesake, Chief Sealth, this day trip
explores the heart of the Kitsap Peninsula. Just close enough to be a relaxing journey, just
far enough to be a getaway, you can walk through Norwegian-influenced Poulsbo, regal
gardens on Bainbridge Island, and the age-old Native American home of the Suquamish at
Old Man House Park.

Museums explore the marine world, Suquamish cultural stories, and local history, while
gardens and parks invite a day outdoors.

bainbridge island

Within such a short distance of Seattle, the hidden back streets of Bainbridge Island still
offer some seclusion despite being a heavily gentrified region of large homes on the water.
But the locals are friendly, and the polish of the island has yielded lovely waterfront dining,
lavish gardens, scrumptious baked treats, and wineries.

getting there

About two dozen times daily, ferries sail for Bainbridge Island from Seattle (terminal at 801
Alaskan Way, Pier 52). The 35-minute crossing is clogged with afternoon rush-hour traffic,
so try to avoid peak travel times (usually about 3 p.m. to 7 p.m.).

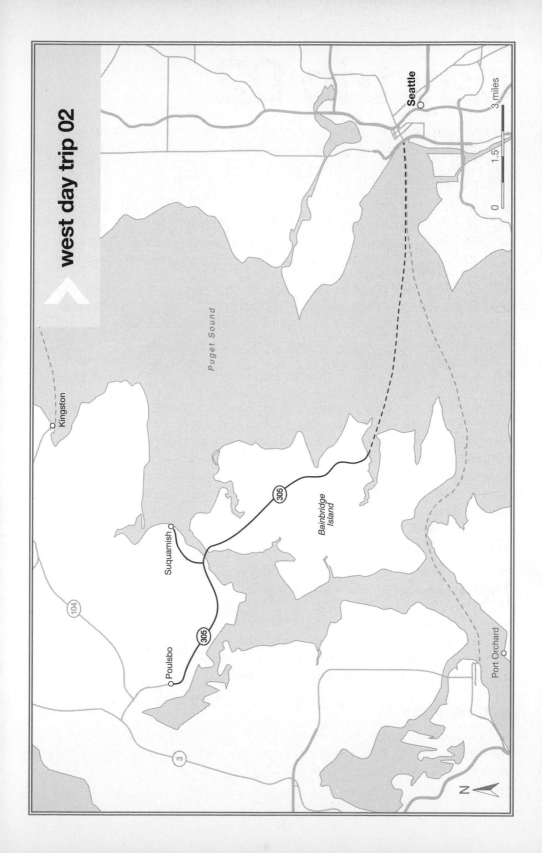

west day trip 02

Seattle

Puget Sound

Kingston

Suquamish

305

Bainbridge
Island

Poulsbo

305

104

3

Port Orchard

N

0   1.5   3 miles

Alternately catch a ferry from Edmonds to Kingston and begin in the Poulsbo area. Driving up from Bremerton is a third option, and avoiding the ferries altogether and arriving by land via Tacoma and Gig Harbor is a fourth. Keep in mind that these alternate routes all add about an hour to the travel time to reach Bainbridge.

where to go

Bainbridge Island Historical Society and Museum. 215 Ericksen Ave. Northeast, Bainbridge Island; (206) 842-2773; www.bainbridgehistory.org. Located in a 1908 schoolhouse, the museum draws on local history from early to modern days of Bainbridge Island. The history of Puget Sound links to shipping, fishing, ferries, and a World War II fort. Open Wed to Mon. $.

Bloedel Reserve. 7571 Northeast Dolphin Dr., Bainbridge Island; (206) 842-7631; www.bloedelreserve.org. The house is purely palatial and the grounds even more so: A human-made waterfall, serene swans, and stooped willows all add a regal note to the Northwest gardens of rhodies and conifers. The reflection, moss, and Japanese gardens all have a sacred air of preservation and veneration. About half of the 150 or so acres remains forested while the rest contains the manicured beds and visitor center. Reservations are advised, but it may be possible to walk in if you drop by early on a non-high-season day. Open Wed to Sun year-round. $$$.

Fort Ward State Park. 2241 Pleasant Beach, Bainbridge Island; www.parks.wa.gov. Checkered with concrete relics of World War II, Fort Ward State Park provides a mix of activities from beachcombing to boating and biking. In the early 1900s the navy established Fort Ward to help protect Puget Sound Naval Shipyard in Bremerton. After serving as a training base and radio station during the war, the navy decommissioned the fort in 1958. Open daily.

Waterfront Park. Off Bjune Drive Southeast. (206) 842-2306; www.ci.bainbridge-isl.wa.us/waterfront_park.aspx. At five-and-a-half acres, Waterfront Park is just a small slice of shoreline. But the playgrounds, boat rentals, and benches make it a lovely spot from which

biking bainbrige

You won't drive far on Bainbridge Island without encountering a cyclist. With its wide road shoulders and off-main routes, the island endears itself to bikers. To join the pedal parade, check in with **Bainbridge Classic Cycle** *(740 Winslow Way East; 206-842-9191 or 206-842-3434; www.classiccycleus.com), which also offers summer rentals from a bike barn near the ferry dock.*

to enjoy the water. For kayak rental information check with **Back of Beyond** (181 Winslow Way; 206-842-9229; www.tothebackofbeyond.com).

where to eat

Blackbird Bakery. 210 Winslow Way East, Bainbridge Island; (206) 780-1322. Vegan chocolate loaf cake doesn't get better than this; it will even have nonvegans calling it yummy. From quiches to cookies, all the baked goods here earn top honors—the only downside is choosing just one. Okay, maybe just two. Cash only. Open daily from about 6 a.m. to 6 p.m. $.

Harbour Public House. 231 Parfitt Way Southwest, Bainbridge Island; (206) 842-0969; www.harbourpub.com. This fun-loving pub offers marina views and well-priced, tasty eats. Organic greens and hearty grains add an atypical edge to the menu. The house salads draw regulars (including a summer-only salad with blackberries) while seafood dishes such as the steamed mussels and clams or salmon bowl fit the marina feel. For hungry eaters, specials include the battered chicken sandwich and a double-digit count on the available styles of burgers, ranging from buffalo to blue cheese or jalapeno. Open daily for lunch, dinner, and late night. $$–$$$.

where to stay

The Eagle Harbor Inn. 291 Madison Ave. South, Bainbridge Island; (206) 842-1446; www .theeagleharborinn.com. Fresh with a European feel, the inn provides self-sufficient stay options in classic comfort. Large patios and well-tended gardens add space and privacy to the guest suites that span hotel rooms and townhouses. Earth tones and natural light provide a serene and quiet escape. $$$–$$$$.

suquamish

The tribal community of Suquamish captures the spirit of the Pacific Northwest before European settlement encroached. A red-cedar festival hall that stretched more than 500 feet along the beach during the 1800s is now commemorated at Old Man House Park. The park also treats with great views of boat traffic and marine life heading through Agate Pass.

In Suquamish, part of a larger area known as Port Madison Indian Reservation, many come to visit the grave of Chief Sealth—the respected leader of the Duwamish and Suquamish tribes.

getting there

From Bainbridge, head north on SR 305 and cross the Agate Pass Bridge. Turn right onto Suquamish Way Northeast. From this main route, Division Avenue leads to the Chief Sealth's grave to the north and Old Man House Park to the south.

where to go

Chief Sealth's Grave and St. Peter's Mission Cemetery. 7076 Northeast South St., Suquamish. The grave of the revered and respected Suquamish leader Chief Sealth draws visitors who come to pay their respects. The headstone reads "Seattle, Chief of Suquamish, and Allied tribes. Died June 7, 1866. The firm friend of the whites, and for him the City of Seattle, was named by its founders." Religious offerings of flowers, trinkets, coins, and tobacco surround the grave site, which is adjacent to the church of St. Peter's Mission. Open daily.

Old Man House Park. Northeast McKinstry Street and South Angeline Avenue Northeast, Suquamish. This small waterfront park marks the former location of a 500-foot-long house and festival hall that lodged dozens of Suquamish families. The house, made of red cedar, stood parallel to the tide lines and featured a sloping roof rather than the more common gabled roof. Open daily.

Suquamish Museum. 15838 Sandy Hook Rd. Northeast, Poulsbo; (360) 394-8496; www .suquamish.org. Although it has a Poulsbo address, the museum is closer geographically and in subject to Suquamish. Just west of the Agate Pass Bridge that connects to Bainbridge Island, the large new museum houses exhibits as well as arts and crafts that illustrate the history, culture, and storytelling of the Suquamish. Open daily May to Sept; Fri to Sun from Oct to Apr. $.

chief sealth

Also called Si'ahl as well as Chief Seattle—which ties him more closely to the city that was named for him—Chief Sealth remains a revered leader for his strong and peaceful leadership. His famed 1854 speech urged respect for Native American land rights and ecological care. But dispute remains, however, over the content of Chief Sealth's Lushootseed-language speech as there is no original written version.

*For a century the Suquamish community has celebrated **Chief Seattle Days** with memorials, songs, dances, fireworks, canoe races, and salmon dinners. The festival occurs in mid-August (360-598-3311; www.suquamish.org).*

poulsbo

The one-time hamlet of Poulsbo attained its Norwegian heritage authentically—from Scandinavian settlers who immigrated here in the 1880s. With Scandinavian bakeries and restaurants, the town's location on a fjord affront the peaks of the Olympic Mountains is a picturesque spot. Admire the pretty white-and-blue First Lutheran Church, walk through the waterfront downtown district, or explore the depths of the ocean at the marine science center.

But perhaps the town festivals are best reason to visit. The Viking Fest celebrates Constitution Day in Norway on May 17 and includes parades, races, and a vendor market, while the Midsommarfest hosts folk dancers for the summer solstice.

getting there

Head 10 minutes west of the Agate Pass Bridge on SR 305 to reach Poulsbo.

where to go

Poulsbo Marine Science Center. 18743 Front St. Northeast, Poulsbo; (360) 598-4460; www.poulsbomsc.org. Touch tanks and aquariums with Puget Sound critters fill the facility. Overlooking the town marina, the center prioritizes education, and kids will especially enjoy the ocean-life exhibits. Open Thurs to Sun.

where to eat

Sluys' Poulsbo Bakery. 18924 Front St. Northeast, Poulsbo; (360) 697-2253. Find baked treats of every kind, including the Norwegian *lefse* flat bread. Open daily. $.

Sogno di Vino. 18830 Front St. Northeast, Poulsbo; (360) 697-8466; www.sogno-di-vino .com. Wine and pizza make a simple and tasty combination. The pizza is baked in a wood-fired oven, and toppings such as fennel sausage, smoked salmon, Gruyere, prosciutto, and rosemary tease the senses. The small but spot-on menu also offers fresh pastas and smaller starters. A warm, friendly vibe permeates throughout. Open daily for lunch and dinner. $$–$$$.

day trip 03

west

hood canal:
shelton, allyn, union and
hoodsport, quilcene

Fishermen awake before dawn to launch their boats where the Olympic Mountains meet a saltwater fjord. While homes overlook a large portion of Hood Canal, state parks with beaches provide access to stretches of waterfront. Every turn delivers understated views of forest, water, and wildlife.

This day trip takes a roundabout route following the C-curve of Hood Canal from its terminus at the Theler Wetlands near Belfair out to the Hood Canal Bridge that marks its connection with Puget Sound. Through the Olympic forests, past waterside restaurants, and beside fishing docks, it's a route of discovery that traces the length of this waterway.

The Hood Canal area also makes a timelessly scenic drive with rewarding activities, whether it's touring a garden nursery, fish hatchery, wine-tasting room, or chainsaw-carving gallery.

shelton

Shelton was established as, and still is, a logging town: The piles of timber at the local Simpson Timber Company, tree slices serving as town greeting signs, and working railroad lines attest to that. But often with a strong industry comes wealth, and Shelton hints at a measure of prosperity with some lovely early-twentieth-century historical architecture in the downtown.

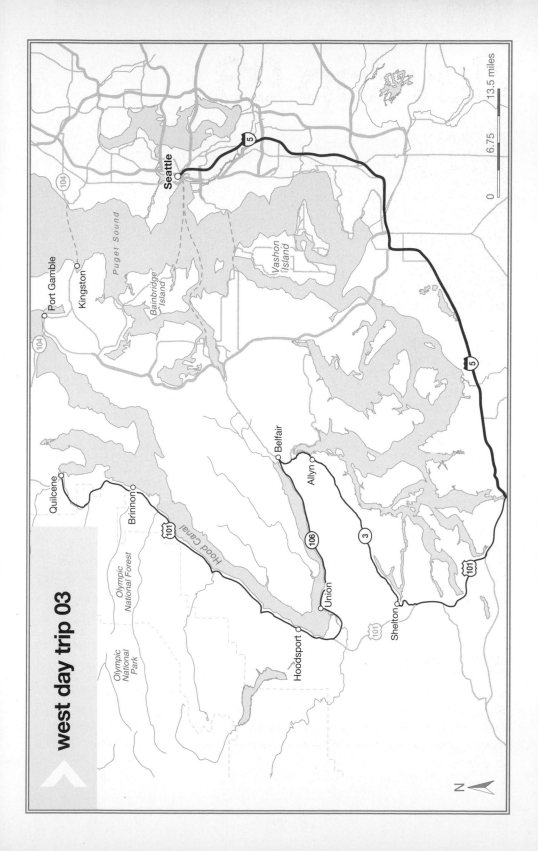

west day trip 03

getting there

From Seattle head south on I-5 to exit 104, which merges with US 101 at Olympia. Just before Shelton, SR 3 spurs off US 101. Take SR 3 to downtown Shelton (80 miles, 1.5 hours). This road trip cuts a leisurely route along SR 3 to the head of the canal then along SR 106 to the lower shore, meeting again with US 101 as it heads north into the Olympic Peninsula. The total tour takes about 2 hours from Shelton to Quilcene.

Alternately begin at the mouth end of Hood Canal by taking the Edmonds-Kingston ferry and traveling along SR 104 as it crosses the Hood Canal Bridge and meets with US 101.

where to go

Shelton Visitor Center. 230 West Railroad Ave., Shelton; (360) 426-2021, (360) 427-8168 or (800) 576-2021; www.sheltonchamber.org. Look for the red caboose on Railroad Avenue for local guidance. Open weekdays, Sat by chance.

Mason County Historical Museum. 427 West Railroad Ave., Shelton; (360) 426-1020. From the pioneers to the logging industry, the museum explores the history of Shelton and Mason County. Sport trophies, documentation of historic barns, and photographs all provide a perspective on the area. Open Tues to Sat.

Squaxin Island Tribe Museum. 150 Southeast K'wuh-deegs-altxw, Shelton; (360) 432-3839; www.squaxinislandmuseum.org. The Squaxin are known as the People of the Water—it's no surprise considering the water that surrounds and laces the Kitsap Peninsula. Murals dominate this beautiful museum, telling the stories of an ancient people. Open Wed to Sun. $$.

where to eat

The Strip Steakhouse. 405 West Railroad Ave., Shelton; (360) 432-5844. A small, well-planned menu befits the intimate dining room. Cozy but with lots of seating, the restaurant serves classic cuts of steak as well as burgers and the odd chicken or seafood dish. Open Mon to Sat for lunch and dinner. $$–$$$.

allyn

The small town of Allyn offers a sheltered vantage of Hood Canal plus a dose of local quirkiness. Visit a chainsaw-carving school, kayak the calm waters, or hike through preserved wetlands and see a whale skeleton. Or just relax on a waterfront patio—the choice is yours.

getting there

SR 3 leads from Shelton to Allyn and Belfair, near the head of the canal.

where to go

George Kenny's School of Chainsaw Carving. 18351 East SR 3, Allyn; (360) 275-9570; www.bearinabox.com. It's nearly impossible to miss this: Just look for the Vikings, eagles, bears, and beavers placed alongside the highway. The school holds classes for chainsaw carvers and exhibits the cedar-carved work for all to enjoy. Each July during Allyn Days it's the center of the competition circuit. Open daily.

North Bay Kayak. 18350 SR 3, Allyn; (360) 535-2198; www.allynkayak.com. Recreational kayaking can be easy and a fun way to explore the calm waters of Hood Canal. Hourly or daily rentals are available with rates starting at about $20 for one hour to about $60 for a full day. From babies to dogs and small children, the company easily accommodates families. $$$.

Theler Wetlands. 22871 Northeast SR 3, Belfair; (360) 275-4898; www.thelercenter .org. An exhibit center, gray-whale skeleton, and diverse wildlife create a surprise escape between the towns of Belfair and Allyn. The wetland spans marsh, farmland, and forest and sits where the Union River meets Hood Canal. No dogs are allowed on the trails. The wetlands are open daily.

where to eat

Lennard K's Boathouse Restaurant. 18340 East SR 3; Allyn; (360) 275-6060; www.lennard ks.com. This fjordside dining room offers a standard pub-style menu. Burgers, salads, pizzas, and sandwiches are bar staples, while pork chops, chicken, meat loaf, and fried seafood provide more substantial options. Open daily for breakfast, lunch, and dinner. $$–$$$.

union and hoodsport

At the "Great Bend" of Hood Canal sit the two towns of Union and Hoodsport, about 15 minutes apart. This area remains a hotbed for commercial fishing, where waking at dawn yields serene shots of fishermen and fisherwomen out early, untangling their nets and pushing off from the dock. With a local fruit winery, access to Olympic National Park, and the area's best accommodations, Union and Hoodsport sparkle.

getting there

Follow SR 106 west along the canal to Union. At the junction with US 101, head north to Hoodsport.

where to go

Shelton-Mason Chamber of Commerce. 150 North Lake Cushman Rd., Hoodsport; (360) 877-2021; www.explorehoodcanal.com. This visitor center opens daily.

Hama Hama Seafood Store. 35846 US 101, Lilliwaup; (360) 877-5811 or (888) 877-5844; www.hamahamaoysters.com. Fresh oysters and smoked salmon reel in visitors to the Hama Hama Seafood Store. The shop sits waterside on the main route, about 15 minutes north of Hoodsport. Open daily.

Hoodsport Winery. 23501 US 101, Hoodsport; (360) 877-9894; www.hoodsport.com. One of the first wineries in Washington, Hoodsport Winery produces delicate fruit wines that sparkle with color. Whether it's the apple, blackberry, pear, or rhubarb wine, or perhaps one of the more traditional varietals such as Syrah, Chardonnay, or Cabernet Sauvignon, there exists no shortage of bottles to uncork for tasting. Open daily.

where to eat

Union Bay Café. 5121 East SR 106, Union; (360) 898-2462; www.unionbaycafeandbar .com. Waterfront views meet hefty portions and simple service. Lemon pepper salmon and sautéed oysters provide tasty seafood dishes and are complemented by fresh salads and substantial roasts. It's the local's spot to catch the game and relax with a drink. Open daily for lunch and dinner; Sun brunch. $$–$$$.

where to stay

Alderbrook Resort. 7101 SR 106, Union; (360) 898-2200; www.alderbrookresort.com. This posh luxury resort and spa on Hood Canal features thoughtfully designed guest rooms as well as private cabins. The warm stone hearth and Northwest feel of the lobby gives way to open, earthy colors in the guest rooms—like traversing forest to meadow. King-size beds, scenic views, and an on-site spa and restaurant all let you tuck in to the experience. $$$–$$$$.

Glen Ayr Resort. 25381 US 101, Hoodsport; (360) 877-9522 or (866) 877-9522; www .glenayr.com. Pull up in your RV, moor your boat, or drive in and grab a motel room—this waterfront resort accommodates many travelers at its Hood Canal location. Balconies allow for excellent morning views with a coffee and panorama of Hood Canal. $$.

quilcene

The wilds begin in Quilcene, which sits beyond the Olympic National Forest. Tucked in the nook of Quilcene Bay, the area (which on first look doesn't present itself as much of a destination) does offer attractions such as a fish hatchery, historical museum, and access to Olympic National Park via Brinnon.

eastern side of olympic national park

Hood Canal trims the southeastern corner of Olympic National Park and a few roads spur into the wilderness providing access. From Brinnon, FSR 2610 strikes up to Dosewallips alongside Dosewallips River, although a road washout necessitates a 5-mile hike to the campground at press time.

SR 119 provides a more-traveled route from Hoodsport to Staircase, where there are hiking, picnic, and camping facilities. For all areas of the park, the central visitor center lies in Port Angeles but is reachable for questions on the area adjacent to Hood Canal as well (3002 Mount Angeles; 360-565-3130; www.nps.gov/olym).

where to go

Olympic National Forest Hood Canal Ranger Station. 295142 US 101, Quilcene; (360) 765-2200; www.fs.fed.us/r6/olympic. For details on exploring the national forest—the lands that ring the national park—stop in to gather guides and guidance. Open weekdays.

Quilcene Historical Museum. 151 East Columbia St., Quilcene; (360) 765-4848. This small community museum provides the Native American and pioneer perspectives on this lumber town. Open Fri to Mon, Apr through Sept. $.

Quilcene River Fish Hatchery. 281 Fish Hatchery Rd., Quilcene; (360) 765-3334; www.fws.gov/quilcenenfh. Adult salmon return in fall, and the autumn is the most active time to see fish spawning in Quilcene River. As with many Washington hatcheries, staff members provide tours to groups, but they are also eager to answer questions as they go about their tasks. Open weekdays.

Whitney Gardens and Nursery. 306264 US 101, Brinnon; (360) 796-4411 or (800) 952-2404; www.whitneygardens.com. Wander the gardens solo or take a guided tour. Rhododendrons, magnolias, and blooming bulbs create a Northwest floral paradise spanning seven acres. Open daily, although Mar through June is the best time for blooms. $.

where to eat

Twana Roadhouse. 294793 US 101, Quilcene; (360) 765-6485. Standard fare includes pizza, burgers, and large breakfasts. But the small restaurant is also a friendly and welcoming spot to start or end a road trip. Open daily for breakfast, lunch, and dinner. $–$$.

northwest

>>>

day trip 01

northwest

whidbey island:
langley, greenbank, coupeville,
oak harbor

The longest island in the contiguous United States boasts a little less landmass than the claim to fame suggests—at its widest Whidbey Island is only about 10 miles across. Throughout the island decommissioned army outposts, historic farms, welcoming gardens, and diverse eateries punctuate the miles of coastline.

On the western front, batten down the hatches for storm watching, oceanside hiking, and views of the snow-capped Olympic Mountains. Historical buildings and mussel farms find a safe harbor in the shelter of the east side of the island. Throughout your visit, you'll hear that you're now "on island"—it means slow down and enjoy the island escape.

Whidbey boasts perhaps the highest density of accommodations in the state. While the prices are encouragingly reasonable, sifting through the hundred-plus inns, B&Bs, cabins, cottages, and vacation rentals takes some work. To ease the effort, visit the lodging section of www.whidbeycamanoislands.com.

getting there

Travel north on I-5 to exit 182, from which Mukilteo Speedway (or SR 525) cuts northwest to the ferry at Mukilteo and I-405 heads south. Running on the hour and half-hour throughout the day, the ferry takes just 20 minutes to transport you to island time.

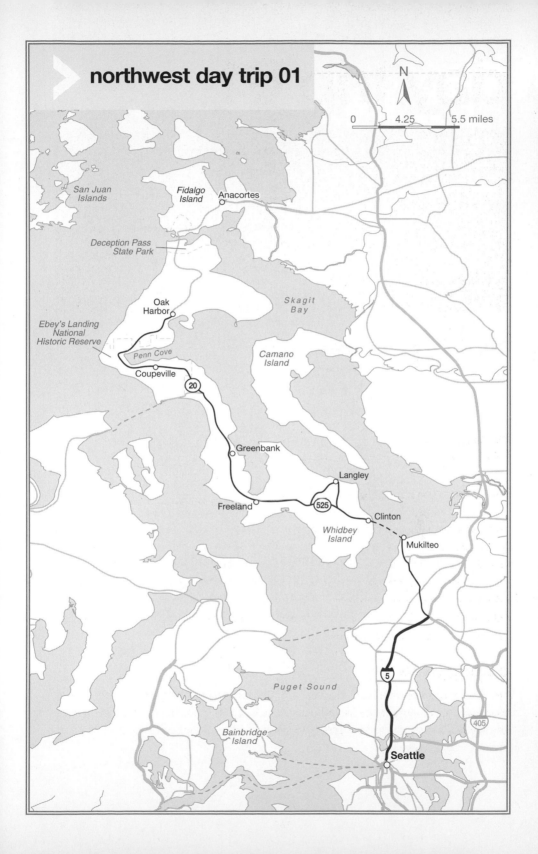

northwest day trip 01

N

0   4.25   5.5 miles

San Juan Islands

Fidalgo Island

Anacortes

Deception Pass State Park

Skagit Bay

Oak Harbor

Ebey's Landing National Historic Reserve

Penn Cove

Coupeville

20

Camano Island

Greenbank

Langley

Freeland

525

Clinton

Mukilteo

Whidbey Island

Puget Sound

Bainbridge Island

5

405

Seattle

langley

A sheltered waterfront town, Langley makes a pretty first destination with its seaside shopping, varied restaurants, and a whale bell that rings when orcas or gray whales are feeding offshore.

getting there

Follow SR 525 from the ferry dock and turn north onto Langley Road to reach Langley— about 15 minutes from the ferry.

where to go

Langley Chamber of Commerce. 208 Anthes Ave., Langley; (360) 221-6765; www .visitlangley.com. Open daily, the visitor center provides the local scoop on events and accommodations.

Island Angel Chocolates. 138 Second St., Langley; (360) 221-2728; www.islandangel chocolates.com. Heavenly crafted truffles and sugary treats aside, the hot chocolate alone is worth the visit. Opt for the thick European-style hot chocolate (a small cup will do) and melt at the taste of the creamy cocoa. Open daily. $.

Seawall. Waterfront, Langley. Watch for whales and shorebirds while looking out over Saratoga Passage. Waterside parks with picnic tables complement the views. A bronze statue of a boy with his dog on the street level marks one of the access staircases. Open daily.

where to eat

The Braeburn. 197 Second St., Langley; (360) 221-3211; www.thebraeburnrestaurant .com. A cute cafe where you can dine on some expected and not-so-expected dishes such as meat loaf, pasta, or catfish BLT. The inviting, warm colors of the decor only enhance the joys of tucking into a fresh apple dumpling—an apple baked to perfection in crisp pastry sided with ice cream. Hours can vary, but generally open daily for breakfast and lunch during spring and summer; closed Wed in fall and winter. No credit cards. $–$$.

Village Pizzeria. 106 First St., Langley; (360) 221-3363. A thin but substantial crust, slices big enough to fold in half, and freshness give Village Pizzeria its top reputation. The dining area is basic, but the waterfront location allows for a quick escape to stroll in the park. While the service can lack charm on occasion, the pizza more than compensates. Open daily. No credit cards. $–$$$.

where to stay

The Boatyard Inn. 200 Wharf St., Langley; (360) 221-5120; www.boatyardinn.com. More spacious than a yacht belowdecks but with all the same waterside appeal, the Boatyard Inn provides well-equipped suites and lofts. Feel the sea breeze from the deck, bunk down in a queen-size bed, prepare local seafood in the kitchen, or hunker down against a winter storm in front of the fireplace. Ten units are independent and self-contained with the true romantic feel of a boathouse. $$$–$$$$.

worth more time

Earth Sanctuary. Newman Rd., Freeland; (360) 331-6667; www.earthsanctuary.org. Between Langley and Greenbank lies perhaps Whidbey's most unique attraction: A woodland pondscape of gardens and stone dedicated to inspiring peace and contemplation. The Cottonwood Stone Circle claims to be the tallest in the world, while the ponds are home to birdlife. Trace the labyrinth, walk beneath the tree canopy, and relax in a green environment. Open daily. $$.

greenbank

The agricultural roots of Whidbey shine in Greenbank. There's no shortage of community passion at Meerkerk Rhododendron Gardens with its vibrant blooms and woodland walks. And there's no hesitation about visiting the pie cafe, wine tasting room, and market at Greenbank Farm.

Also look for the elephants, giraffes, and other exotic animals at Animal House II, a shop on SR 525 that sells large fiberglass animals. It makes a great stop for photos.

getting there

Travel 13 miles along SR 525 from the intersection with Langley Road to Greenbank.

where to go

Greenbank Farm. 765 Wonn Rd., Greenbank; (360) 678-7700; www.greenbankfarm.com. Long a focal point of the island and situated at its narrowest point, this historic farm has transformed from a large producer of loganberries (a raspberry-blackberry hybrid) into a community gathering point. A wine-tasting room is the easiest way to sample the island's wine varietals ($1 per sample), and the shop stocks bottles from the nearby Greenbank Cellars as well as Whidbey Island Vineyards and Winery. Open daily.

Meerkerk Rhododendron Gardens. 3531 Meerkerk Lane (off Resort Road), Greenbank; (360) 678-1912; www.meerkerkgardens.org. Of course the highlight of these gardens is the peak rhododendron bloom from late April to May, but with beds of daffodils (the local deer eat the tulips) and woodland trails the gardens become can be a year-round destina-tion. A gatehouse reminiscent of fairy tales serves as the departure point for guided tours, botany hunts, and photography expeditions. Open daily in summer; Wed to Sun in off-peak season. $$.

where to eat

Whidbey Pies Cafe. 765 Wonn Rd., Greenbank; (360) 678-1288; www.greenbankfarm .com. Come for the pies, stay for lunch. Loganberry, gooseberry (my favorite), rhubarb, marionberry, and apple pies are some of the classic double-crust offerings at this small but busy cafe. While the menu also offers sandwiches, soups, and quiches, I'm partial to simply indulging in a second slice. Open daily for lunch. $–$$.

coupeville

As the heart of Ebey's Landing National Historical Reserve, Coupeville and its historic charm may be the strongest pull of the island. Walk out on the pier to see Rosie—the skeleton of a male gray whale—or visit one of the many nearby state parks that feature army barracks and hillside batteries.

A downtown museum, restaurants with deliciously fresh seafood (including local Penn Cove mussels), and plenty of historic accommodations make the town an excellent stopover.

getting there

From Greenbank, SR 525 continues for 5 miles before becoming SR 20. The route journeys another 5 miles before it intersects with Coupeville's Main Street.

where to go

Ebey's Landing National Historical Reserve. Coupeville; (360) 678-6084; www.nps .gov/ebla. The reserve encompasses the historic town of Coupeville, the battlements of Fort Casey and Fort Ebey State Parks, and the still-producing farming community. Established in 1978, the historic reserve treasures eighteen working farms and Washington's second oldest town.

Fort Casey State Park. 1280 Engle Rd., Coupeville; (360) 240-5584 (lighthouse tours); www.parks.wa.gov. With the larger battery of the two coastal defense parks near Coupe-ville, Fort Casey makes a fun and eerie destination to explore. Adjacent to Keystone ferry, roam along the coastline while viewing the Olympic Mountains in the distance. Visit Admi-ralty Head Lighthouse, the guns at the artillery post, or the underwater dive park. Open daily.

Fort Ebey State Park. 400 Hill Valley Dr., Coupeville; www.parks.wa.gov. The battery and concrete gun platforms tell the story of the World War II coastal defense station. Trails snake along the bluffs with more options for hiking and biking inland. Walk, camp, surf, or simply admire the views of the Olympic Mountains. Open daily.

Island County Historical Society Museum. 908 Northwest Alexander St., Coupeville; (360) 678-3310; www.islandhistory.org. The warmth of carved cherrywood doors welcomes you to the museum and provides the first glimpses of Whidbey Island history. Venture inside to unearth the past of this agricultural and ocean-bound island. Open daily year-round. $.

Lavender Wind Farm. 2530 Darst Rd., Coupeville; (877) 242-7716; www.lavenderwind .com. Find out what the color purple smells like each summer at this lavender farm. The horizon teases with mountains and ocean, while the gift shop offers the fragrant lavender in many forms including ice cream, soaps, and oils. Open daily. $.

Rosie the Whale. Coupeville Wharf, Coupeville; www.beachwatchers.wsu.edu/island/ bones/rosie.htm. The skeleton of a nearly three-year-old male gray whale hangs from the rafters of the boat shed at the end of Coupeville wharf. Read the exhibits, grab a drink at the coffee shop, or watch the gulls circling overhead. Open daily.

where to eat

Christopher's. 103 Northwest Coveland St., Coupeville; (360) 678-5480; www.christophers onwhidbey.com. A modern dining room serves seafood with tender care. The crab cakes are delectably buttery and house salads crisp with a tasty dressing. Plates arrive freshly prepared by a trained hand. Open Mon to Sat for lunch and dinner. $$–$$$.

Knead & Feed Restaurant. 4 Northwest Front St., Coupeville; (360) 678-5431; www .kneadandfeed.com. Salads and sandwiches are served in the country-kitchen dining room that looks out over the water and echoes the farming heritage of Ebey's Landing. For more than three decades this family-run restaurant has prepared food with love. Open for week-day lunch; weekends for breakfast and lunch. $–$$.

where to stay

Anchorage Inn. 807 North Main St., Coupeville; (360) 678-5581 or (877) 230-1313; www .anchorage-inn.com. Seven rooms range from the attic Crow's Nest with a spacious layout to a main-floor budget room with a queen-size bed. All have private baths, and the floral decor adds a Victorian elegance without too much frill. Hosts Dave and Dianne teach courses on inn keeping and welcome guests with the perfect balance of charm and profes-sionalism. $$–$$$.

Compass Rose Bed and Breakfast. 508 South Main St., Coupeville; (360) 678-5318 or (800) 237-3881; www.compassrosebandb.com. Step inside the historic Victorian home and enter a world of curiosities and worldly treasures. Silver tea services, throne-like chairs, original art, and rescued wood carvings all add a distinct historical charm that is unmatchable. Two rooms each have a private bath. $$.

oak harbor

Best known for its naval base (watch for the planes zooming over head and jet airplanes mounted alongside the highway), Oak Harbor also serves as a base from which to explore Washington's most popular state park. Head to Deception Pass by land or approach by water—regardless, the views of the bridge spanning surging waters will delight.

getting there

Oak Harbor sits 10 miles and about 20 minutes from Coupeville along SR 20.

where to go

Deception Pass State Park. 41020 SR 20, Oak Harbor; (360) 675-2417; www.parks wa.gov. Rugged cliffs, plentiful (albeit sometimes noisy) camping, and photo-worthy views define this popular state park. The small passageway separating Whidbey and Fidalgo Islands is the bottleneck for tidal surges. While outlooks offer picturesque vantages on both sides of the bridge, jet-boat rides with Deception Pass Tours provide more stunning pictures (888-909-8687; www.deceptionpasstours.com). The park is open daily.

where to eat

Seabolt's Smokehouse and Deli. 31640 SR 20, Suite 3, Oak Harbor; (800) 574-1120; www.seabolts.com. Most of the seafood is deep fried, but indulge in the chowders and stash away some of the smoked delicacies for a picnic in the park. The atmosphere is a bit coarse, but the tried-and-tested recipes hold true as local favorites. Open Mon to Sat for lunch and dinner; Sun for lunch only. $–$$.

worth more time

San Juan Islands. North of Oak Harbor lies Anacortes—the departure point for ferries to the San Juans. A one-way trip from Seattle takes 2.5 to 3 hours, and there are three major islands in the group: San Juan, Orcas, and Lopez Islands.

A favorite summer destination, take a weekend in the San Juans to relax, whale watch, swim, kayak, bicycle, nap, bird watch, paint, and dine. The island time is truly yours. (888) 468-3701; www.visitsanjuans.com.

day trip 02

northwest

>>> **port towns:**
port gamble, port townsend

From the New England streets of Port Gamble to the Victorian alleys of Port Townsend, this charming day trip boasts a civilized tour of northern Kitsap and the eastern tip of the Olympic Peninsula. Museums highlight everything from seashells to Art Deco light fixtures, while a state park provides the chance to bunk in army barracks and explore the undersea world.

port gamble

Built by New Englanders as a company town for lumber workers, Port Gamble is perhaps Washington's quaintest historic small town. A seashell museum and an insightful community museum both deliver surprisingly good exhibits. Across the street the local tearoom serves finely cut sandwiches during high tea. Rent a bicycle and explore a little further. And if the Maine charm enchants you, the houses are still company owned and occasionally available for lease.

getting there

Catch a ferry from Edmonds to Kingston, which is just southeast of Port Gamble. Follow SR 104 northwest for about 8 miles into Port Gamble. The journey takes about 15 minutes. From Port Gamble, Port Townsend lies further north.

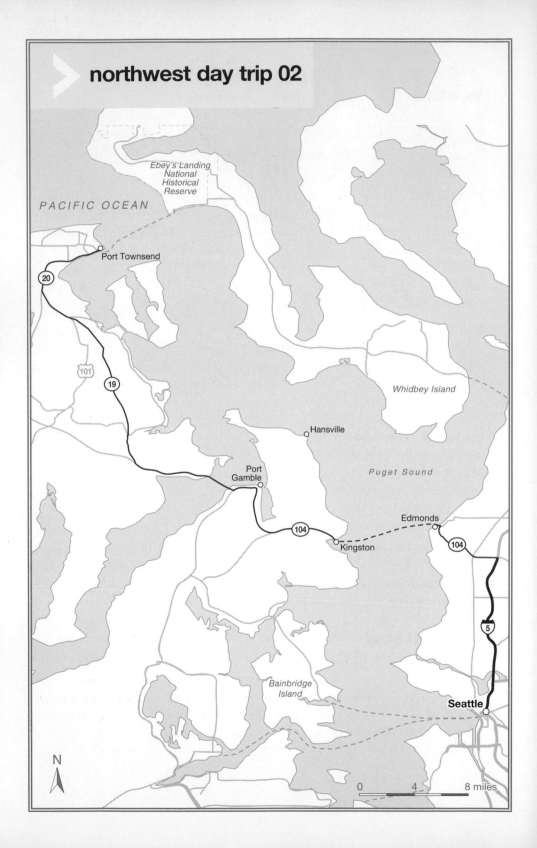

Ebey's Landing
National
Historical
Reserve

PACIFIC OCEAN

Port Townsend

20

101

19

Hansville

Port
Gamble

Puget Sound

Whidbey Island

Edmonds

104

Kingston

104

5

Bainbridge
Island

Seattle

N

0   4   8 miles

where to go

Kitsap Peninsula Visitor Information. 32220 Rainier Ave. Northeast, Port Gamble. Located in Dauntless Bookstore, which also offers bicycle rentals, the visitor center displays standard-yet-useful brochures. The bookstore is open Tues to Sun although hours change with the seasons.

Of Sea and Shore Museum. 32400 Rainier Ave. Northeast, Port Gamble; (360) 297-7636 (Port Gamble General Store); www.ofseaandshore.com/museum/museum.php. Whether it's the giant mollusks, thorny oysters, horseshoe crabs, Thailand land snails, or flowers dipped in a mineral spring, the treasures at this museum delight and surprise. The first floor of the building includes a gift shop and cafe, while the second level displays thousands of shells that are part of a private collection. All the displays are informatively labeled, and the bright natural light creates a refreshing museum experience. Open daily.

Port Gamble Historic Museum. 32400 Rainier Ave. Northeast, Port Gamble; (360) 297-8074; www.portgamble.com. Retracing the journey of Maine businessmen Andrew Jackson Pope and Frederick Talbot, who established a long-successful lumber mill at Port Gamble, the museum features excellent exhibits that succinctly tell the town's history. Discover why Port Gamble has a New England look, what happened before women arrived in town, or see Abraham Lincoln's signature on a land deed. Open daily May to Oct; Fri to Sun from Nov through Apr. $.

where to eat

Tea Room at Port Gamble. 32279 Rainier Ave. Northeast, Port Gamble; (360) 297-4225; www.tearoomatportgamble.com. Sit down for breakfast tea, high tea, or a sandwich plate in this Victorian dining room. Carefully quartered sandwiches are served on tiered chinaware with any variety of tea blends. A small gift shop and case of handmade chocolates greet visitors and tempt you to indulge in dessert first. The Mayan chocolate truffle is spicy, complex, and particularly tasty. Open daily for lunch and afternoon tea; closed Mon during fall and winter. $$–$$$.

where to stay

Port Gamble Guest Houses. Puget Avenue Northeast, Port Gamble; (360) 297-5114; www.portgambleguesthouse.com. Experience the New England charm with a room or entire house in one of the former company properties. The Port Gamble Guest Houses sit on a grassy meadow overlooking the water, and amenities include stocked kitchens, fireplaces, and patios. $$–$$$.

port townsend

This Victorian village combines a picturesque cliffside setting with historic buildings, a vibrant shopping district, and dining ranging from soda shops to bistros. Across the water from the defense forts on Whidbey Island, Fort Worden State Park preserves the World War II buildings and barracks, while various former military buildings see reincarnations as museums, community centers, and accommodations.

On the waterfront, catch a glimpse of the local wooden boat culture with the working woodshops and moored boats.

getting there

Traveling from Port Gamble, cross the Hood Canal Bridge via SR 104. Follow SR 19 (Beaver Valley Road) until it merges with SR 20 for a short stretch before reaching Port Townsend — about 30 miles or 45 minutes from Port Gamble, or 60 miles and 2 hours from Seattle.

where to go

Fort Worden State Park. 200 Battery Way, Port Townsend; (360) 344-4400; www.parks .wa.gov/fortworden. North of town venture into a gated world of army barracks and waterfront batteries. A miscellany of museums includes the **Commanding Officer's Quarters Museum** (under the wing of the Jefferson County Historical Society), **Puget Sound Coast Artillery Museum, Port Townsend Marine Center** (360-385-5582; www.ptmsc.org), and **Point Wilson Lighthouse.** Thankfully the **Guardhouse Visitor Center** (360-344-4459) provides details on each. Open daily.

Jefferson County Museum. 540 Water St., Port Townsend; (360) 385-1003; www .jchsmuseum.org. In a grand downtown building that was the city hall (built in 1892), this museum relates the diverse history of the Victorian port. Open daily. $.

Kelly Art Deco Light Museum. Vintage Hardware, 2000 Sims Way, Port Townsend; (360) 379-9030; www.vintagehardware.com/deco_museum. The store is as much a museum as the exhibits are: Heavy wooden doors with brass plates (sourced from a Manhattan bank) lead to two floors of light fixtures, furniture, and miscellaneous vintage wares. In the museum, elegant displays of Art Deco light fixtures demonstrate the era's distinct style. Open daily. $.

Wooden Boat Chandlery. 380 Jefferson St., Port Townsend; (360) 385-3628; www .woodenboat.org. From the polished brass of the chandlery to the smell of cedar shavings and drone of saws at the demonstration boathouse, the Wooden Boat Foundation provides visitors an authentic and thrilling experience at this location. Newly built in 2009, the boathouse offers a third-floor observation area as well as in-progress vessels on the ground level. Open Mon to Sat.

where to eat

Hudson Point Cafe. 130 Hudson St., Port Townsend; (360) 379-0592. Cajun catfish, oysters, mussels and clams, or crab cakes all provide a superb taste of the ocean. The dockside location provides access to the boardwalk for an after-meal stroll. Open for breakfast and lunch daily. $$–$$$.

Nifty Fiftys. 817 Water St., Port Townsend; (360) 385-1931. Jukeboxes, Hamilton Beach milk-shake mixers, and syrupy cola create an iconic soda shop. Whether it's just a shake at the bar, a corn dog, or the halibut-and-chips, the friendly service and focus on authenticity will have you putting another quarter in the jukebox. Open daily in summer, closed Tues during off-peak season. $–$$.

Public House Grill. 1038 Water St., Port Townsend; (360) 385-9708; www.thepublic house.com. The bistro feel of the dining room matches an eclectic menu that goes beyond pub grub. Smoked trout, duck, and chicken Dijon balance off the salads, fish-and-chips, and burgers. Open daily for lunch and dinner. $$–$$$.

where to stay

The Palace Hotel. 1004 Water St., Port Townsend; (360) 385-0773 or (800) 962-0741; www.palacehotelpt.com. It's best to be up front about these things: The Palace Hotel is not the place to stay if a few ghost stories rattle your chains. But if historic rooms with vaulted ceilings (some with private baths) and the elegance of a Victorian-era hotel do tempt you, then by all means book a night's stay. The 1889 Captain Tibbals building has a storied history as a brothel, and the rooms are named after the girls. $$–$$$$.

Port Townsend Hostel. 272 Battery Way, Port Townsend; (360) 385-0655; www.olympic hostel.org. While the hostel is a bit overpriced if not traveling solo (snag a similarly priced room for two at the downtown Palace Hotel during the off-peak season), the hostel provides an excellent launching point from which to explore the state park. Museums, a marine science center, and conference center all sit within the park's boundaries, not to mention beachcombing and hiking opportunities. Thankfully there's no 5 a.m. wake-up call, but there is free breakfast. $.

day trip 03

northwest

In the rain shadow of 7,980-foot Mount Olympus, the dry agricultural fields around Sequim are perfect for growing lavender. Oh, and add fruits, grains, and vegetables to the crop list too. Agriculture is so important to the town that there's an annual Irrigation Festival that celebrates harnessing the Dungeness River to water the fields more than one hundred years ago. But despite the pastoral life, the wilds of the Pacific sit just north of town along Dungeness Spit—the longest natural sand spit in the United States.

West along the coast, Port Angeles mixes the modern lore of the *Twilight* vampire book-and-movie series with its proximity to Olympic National Park. In town, museums and quirky art parks are perfect for families, while romantic restaurants cater to couples. Port Angeles is the departure point for ferries to Victoria, Canada, and the views over the Strait of Juan de Fuca tease you to explore further.

sequim

Downtown Sequim (pronounced *S-qwim,* like *swim* with a q thrown in) offers a museum, small shopping district, and tasty dining. But the true magic of this nearly rainless town can be found in the fields and along the shore. Head north to the ocean where a lighthouse marks the arc of the country's longest natural sand spit. Nearby an animal park, lavender farms, and organic markets hold true to the area's agricultural heritage.

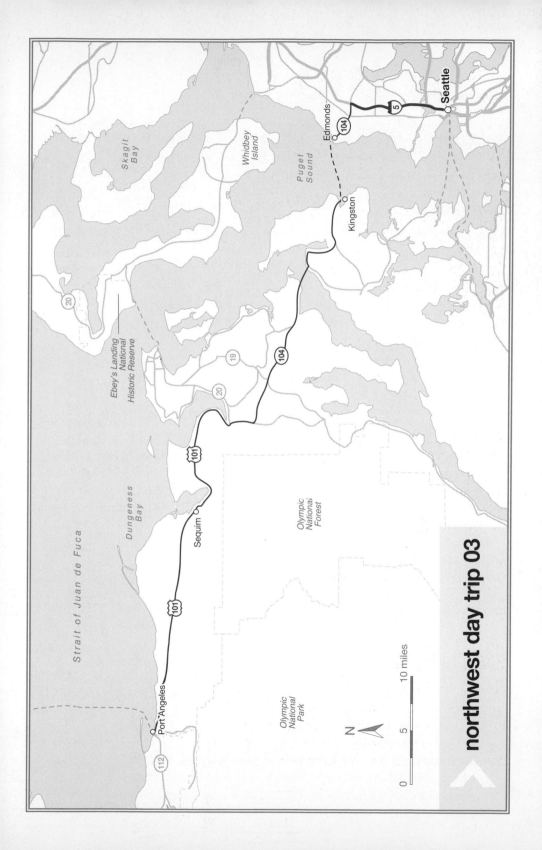

Skagit Bay

Whidbey Island

Puget Sound

Seattle

Edmonds

104

5

Kingston

104

19

20

Ebey's Landing National
Historic Reserve

20

101

Dungeness Bay

Sequim

Strait of Juan de Fuca

101

Olympic National Forest

112

Port Angeles

Olympic National Park

N

10 miles

5

0

northwest day trip 03

getting there

Head north on I-5 and take the Edmonds-to-Kingston ferry, which makes about two dozen trips daily. SR 104 cuts across north Kitsap, crosses the Hood Canal Bridge, and connects with US 101. Also known as the Olympic Loop Highway, this route leads to Sequim for a total travel time of about 2 hours or 70 miles.

where to go

Dungeness National Wildlife Refuge. Voice of America Road, off Lotzgesell Road, Sequim; www.fws.gov/washingtonmaritime/dungeness. A shoelace of sand, beach cobbles, and grasses nearly closes off Dungeness Harbor. This area teems with birdlife and seals. A 5-mile hike (one-way) trips to the end of the sand spit, while lookouts provide ocean and sandy views just 10 minutes down the trail. The reward for the longer journey is seeing the isolated New Dungeness Lighthouse, built in 1857. Open daily. $.

become a lighthouse keeper

Becoming a volunteer lighthouse keeper at New Dungeness Lighthouse affords a unique opportunity. For a moderate weekly fee, live on the sand spit and complete the daily tasks that include polishing the brass, cleaning the restrooms, and raising the flag.

The lighthouse is open to tours daily so it won't be quite such a lonely task, and the keeper's quarters accommodate up to seven people. Visit www.new dungenesslighthouse.com for more details.

Museum & Arts Center. 175 West Cedar St., Sequim; (360) 683-8110; www.mac sequim.org. See the bones of the Manis Mastodon: The first (although disputed) evidence that 14,000 years ago, humans hunted mastodons and lived on the Northern Olympic Peninsula—4,000 years earlier than thought. Digging a pond in his yard, Emanuel Manis discovered the tusks and bones of a mastodon that had a spear point lodged in its ribs. The museum delves into the mystery as well as local history. On the first Friday of each month Sequim hosts an art walk creating a vibrant atmosphere for visiting local merchants. Open Tues to Sat.

Olympic Game Farm. 1423 Ward Rd., Sequim. (360) 683-4295 or (800) 778-4295; www .olygamefarm.com. A driving tour takes visitors through the animal lands of the privately held park where feeding the animals whole-wheat bread prompts fun encounters with pastures of yak, grazing zebras, and munching llamas. After driving past the bears, emus, and elk, take a walking tour through the wolves, tigers, and cougars. The farm was once connected with Walt Disney Studios and started out caring for animal actors during their off-set time. Open daily. $$$.

where to eat

Bell Street Bakery. 175 West Bell St., Sequim; (360) 681-6262; www.bellstreetbakery .com. A polished, new bakery allows the hungry to watch bread being baked or to head next door to the retail shop that serves ready-made sandwiches, quick breakfast foods, coffee, and baked treats. Open as a retail location as well as for breakfast and lunch hours daily; closed Sun in off-peak season. $.

Dockside Grill. 2577 West Sequim Bay Rd., Sequim; (360) 683-7510 or (888) 640-7226; www.docksidegrill-sequim.com. Overlooking John Wayne Marina, this wharf-perched restaurant serves the area's bountiful seafood. Cedar planking is used to add subtle flavors to steaks and vegetables as well as the usual salmon. From baby-clam pasta to calamari steak, the ocean meets table at the Dockside. Open Wed to Sun for lunch and dinner. $$$–$$$$.

where to stay

Red Caboose Getaway. 24 Old Coyote Way, Sequim; (360) 683-7350; www.redcaboose getaway.com. "All it needs is a bullet hole!" I exclaimed walking up to the Western-themed caboose. Lo and behold the three layers of glass on the back door of caboose number four had spiderweb cracks where a bullet hit—likely from a farm boy's gun during a cross-country trek. From the fine china and historic train photos in the dining car to each of the themed cabooses, the stationmasters roll out a fun overnight destination. $$$.

port angeles

Choose your Port Angeles: the *Twilight* locations of Bella Italia, Lincoln Theater, and Odyssey Bookshop, the accessibility of Olympic National Park with its mountain views and hot-springs hiking, the wine tasting and fine dining, or storm watching from oceanside inns.

getting there

The 16-mile journey from Sequim to Port Angeles takes about 30 minutes on US 101.

where to go

Port Angeles Visitor Center. 121 East Railroad Ave., Port Angeles; (360) 452-2363; www .portangeles.org. Well-signposted when arriving in town from the east, the visitor center can provide maps and recommendations for Port Angeles as well as Victoria across the Strait of Juan de Fuca. Open daily.

Feiro Marine Life Center. 315 North Lincoln St., Port Angeles; (360) 417-6254; www .olypen.com/feirolab. On the Port Angeles waterfront, touch tanks, aquariums, and exhibits invite you into the ocean world. Open daily during summer; weekends only in off-peak season. $.

Museum at the Carnegie. 207 South Lincoln St., Port Angeles. (360) 452-2662, www .clallamhistoricalsociety.com. A delightful local museum introduces the strong characters of the Olympic Peninsula. Lighthouse keepers, female politicians, and New York artists all stir up history. Photos, video, and exhibits fill the historic building. Open Wed to Sat. $.

olympic national park

Although it's longer than a day trip to venture to the Hoh Rain Forest, Forks, and the west coast of the Olympic Peninsula, the national park offers stunning destinations within an easy reach of Port Angeles:

- *Hurricane Ridge: Drive 45 minutes south of Port Angeles up Hurricane Ridge Road. A visitor center and hiking trails complement the wildflower meadows and views of Mount Olympus. Open daily during summer and Fri to Sun in winter, although snow is common in the colder months.*

- *Olympic Hot Springs: About 45 minutes along Hot Springs Road west of town and then a further 2.5-mile one-way hike lie some clothing-optional hot springs. Stagnant water is unappealing in summer, but with a light snow on the ground the destination is serene. The hot springs are waist deep (when sitting) and vary in temperature—dip a toe in first. For more polished hot springs,* **Sol Duc Resort** *(www.visitsolduc.com) is located west of Lake Crescent.*

- *Lake Crescent: Thirty minutes along US 101 west of Port Angeles, Lake Crescent is a summertime favorite. A glacier-carved lake serves as a base for hikes to waterfalls and other viewing points.*

For further information on these destinations, check with the **Olympic National Park Visitor Center** *(3002 Mount Angeles Rd., Port Angeles; 360-565-3130; www.nps.gov/olym).*

Olympic Cellars. 255410 US 101, Port Angeles; (360) 452-0160; www.olympiccellars .com. The gambrel roof of an 1890 barn shelters wine cellars and a restaurant. Whether it's for wine tasting or an event, the winery is a welcoming host. Open daily for wine tasting.

Olympic National Park Visitor Center. 3002 Mount Angeles Rd., Port Angeles; (360) 565-3130; www.nps.gov/olym. Maps, advice, and permits for Olympic National Park are available from this visitor center on the south edge of town. The road continues into the hills, leading to Hurricane Ridge. Open daily. Park admission is $15 per car. $$$.

Port Angeles Fine Arts Center and Webster's Woods Art Park. 1203 East Lauridsen Blvd., Port Angeles; (360) 417-4590; www.pafac.org. Alongside Port Angeles Fine Arts Center, Webster's Woods Art Park creates a vibrant forest world to explore. The art pieces integrate with nature, whether it's the path of safe-shatter glass, suspended orbs, or re-envisioned tree fungi. The art park is open daily; the arts center opens Wed to Sun.

where to eat

Bella Italia. 118 East First St., Port Angeles; (360) 457-5442; www.bellaitaliapa.com. Now best known as the location of Bella and Edward's first date in *Twilight,* Bella Italia also serves warming, classic dishes. Pizzas, pastas, seafood, and steaks shape a wide-reaching menu with a few surprises. While you can order up the *Twilight*-famous mushroom ravioli in the cozy dining room, the porterhouse chop with its roasted garlic may be best for warding off the vampires. Open daily for dinner. $$–$$$.

Michael's Seafood and Steak House. 117B East First St., Port Angeles; (360) 417-6929; www.michaelsdining.com. The casual atmosphere is fun, intimate, and cozy. Look for the battered chanterelle mushrooms in season and regular happy-hour specials. While the pub-fare offerings (mainly burgers, appetizers, and quick bites) rate as very good, it was a challenge to get a steak cooked to order. At the intimate, basement-level dining room it may be best to stick to the more casual fare. Open daily for dinner. $$–$$$$.

Toga's Soup House. 122 West Lauridsen Blvd., Port Angeles; (360) 452-1952. Emerging from the mountains of the national park, a home-simmered bowl of soup and perhaps a grilled sandwich are the ideal warm-up treats. Add friendly service, a casual country dining area, and efficient take-out service to quickly please hungry hikers. Open weekdays only. $–$$.

where to stay

Domaine Madeleine. 146 Wildflower Lane, Port Angeles; (360) 457-4174; www.domaine madeleine.com. A cliffside bed-and-breakfast offers more privacy than most inns. The Renoir Room features a grand sitting area with a basalt stone fireplace, while the upstairs Ming Room offers a private balcony. Separate from the main house, cottages offer more privacy, although all the rooms suggest the feeling of a secluded retreat. $$$–$$$$.

port angeles twilight

If hunting for vampires, these Twilight *locations are popular haunts in Port Angeles:*

- *The site of Edward and Bella's first date,* **Bella Italia** *is at 118 East First St.*

- *The* **Lincoln Theater** *(132 East First St.) is where Bella heads to watch a horror film in* New Moon.

- *Book shops are pivotal to the* Twilight *plot, and Port Angeles has two:* **Port Book & News** *(104 East First St.) and* **Odyssey Bookshop** *(114 West Front St.).*

Dazzled By Twilight *(135 East First St., 360-452-8800; www.dazzledbytwilight .com) is easy to spot thanks to the T-shirts and character cutouts in the window. They also host tours.*

Downtown Hotel. 101½ East Front St., Port Angeles; (360) 565-1125 or (866) 688-8600; www.portangelesdowntownhotel.com. Basic, clean, and centrally located, this small second-level hotel has rooms with private or shared baths. Even those rooms with a shared bath are European style and include an in-room sink. It's the perfect balance of comfort, convenience, and price. $–$$.

day trip 04

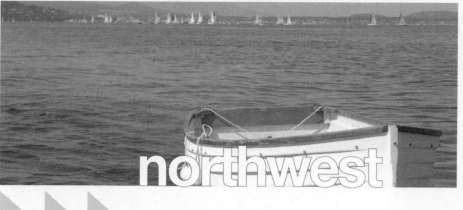

northwest

>>> **royal city:**
victoria

victoria

As Western Canada's royal city, Victoria features grand hotels, government houses, legislature buildings, and even the royal family—in wax that is. A long waterfront walk around Victoria's Inner Harbor bustles with performers, vacationers, and government employees on lunch during the summer.

But aside from its history—which includes coal barons, ghosts, and internationally famous artists—there are lush gardens, parks, and butterfly sanctuaries. For shopping head to the character-filled shops that line Government and Lower Johnson Streets and fill Chinatown.

getting there

A direct-from-Seattle passenger ferry makes the cross-border trip during the summer months for a total travel time of about 2 hours. Contact the Victoria Clipper for schedules (250-382-8100 in Victoria or 206-448-5000 in Seattle; www.victoriaclipper.com).

Alternately if you'd rather travel with a vehicle (although the attractions listed in this chapter are almost exclusively accessible by walking or public transit), drive to Port Angeles (2.5 hours) and board the MV *Coho* ferry (250-386-2202 in Victoria or 360-457-4491 in Port Angeles; www.cohoferry.com) to cross the Strait of Juan de Fuca for a total travel time of about 4 hours.

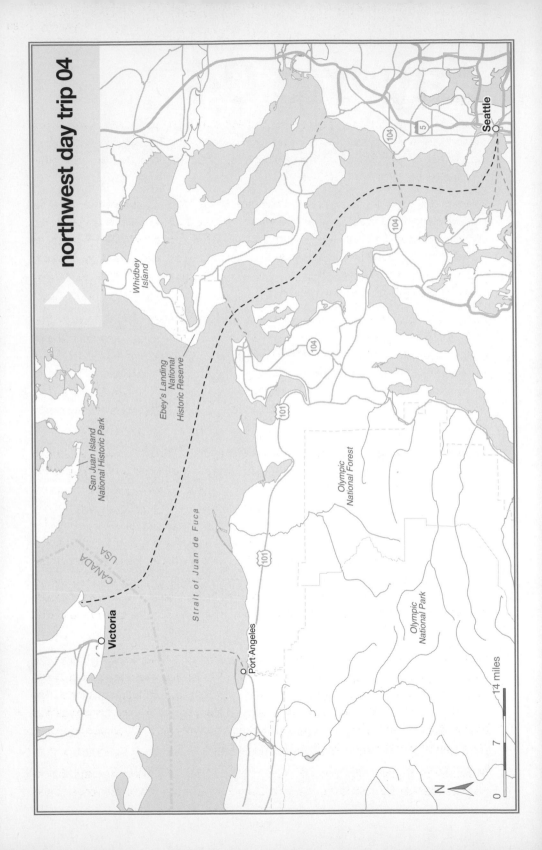

where to go

Tourism Victoria. 812 Wharf St., Victoria; (250) 953-2033 or (800) 663-3883; www.tourism victoria.com. A harborside information center provides maps, brochures, and details for local attractions, events, and accommodation. Plus, the location is handy to the ferry terminals and floatplane docks. Open daily.

Beacon Hill Park. Douglas Street at Southgate Street, Victoria; www.victoria.ca. At its northwest end, Beacon Hill Park lies close to the museums and attractions of downtown. But follow the wooded paths deeper into the park to climb over rocky hillocks, through groves of trees planted by city mayors from around the world, past rare Garry oak ecosystems, and into a petting zoo. Victorian gardens and Northwest plants lace the grounds creating a lush land of discovery. Open daily.

Butchart Gardens. 800 Benvenuto Ave., Brentwood Bay; (250) 652-4422, (250) 652-5256 or (866) 652-4422; www.butchartgardens.com. At Butchart Gardens, Christmas is a season with dainty lights, ice skating, and holiday garlands. But perhaps more magical is the Sunken Garden where ivies climb down the stone walls of an old quarry. Japanese, Italian, and rose gardens create outdoor banquet-like spaces—a feast for the senses. Open daily year-round with calendars available that detail the blooms, foliage, and special events to anticipate. $$$.

Craigdarroch Castle. 1050 Joan Crescent, Victoria; (250) 592-5323; www.craigdarroch castle.com. What would a royal city be without its castle? Craigdarroch Castle delivers the opulence of a throne seat but with a tumult of a history befitting Hamlet. Robert Dunsmuir, a man made wealthy from coal mining, commissioned construction on a new house in 1887, but he died in 1889 before the home was finished. Bitter disputes resulted from Dunsmuir's will, causing on-going friction between his two sons, James and Alex, and their mother Joan. When son Alex Dunsmuir died ten years later, another inheritance dispute escalated into a lawsuit between Joan and James—who was then premier of British Columbia. A headline in the *New York Times* read: "Premier sued by his Mother." There's little wonder that with so much family turmoil, Robert Dunsmuir is said to haunt the halls of the castle. Open daily. $$$.

Emily Carr House. 207 Government St., Victoria; (250) 383-5843; www.emilycarr.com. As an artist and anthropologist, Emily Carr painted First Nations villages throughout British Columbia. Her depictions of totems, longhouses, and BC's towering trees are iconic. This yellow home, built in 1863, was Carr's birthplace and now includes Victorian furnishings and artifacts from the artist's life. A People's Gallery features work by both Carr alongside that of local artists. Open Tues to Sat from May to Sept. $.

Government House. 1401 Rockland Ave., Victoria; (250) 387-2080; www.ltgov.bc.ca. Because Canada still retains the role of a Commonwealth nation and allegiance to the

British monarchy, the lieutenant governor of British Columbia represents the head of state at the provincial level. Tours of the modern house are available to organized groups and the gardens are open to all daily.

Legislative Assembly of British Columbia. 501 Belleville St., Victoria; (250) 387-3046; www.leg.bc.ca/info/2-2.htm. The waterfront stone building makes a favorite photo back-drop. Tour guides explain the role of the Legislative Assembly and provide history on the building and province. Free tours run daily from mid-May through Aug; weekdays only from Sept to mid-May.

Maritime Museum of British Columbia. 28 Bastion Sq., Victoria; (250) 385-4222; www .mmbc.bc.ca. More haunting tales fill these halls. The museum sits on the former location of a gallows, and the building also served as a jail and courthouse. But only the collections of maritime exhibits are guaranteed sightings with admission. From pirates to fishing and shipwrecks, the museum brings the high seas to dry land. Open daily. $$.

Observatory at the NRC Herzberg Institute of Astrophysics. 5071 West Saanich Rd., Victoria; (250) 363-8262; www.nrc-cnrc.gc.ca/eng/services/hia/centre-universe.html. Although situated outside of downtown (which is necessary to escape some of the light pollution), the observatory makes a unique destination. Stargaze with the 5.9-foot Plaskett telescope. Open Tues to Sat from spring to Oct. Call for updated hours and a sky report before making the trip. $$–$$$.

Royal BC Museum. 675 Belleville St., Victoria; (250) 356-7226 or (888) 447-7977; www .royalbcmuseum.bc.ca. This museum rates as the city's must-see attraction. From the mystical towering totems to the house of a chief, the First Peoples Gallery tells the story of the Pacific Northwest's First Nations in living detail. Enter a Chinatown herbalist's shop, lock eyes with a grizzly, or admire a replica of Captain George Vancouver's ship. Open daily. $$$.

Royal London Wax Museum. 470 Belleville St., Victoria; (250) 388-4461; www.waxmu seum.bc.ca. As with any royal city, a queen presides over Victoria. In fact, there are more than a dozen monarchs including the Elizabeths, Victoria, and the six wives of Henry VIII. Besides royalty, displays also put a wax face to Captain George Vancouver; President Franklin Roos-evelt; and, Sherpa Tenzing Norgay, who summited Mount Everest with Sir Edmund Hillary. Open daily. $$$.

Victoria Butterfly Gardens. 1461 Benvenuto Ave., Brentwood Bay; (250) 652-3822 or (877) 722-0272; www.butterflygardens.com. More than 3,000 butterflies flit through the tropical conservatory. While butterflies are the highlight at the gardens, koi, flamingos, and parrots also inhabit the animal house. Open daily Feb through Dec; closed during Jan. $$$.

where to shop

For souvenirs, a walk down Government Street will yield all the Canadian-flag T-shirts you'll ever need. Look for **Cowichan Trading Company** at 1328 Government St., featuring the original versions of the cozy woolens donned by the Canadian Winter Olympic team at the 2010 Games.

Off Government Street, **Bastion Square** features vendors selling at an open-air market, Wed to Sun and holidays from May through mid-Oct. For boutique shopping, urban fashions, and cool finds, head to Lower Johnson Street and Market Square.

A small **Chinatown district** starts at the bold gateway at Fisgard and Government Streets. Shops selling broad selections of Asian goods are stocked to the roof, and prices are generally reasonable. Look for the narrow Fan Tan Alley that branches off Fisgard. The district is one of the oldest Chinatowns in North America and grew as a result of the gold rush.

where to eat

Bard & Banker. 1022 Government St., Victoria; (250) 953-9993; www.bardandbanker .com. This Scottish-style pub certainly rises above beer-sticky floors and packets of crisps. The dinner menu includes the name-brand British fare including bangers and mash, shepherd's pie, and fish-and-chips. But with a streetside patio and hidden delicacies like liver with wild boar or seafood sliders, the pub is worth visiting for more than a pint of stout. Open daily for lunch and dinner. $$–$$$.

ReBar Modern Food. 50 Bastion Square, Victoria; (250) 361-9223; www.rebarmodern food.com. Modern comfort food at its best and healthiest: This brightly decorated café has spawned cookbooks and an avid local following. The almond burger persists as a highlight while the salads and brunch items make excellent weekend fare. Open Mon to Sat for breakfast, lunch, and dinner; Sun for breakfast/brunch and lunch. $$.

Red Fish Blue Fish. 1006 Wharf St., Victoria; (250) 298-6877; www.redfish-bluefish.com. Tacones—"taco cones"—are the specialty here and the easiest thing to eat from a plate balanced on your knee. This wharfside food stand serves fresh seafood, crisp fries, and immense sandwiches. The fish-and-chips can be made with halibut, salmon, or cod, while the tacones offer edamame, shrimp, or salmon as some of the many fillings. Hours change with the seasons, but expect the stand to be open most lunch hours when the weather is nice. $$–$$$.

Sam's Deli. 805 Government St., Victoria; (250) 382-8424; www.samsdeli.com. For more than thirty years the sandwiches have been stacked a figurative mile high. While the menu doesn't venture much beyond soups, sandwiches, and salads, these are all done well and with freshness as the focus. For a budget bite on the waterfront, Sam's is a tough deal to beat. Open for breakfast, lunch, and an early dinner daily. $–$$.

where to stay

Andersen House Bed-and-Breakfast. 301 Kingston St., Victoria; (250) 388-4565 or (877) 264-9988; www.andersenhouse.com. With dozens of bed-and-breakfasts in Victoria, this one breaks from Victorian frilliness and melds historic architecture with vibrant art and deluxe comfort. The charming garden studio looks out through antique stained glass at a lush Northwest garden. The upper-level captain's apartment can sleep up to four. Throughout the house, original artwork, vaulted ceilings, and character woodwork create a special destination. $$$$.

The Fairmont Empress. 721 Government St., Victoria; (250) 384-8111 or (866) 540-4429; www.fairmont.com/empress. The ivy-covered building competes with the legislature for the title of most grandiose waterfront building. From the rich woodwork in the breakfast dining hall to the afternoon tea served on fine china, a stay at the Empress truly gives that regal feeling. Rooms range from standard to luxurious. $$$$.

James Bay Inn. 270 Government St., Victoria; (250) 384-7151 or (800) 836-2649; www.jamesbayinn.bc.ca. Clean rooms with basic furnishings provide a budget option in town (with a little more space than the hostel listed below). Rooms vary in size and amenities and occasionally have a quirky feature, like a double-headed shower. Bed sizes range from twin to king. $$–$$$.

Ocean Island Backpackers Inn. 791 Pandora Ave., Victoria; (250) 385-1788 or (888) 888-4180; www.oceanisland.com. Although the private rooms are tiny, the central location, lots of advice on local day trips, Internet cafe, and on-site eatery make the hostel a fabulous budget deal. Rooms are clean, and bathrooms, although shared, are private. For increased privacy, opt for a pricier suite in the inn's off-site 1907 heritage house. $–$$.

>> festivals and celebrations

february

Well-timed to coincide with Valentine's Day (although officially on Presidents' Day week-end), this event appeals with simple romance. The Yakima Valley's annual **Red Wine and Chocolate Festival** pairs local fine wines with blends of dark chocolate. A tip from the festival: Taste the wine first then let the chocolate melt in your mouth. (509) 965-5201 or (800) 258-7270; www.wineyakimavalley.org.

Who wouldn't want to hang out with a group of cowboys? The **Spirit of the West Cowboy Gathering** in Ellensburg rounds up the folks in ten-gallon hats for a campfire sing-along of sorts in mid-February. Poets, musicians, and artists arrive in town to entertain. (888) 925-2204; www.ellensburgcowboygathering.com.

Vancouver celebrates **Chinese New Year** with parades, costumes, food, and dances. The date changes annually and is based on the lunar calendar, although the date is usually in late January to mid-February.

march

Things get steamy at the **Penn Cove Mussel Fest** in early March. Eating contests, cooking contests, and demonstrations comprise the weekend festival in Coupeville, Whidbey Island. www.thepenncovemusselfestival.com.

april

The **Skagit Valley Tulip Festival** features a whole month of tulip, daffodil, and iris blooms—although just when the flowers will bloom only Mother Nature knows. (360) 428-5959; www.tulipfestival.org.

In mid-April go birding at the **Olympic Peninsula BirdFest** when the Audubon community gathers to stake out the sand spits, tidal flats, and shoreline on the peninsula. (360) 681-4076; www.olympicbirdfest.org.

The **Spring Barrel Tasting** in Yakima is a preview event for that season's wines. Dozens of wineries participate in the late-April event. (509) 965-5201 or (800) 258-7270; www.wineyakimavalley.org.

Running late April into early May, the **Washington State Apple Blossom Festival** in Wenatchee celebrates the spring blooms with parades, carnivals, and contests as well as square dancing, airplane flyovers, and a bocce ball tournament. (509) 662-3616; www .appleblossom.org.

During the last weekend in April (although it's timed with the birds and tides and can sometimes stretch into May), the **Grays Harbor Shorebird Festival** celebrates the stopover and return of migratory birds. Flocks gather on the mudflats of Grays Harbor affording excellent viewing opportunities. (800) 303-8498; www.shorebirdfestival.com.

may

Celebrating water and the agricultural life it brings to Sequim, the **Irrigation Festival** runs in early May. The festival is the oldest in the state, and you'll see everything from a strong-man competition to fireworks and a parade. www.irrigationfestival.com.

For Mother's Day weekend, **Buds and Blooms** features the gardens of Federal Way, including the Rhododendron Species Botanical Garden. (253) 835-6868; www.federalway .org.

May 17 is Norwegian Constitution Day and time to visit Poulsbo for **Viking Fest.** There's a lutefisk-eating contest, Norwegian entertainment, and road race. (360) 697-7450; www .vikingfest.org.

On May 18, **Mount St. Helens** remembers the lethal volcanic eruption that occurred in 1980. www.visitmtsthelens.com.

Canadian Victoria Day weekend (Monday on or before May 24) looks very tartan with the **Victoria Highland Games and Celtic Festival.** www.victoriahighlandgames.com.

june

Edmonds Arts Festival, Edmonds. A three-day family festival makes a great destination for Father's Day weekend. (425) 771-6412; www.edmondsartsfestival.com.

Head to Poulsbo around June 21 for **Skandia Midsommarfest.** Of course there's folk dancing, but this Swedish summer solstice celebration also features the traditional raising of the Midsommar pole. (206) 784-7470; www.skandia-folkdance.org.

Sand-castle builders construct impressive sand structures beachside, while in the forest chainsaw carvers create cedar masterpieces. The **Sand and Sawdust Festival** runs in late June. www.oceanshoresact.com.

All summer long **Olympic Music Festival** hosts classical musical acts at a dairy farm in Quilcene on Hood Canal. (360) 732-4800; www.olympicmusicfestival.org.

july

Defect for **Canada Day** (July 1) and take in a parade, entertainment, and fireworks in downtown Victoria. www.victoria.ca/canadaday.

Fourth of July weekend is big in most towns and cities around the state—with too many festivities to list here. Some that host the nation for a party include Leavenworth, Bainbridge Island, Everett, Port Orchard, Edmonds, and Bellevue, to name a handful. The Washington Tourism Web site (www.experiencewa.com) is a central spot to search for event listings.

Bellingham Festival of Music runs in early July and welcomes artists for orchestral and chamber concerts. (360) 201-6621; www.bellinghamfestival.org.

In mid-July the countryside is a shade of purple during the **Sequim Lavender Festival.** Tour local lavender farms and then head to town for the party. (360) 681-3035 or (877) 681-3035; www.lavenderfestival.com.

The **Bellevue Arts Museum's Artsfair** becomes the center of the state for a rich marketplace of art and craft. The juried arts show runs around the third week of July. (425) 519-0770; www.bellevuearts.org/fair.

august

You won't find a more colorful parade in British Columbia than **Vancouver Pride Festival.** The first weekend in August, a Sunday parade takes over the "gayborhood" near Denman at Davie streets in Vancouver, British Columbia. 604-687-0955; www.vancouverpride.ca.

In mid-August the Suquamish community hosts **Chief Seattle Days** with memorials, songs, dances, fireworks, canoe races, and salmon dinners. (360) 598-3311; www.suquamish.org.

Mid-August brings the tastiest of foods plus family activities to the shores north of Seattle with the annual **Taste of Edmonds.** (425) 776-6711; www.edmondswa.com/Events/Taste.

september

Olympia Harbor Days celebrates Labor Day wharfside in the state capital with tugboat races and ships on site. www.harbordays.com.

The **Ellensburg Rodeo** gets rowdy over Labor Day weekend. (509) 962-7831 or (800) 637-2444; www.ellensburgrodeo.com.

Although there are also crab and oyster festivals, the Labor Day–weekend **Seafood Festival** has been held for more than sixty years in Westport. The Westport-Grayland Chamber of Commerce can provide details. (360) 268-9422 or (800) 345-6223.

Kilts fly at the **Kelso Highlander Festival** held in mid-September. It's Scottish-and-Celt everything with music, food, competitions, and activities. www.highlander.kelso.gov.

In mid-September more than 200 wooden vessels launch in, sail to, and dock at Port Townsend for the **Wooden Boat Festival.** Expect sailing races, rowing competitions, and maritime music. Contact the Wooden Boat Foundation for details. (360) 385-3628; www .woodenboat.org.

The **Puyallup Fair**—it's one of the largest fairs in the country with a carnival, rodeo, monster trucks, food, and entertainment. Running in mid-September, the fair attracts more than one million visitors each year. (253) 841-5045; www.thefair.com.

october

Issaquah Salmon Days honors the annual return of the salmon to Issaquah Creek. (425) 392-0661; www.salmondays.org.

Port Townsend Kinetic Race features participants charting a course through town in human-powered vehicles that display engineering and artistic merit. Through mud, up hills, and around the course, the wacky race runs the first weekend in October and makes for great entertainment. The town's race is the second-oldest version of worldwide kinetic race events—behind only the founding town of Ferndale, California. www.ptkineticrace.org.

Also in early October, Everett celebrates Oktoberfest with the **Everett Sausage Festival.** www.everettsausagefest.com.

Apple Days offers no surprises but a delicious look at the locally grown fruit as well as entertainment. The Cashmere Museum, for which the event is a fundraiser, has the details on the early-October event. (509) 782-3230; www.cashmeremuseum.org.

Whatcom Artist Studio Tour highlights the talented local artists at work in the county. During the first two weekends in October, admire, browse, and purchase the work of more than fifty artists. (360) 650-9691; www.studiotour.net.

It's crab season in October and a fitting reason to celebrate with a festival in Port Angeles: enter the **Dungeness Crab & Seafood Festival.** (360) 452-6300; www.crabfestival.org.

Mid-October the **Cranberry Harvest Festival** coincides with the harvest of the tart berry. The Cranberry Coast Chamber of Commerce provides details on the event. (360) 267-2003 or (800) 473-6018; www.cranberrycoastcoc.com.

Leavenworth Oktoberfest means bottoms up the first three weekends in October. The keg-tapping ceremony is the center of the festivities, but there's also food, crafts, and entertainment. www.leavenworthoktoberfest.com.

november

Thanksgiving in Wine Country centers on Yakima's wines and their pairings with traditional and inspiring holiday cuisine. (509) 965-5201 or (800) 258-7270; www.wineyakima valley.org.

Late November through the New Year, **Zoolights** brightens Point Defiance Zoo & Aquarium in Tacoma. The zoo even has a recycling program for old strings of holiday lights—so bring yours along. (253) 591-5337; www.pdza.org.

december

The **Leavenworth Christmas Lighting** is the town's iconic holiday festival. Over the first three weekends in December, carols, white lights, and Christmas cheer fill the Bavarian town. The local chamber will have the exact details. (509) 548-5807; www.leavenworth.org.

index